LUXURY FASHION MARKETING AND BRANDING

T0299758

Luxury Fashion Marketing and Branding offers a comprehensive analysis of the key theories and concepts needed to understand the promotion of luxury fashion products. It covers subjects including luxury fashion retailing, digital marketing and communication, data analytics, emerging technologies, consumer behaviour and PR. The textbook also offers a focused discussion of the challenges faced by luxury fashion brands to meet growing customer demand for ethical and sustainable practice, including concerns related to diversity, inclusivity and cultural sensitivity.

This textbook is grounded in business practices, featuring real-world examples and international case studies from both established and modern brands. Chapter objectives and summaries aid comprehension, whilst end-of-chapter questions and activities enable further research and discussion.

Luxury Fashion Marketing and Branding is ideal for advanced undergraduate and postgraduate students of fashion marketing and communications, luxury fashion business and luxury brand management. Its applied approach will also make it suitable for those studying for an Executive MBA in Fashion and Luxury Management. Online resources include an instructor's manual, lecture slides and a test bank.

Alice Dallabona is a Lecturer in Fashion Marketing at the University of Leeds, UK.

Mastering Fashion Management

The fashion industry is dynamic, constantly evolving and worth billions worldwide: it's no wonder that Fashion Business Management has come to occupy a central position within the Business School globally. This series meets the need for rigorous yet practical and accessible textbooks that cover the full spectrum of the fashion industry and its management.

Collectively, *Mastering Fashion Management* is a valuable resource for advanced undergraduate and postgraduate students of Fashion Management, helping them gain an in-depth understanding of contemporary concepts and the realities of practice across the entire fashion chain – from design development and product sourcing, to buying and merchandising, sustainability, and sales and marketing. Individually, each text provides essential reading for a core topic. A range of consistent pedagogical features are used throughout the texts, including international case studies, highlighting the practical importance of theoretical concepts.

Postgraduate students studying for a Masters in Fashion Management in particular will find each text invaluable reading, providing the knowledge and tools to approach a future career in fashion with confidence.

Luxury Fashion Brand Management
Unifying Fashion With Sustainability
Olga Mitterfellner

Fashion Business and Digital Transformation
Technology and Innovation across the Fashion Industry
Charlene Gallery and Jo Conlon

Customer Experience in Fashion Retailing
Merging Theory and Practice
Bethan Alexander

Luxury Fashion Marketing and Branding
A Strategic Approach
Alice Dallabona

For more information about the series, please visit https://www.routledge.com/Mastering-Fashion-Management/book-series/FM

LUXURY FASHION MARKETING AND BRANDING

A Strategic Approach

Alice Dallabona

LONDON AND NEW YORK

Designed cover image: © Matthias Clamer / Getty

First published 2025
by Routledge
4 Park Square, Milton Park, Abingdon, Oxon OX14 4RN

and by Routledge
605 Third Avenue, New York, NY 10158

Routledge is an imprint of the Taylor & Francis Group, an informa business

© 2025 Alice Dallabona

British Library Cataloguing-in-Publication Data
A catalogue record for this book is available from the British Library

ISBN: 978-1-032-20707-0 (hbk)
ISBN: 978-1-032-20688-2 (pbk)
ISBN: 978-1-003-26481-1 (ebk)

DOI: 10.4324/9781003264811

Typeset in Interstate
by codeMantra

Access the Support Material: www.routledge.com/9781032206882

CONTENTS

Introduction

The luxury fashion industry is a multifaceted entity that features a variety of players, in 2020 it was reported that the top ten luxury fashion brands dominated the market, and made over 90% of sales. The industry features a mix of independent labels and brands belonging to conglomerates and groups, but they all share similar characteristics in terms of brand management, marketing and communication. This book examines such characterising traits of luxury fashion brands through theory, examples and detailed case studies.

Chapter One introduces key concepts that will be discussed throughout the book, considering themes that will be examined later on in more detail. The chapter investigates the problematic definition of luxury through the comparison of different models, offering a historical overview, and focuses on its characterising traits whilst also considering its ethical dimension, that is still salient in today's market. Moreover, a number of theories are explored to provide a definition of luxury fashion and to clarify the problematic issues concerning the presence of different levels of luxury within the industry. In this sense, the rationale for expanding into lower-priced products, which implies a widening of the brands' customer base, is examined, addressing the significant benefits but also identifying the risks involved in terms of brand dilution. Moreover, the chapter examines recent strategies of brand elevation aimed at supporting the status and prestige of luxury fashion brands. The chapter features a number of examples and a case study reviewing the successful strategies employed by Armani to develop and maintain several diffusion lines and sub-brands that sell at different price points.

Chapter Two opens with a historical overview of luxury fashion brands, focusing in particular on France and Italy and the different ways their luxury fashion brands have evolved in terms of brand management. Moreover, the chapter addresses the development of luxury conglomerates. Then, the chapter explores the problematic definition of luxury fashion brands. Similar to conceptualisations of luxury, the notion of a luxury fashion brand appears to be a self-evident concept but it hides, under the surface, a much more complex nature. Several theories and models of luxury fashion brands are examined and compared, considering situations of dialogue and contradictions and, moreover, the chapter proposes a new model of luxury fashion brand. Furthermore, the chapter investigates the growing phenomenon of luxury fashion brands extending into different product categories, from cosmetics to furniture. The notion of brand extension and the way it is implemented by luxury fashion brands are discussed, identifying different contractual agreements and the advantages and

DOI: 10.4324/9781003264811-1

downsides involved in such a strategy. The latter issue is discussed through the case study of hotels associated with luxury fashion brands, with a particular focus on luxury fashion flagship hotels.

Chapter Three focuses on the challenges involved in maintaining brand equity and brand value in the luxury fashion industry. First, the chapter examines definitions of brand equity and a number of models that theorise how value can be created, maintained and increased. The chapter addresses how fashion brands have to navigate a series of challenges originating in business practices. In this sense the chapter considers the rise of ready-to-wear and the development of different strategies to manage brand equity emerging in France, Italy and the USA, and how conglomerates are reshaping the industry. The chapter further discusses the expansion of luxury fashion brands into international markets, and the challenges and opportunities involved in such strategy. Moreover, it is examined how extensions into the lower market segments and the rise of premium labels have changed the face of competition within the industry. Furthermore, the chapter investigates the importance of adapting to changes in society in order to remain relevant and attract customers, and discusses how notions such as customisation or insperiences nowadays are pivotal in responding to people's values. The last section of the chapter focuses on what happens when luxury fashion brands are unable to respond effectively to change or to capitalise on opportunities, leading to a decline in brand equity. In this sense different strategies such as brand rejuvenation, repositioning and rebranding are explored with regards to their role in fighting brand decline. The theoretical concepts outlined with regards to the latter are illustrated through the case study of Burberry.

Chapter Four focuses on the luxury fashion brand consumer, arguing that the peculiarities of the industry, with its extensive offerings and different levels of luxury, alongside the international presence of labels and the socio-economic disparities between established and emerging markets, contribute to problematise the notion. The luxury fashion brand consumer is a multifaceted entity and the chapter examines the issue through a historical overview, investigating different theories and models of luxury consumption and discussing how notions of class have been challenged by the emergence of the concept of lifestyle. Moreover, contemporary drivers of luxury fashion consumption are explored, discussing their features and their roles in supporting the purchase of luxury fashion goods and their desirability. Furthermore, differences between geographical areas, and, in particular, the divide between mature and emerging markets such as China and India are also examined. With regards to this, a case study is proposed, investigating the characteristic traits of Millennial consumers.

Chapter Five discusses luxury fashion retail, with a particular focus on the customer experience. First, the different channels luxury fashion brands use to reach their customers are examined. Limited availability and controlled distribution within the luxury fashion industry are discussed, also considering issues related to parallel markets. A case study focusing on Off-White then examines the rationale and marketing strategies employed when luxury fashion brands collaborate with mass-market retailers, and how notions of exclusivity are maintained in this scenario. Then the chapter discusses how, when it comes to luxury fashion, customers have high expectations at every stage of their shopping experience, from packaging to retail environment and customer care. In this sense, the pivotal role of flagship stores is investigated. Furthermore, the chapter addresses and contextualises the reluctance of luxury fashion brands in joining the e-tail revolution, examining the strategies adopted when it comes to selling online products associated with luxury fashion brands and the problematic issues arising from that. In this sense, omnichannel strategies and the evolution of e-commerce and m-commerce are discussed.

Chapter Six focuses on how luxury fashion brands can use different sources of brand identity to create and disseminate narratives about what the brands stand for through their marketing and communication strategies. The narratives proposed are intrinsically selective and often present a mix of fact and fiction aimed at supporting the brands' prestige and desirability through storytelling. The chapter examines several sources of identity such as typical products and visual symbols, before addressing some elements in more detail. First, the role of country of origin as a source of differentiation and competitive advantage is explored. In this sense, the problematic issues concerning the production practices and business structure of luxury fashion brands are also discussed. Second, the case of historical roots and heritage of luxury fashion brands is investigated, focusing in particular on how narratives of handmade craftsmanship are reinforced through different marketing and communication strategies. Last, the chapter discusses the myth of the designer as a powerful communication tool. This is further investigated through a case study focusing on the figure of Coco Chanel.

Chapter Seven examines the different tools used by luxury fashion brands to promote and advertise their products. The role of fashion shows in promoting luxury brands is examined, offering a historical overview of the phenomenon and mapping its evolution from an event aimed at fashion insiders to a spectacle for the wider public, and the consequences arising from the latter. Moreover, the multifaceted issue of advertising in luxury fashion is investigated, also considering the challenges and opportunities arising from brand extension in this sense. Furthermore, the role of celebrity endorsement within the marketing strategies of luxury fashion brands is also discussed, and the concepts outlined are illustrated through the case study of Fear of God. Last, the key role of public relations in managing the relationships between luxury fashion brands, the media, and the wider public is explored, discussing the different techniques and strategies available. Moreover, the chapter also explores the pivotal role of PR in terms of crisis management, addressing a number of recent controversies.

Chapter Eight addresses the challenges and opportunities for luxury fashion brands arising from recent changes in the media landscape affecting marketing and communication practices. Luxury fashion brands, although initially reluctant to embrace the digital revolution, are now fully engaging with digital and social media and adopt a variety of strategies in this sense. First, the chapter addresses the issue of digital marketing, discussing a number of tools and techniques, before focusing on social media marketing. In this sense, the opportunities but also the challenges involved in balancing exclusivity with reaching a wider audience are explored. This is further investigated through a case study focusing on Cyber Valentine's Day (also known as 520 festival), a digitally native celebration of love that luxury fashion brands are using to connect with Chinese consumers. Last, the chapter examines how digital and social media do not only offer luxury fashion brands platforms to reach the wider public, but also to gather valuable data that can inform and drive marketing and communication alongside branding and management strategies.

Chapter Nine focuses on the role of new technologies in the marketing and communication strategies of luxury fashion brands. First, the chapter addresses the issue of how to support and increase consumer engagement through digital means, discussing in particular the use of augmented reality (AR), virtual reality (VR), RFID and QR codes but also chatbots and AI through a series of examples regarding both older and more recently established luxury fashion brands, such as Gucci and Off-White. Moreover, the chapter examines the issue of dematerialisation in luxury fashion, which sees brands associating their names to virtual products, and explores the different tools, such as NFTs, and strategies employed in this sense. This topic is further explored through a case study focusing on luxury fashion brands and gaming. Last, the chapter discusses the role of AI and blockchain in supporting luxury fashion brands in their constant fight against fakes and counterfeits, an ever-present issue for labels that has become even more prominent since the advent of social media and e-commerce.

Chapter Ten focuses on issues that have become more and more topical in the last few years as a function of changes in societal values, and that are rapidly becoming major sources of scandals and controversies in the luxury fashion industry, causing a seismic shift in communication and marketing practices. First, the chapter examines the concept of diversity and investigates how luxury fashion brands are engaging with this dimension through a variety of strategies both in front of the camera and behind the scenes. In this sense, the notion of tokenism is also considered. The latter is also considered when it comes to inclusivity, exploring the steps undertaken by brands in order to foster change but also highlighting areas for improvement. Moreover, the chapter examines the issue of cultural sensitivity addressing how the growing internationalisation of luxury fashion brands and the role of new media have made labels more vulnerable to criticism when issues of cultural appropriation arise, or when local cultures and values are not respected. In this sense, the case study of the Dolce & Gabbana Love China scandal is explored.

Chapter Eleven examines a series of ethical issues that have become relevant in today's society and that luxury fashion brands cannot ignore in their quest to remain relevant and desirable, affecting a variety of areas from marketing and communication to management. Nowadays more and more people are exposed to information about the impact of their consumption practices and the fashion industry has been harshly criticised for not doing enough in this sense. The chapter first discusses the debates concerning the morality of luxury consumption and its production practices in terms of their social impact. Then the issue of animal welfare is considered, exploring how fur and exotic skins that used to characterise the luxury fashion industry have now become controversial and are being progressively abandoned, leading to the development of new cruelty-free alternatives. Furthermore, the chapter examines how luxury fashion brands address the issue of the environmental cost of their products and the strategies they can employ to engage with sustainability. The case study of Stella McCartney is then investigated, exploring how the brand addresses all of the elements discussed above.

Part I

Luxury Fashion Branding

1 What is Luxury

Case study: Armani

CHAPTER OBJECTIVES

This chapter:

- explores the definitions of luxury
- discusses the characteristics of luxury goods
- examines the different levels of luxury within the luxury fashion industry

---

1.1 Chapter summary

Chapter One introduces key concepts that will be discussed throughout the book and explores the problematic relationship between the luxury fashion industry and the concept of luxury. In this sense, the chapter examines the definition of luxury and discusses the characteristics of luxury goods, highlighting situations of dialogue and contradiction with the strategies adopted by luxury fashion brands. In this sense the rarity principle of Phau and Prendergast and the luxury paradox theorised by Dubois and Paternault are considered. Moreover, the chapter addresses the problematic issues concerning the presence of different levels of luxury within the industry. In this sense the conceptualisations created by Okonkwo, Alleres and Silverstein and Fiske are examined. The chapter also examines recent strategies of brand elevation that emerged in response to brand extension in the lower market segments, and that aim to strengthen the exclusivity and prestige of luxury fashion brands. Those elements are also discussed through a case study reviewing the successful strategies employed by Armani in this sense.

1.2 Introduction

Some may think that it would be unnecessary to discuss what constitutes luxury, as luxury is often regarded as a self-evident concept that requires no explanation as people instinctively know what it is. Others may add that it would be similarly unrequired to examine the

DOI: 10.4324/9781003264811-3

relationship between notions of luxury and luxury fashion, as those concepts are perceived by many as synonymous. However, the different traits of luxury, its evolution and society-related nature help to understand how luxury fashion brands are created and how they support their aura and prestige. At the same time, to consider the intrinsically controversial nature of luxury can offer important tools to support brand management and guide brand communication. Moreover, this discussion helps to conceptualise the fact that actually within the luxury fashion industry nowadays one is faced with products that hold a problematic relationship with notions of luxury, as they are simply not as luxurious as one might imagine. If in the past luxury fashion brands were solely associated with exclusive pieces that remained accessible only to the very rich, nowadays they have extended their ranges to include mass-produced goods available to a wider clientele. This situation has led many to question whether the luxury fashion industry has lost its lustre (Thomas 2007) and to challenge its association with the concept of luxury.

For a number of years, the identification of the luxury fashion industry with the concept of luxury was a given. However, the industry faced dramatic changes as from the 1980s onwards luxury fashion brands started to associate their names more and more with cheaper products that could appeal to a wider public, expanding their customer base to include not only extremely wealthy individuals. This has led to a problematic relationship between the luxury fashion industry and the concept of luxury (section 1.3), to issues in defining what the characteristics of luxury fashion products are (section 1.4) and the need to create new definitions of luxury to reconcile the contradictions within the business (section 1.5).

1.3 Defining luxury

Notions of luxury have a long-standing association with specific sectors. As discussed by Chevalier and Mazzalovo (2008: vii–x), those include primarily fashion (haute couture and ready-to-wear), but also jewellery and watches, perfumes and cosmetics, fashion accessories, wines and spirits, alongside luxury cars, hotels, tourism and private banking. Okonkwo (2007: 131) adds furniture and home decoration, as well as museums and galleries to the list, whereas Corbellini and Saviolo (2009: 25) also argue that the demand for experiences has shaped the recent development of the luxury sector into the areas of exclusive services (like personal shoppers or medical professionals) and real estate.

Luxury is commonly associated with ideas of opulence, pleasure, desirability, superfluity but also inappropriateness. The latter is particularly relevant for the contemporary luxury fashion industry, as it deals with fierce criticism about its production practices and controversies surrounding its consumption.

Examining the etymology of luxury, Calefato (2014: 10) discusses how the positive connotations of abundance and opulence that characterise the term derive from the Latin 'luxus'. Other positive traits associated with luxury are notions of pleasure and enjoyment concerning the way luxury goods are experienced and their sensory appeal. As observed by Dubois, Laurent and Czellar (2001: 13) luxury goods appeal to the senses, as, for example, an iconic bag manufactured by a luxury fashion brand would showcase striking aesthetic qualities and good design, would appeal to the sense of touch through the softest leather and quality packaging, to the sense of hearing as hands free the object from boxes and layers of materials and finally touch the delicate surface, to the sense of smell through the aroma of leather. In opposition, the sensory experience of mass manufactured goods couldn't be more different, as, for example, flimsy and poorly designed packaging do their best to protect items manufactured from cheap plastic leading to a pungent smell and a characteristic sound as it rubs together. Desirability is another trait that characterises luxury, and revolves around who has access to luxury and the way people acquire the goods that they aspire to. In fact, the less people have access to luxury the more desirable it becomes, as similar restrictions and difficulties in acquiring it also support its appeal.

It has been noted that superfluousness is what characterises luxury in contrast to economic necessity. However, to define luxury as something that is not necessary is problematic because of the role that luxury has played, and still plays, in societal practices. In fact, luxury consumption has been historically used by the ruling classes and elites as a tool to display their power and prestige, in this sense almost representing a necessity for them (Mortelmans 2005: 501). In this respect the case of French King Louis XIV is exemplary, as he spent incredibly large amounts of money to create the luxurious Château de Versailles and a sumptuous way of life with the purpose to both exhibit and enhance his political power (Williams 1982: 28). Such practices are still relevant today because, as the artistic director of Christian Dior noted, luxury is a necessity if you can afford it (Bourdieu 1984: 280).

Moreover, to define luxury as superfluous in terms of opposition to necessities is also problematic because notions of the latter are far from fixed but imbued with ideology. As argued by Barthes (1977: 41-2), to define luxury in terms of function of goods is limiting as that is only one of the possible meanings that things can convey, and not one of their natural attributes. For example, any bag could be used to carry one's possession, but to showcase a Birkin bag by Hermès would signal wealth and status in a way that a bag bought cheaply on a market stall wouldn't. Similarly, Baudrillard (1981: 82) also criticises the notion of necessity because of its ideological nature, as he discusses that notions of needs change in time and from culture to culture, showing their nature of cultural constructions that are needed because the system needs them in order to convince people to consume (Mortelmans 2005: 503).

Notions of inappropriateness in luxury etymologically originate from the Latin 'luxuria' (Calefato 2014: 10). As discussed by Berry (1994) in his seminal book on the history of luxury, in the Western World the concept of luxury has been characterised by a long-standing criticism about how its consumption is inappropriate, as for example Greek philosopher Plato accused luxury consumption of bringing political instability by weakening society. This criticism was also shared by philosopher Aristotle, and is at the base of the widespread idea that luxury consumption by the elites was one of the main causes for the fall of the Roman empire (Mortelmans 2005). Notions of inappropriateness of luxury were also appropriated by Christianity, that associated luxury with corruption and sin and argued for its eradication. It was only centuries later, in the 18th century, that luxury started to be associated with more positive narratives, as notions of personal liberty and the value of pursuing one's desires emerged (Berry 1994).

However, luxury only partially lost connotations of moral taints, as at the time the debate over its inappropriateness continued, although not any more from a moral point of view but in political terms. For example, philosopher Jean-Jacques Rousseau argued that inequality within societies was a function of the fact that wealthy people were indulging in luxury, which he saw as the cause of the poverty of the majority of the population (Williams 1991: 43). The political debate over luxury continued until the 19th century (Jennings 2007) and it appears that the controversial nature of luxury consumption is still topical, playing an important role with regards to marketing luxury brands and products amid accusation of moral taint and inappropriateness (Danziger 2005). In actuality, and especially in times of economic crisis, the fact that some can purchase luxury goods costing more than what the majority of the population earns in a year has been accused of being an immoral and tactless act.

Notions of luxury are also associated with specific characteristics of goods, which are discussed in the next section. However, when it comes to luxury fashion brands, the material characteristics of products are not the only salient trait because, as examined in section 1.5, the variety of products offered results only in a partial convergence between notions of luxury and luxury fashion goods, and this leads to some problematic negotiations that see the label as the creator and guarantor of value and desirability.

1.4 Characteristics of luxury goods

Luxury goods, including those associated with luxury fashion brands, need to possess a series of characteristics to be deemed as such. In some languages different words are used to express what specific traits of luxury are meant, as, for example, Kapferer (2014: 717) observes how in Japanese the word 'Koukyuu' is used to indicate high quality and craftsmanship, but the term 'Zeitaku' is used to signify something indulgent and unnecessary, whereas 'Goukana' refers to lavishness and 'La-gu-ju-ri' represents a phonetic adaptation of the word 'luxury' and refers to the world of luxury fashion brands.

This section will address such issues and explore the different attributes that academic literature has considered to be essential for the definition of luxury goods. They are:

- rarity, scarcity and restriction
- high quality, good design and aesthetic value
- craftsmanship and uniqueness
- exclusivity and high price.

Luxury goods have been associated with issues of rarity, scarcity and restriction in a large number of works. It has been observed that luxury has been historically associated to issues of rarity and scarcity of extraordinary commodities, such as pearls for example. In fact, pearls were in the past much more expensive than they are today, as difficulties in acquiring them and issues affecting regularity were the norm before the advent of cultivated pearls, when they became more easily available and their value dropped. However, whilst rarity is considered by many academics as an essential characteristic of luxury goods, Berry (1994: 5) argues that *per se* rarity is not a sufficient condition to define luxury goods, because the fact that a product is scarce does not necessarily make it a luxurious one as other factors need to be at play in order to support desirability and appeal.

After all there are many leather workshops that produce handbags in very limited numbers, but they don't share the same reputation and aura of Bottega Veneta, and are not pursued and valued by consumers in the same way. In this sense traits related to scarcity and rarity contribute but are not solely responsible for making something a luxury good. It is also important to observe that rarity requires knowledge in order to be recognised, as only a connoisseur would be able to distinguish a scarce good and truly appreciate it for this reason (Bourdieu 1984: 279).

Appadurai (1986: 38) argues that luxury goods are characterised by restriction, in the sense that they are limited to the elites because of price or law, and that for centuries the consumption of luxury goods has been controlled through sumptuary regulations. Thinking of fashion, in the past certain colours or garments were reserved for certain individuals only, as, for example, in Ancient Rome where only the Emperor could wear a specific shade of purple, whereas in the Elizabethan era there were limitations on items such as fur and silk. Moreover, Appadurai argues that luxury goods are characterised by complexity of acquisition which can be a function of the real scarcity of the goods but that may also be retained when they are not really scarce if a series of conditions are respected. In the luxury fashion industry, the complexity of acquisition of the goods is actively pursued by companies that employ strategies of limited distribution in order to create forms of well-controlled scarcity (Chevalier and Mazzalovo 2008: 14) in order to maintain their prestigious reputation (Okonkwo 2007: 105). This is the rationale behind selling goods only through selected and sophisticated retailers, as luxury fashion brands control how many units are available and regulate access to their products (see section 5.3 for more information). In some cases luxury fashion brands have introduced waiting lists for the most desirable items, further restricting access and supporting desirability. Mortelmans (2005: 507) observes how scarcity, be that real or created ad hoc, supports higher prices when combined with high demand for the goods in question.

It has to be noted that real rarity and scarcity is only seen in a fraction of the goods associated with luxury fashion brands, as those traits are only suitable to describe their most high-end items. On the other hand, the majority of products associated with those labels, from diffusion lines to cosmetics for example, are produced in large numbers, so that connotations of rarity are solely the result of impressions of scarcity created through a variety of strategies like limited production and availability (Chevalier and Mazzalovo 2008: 49). For example, when it comes to beauty products this translates into carefully managing distribution so that goods are not available through discount shops or less than reputable outlets, but the adoption of strategies aimed at supporting narratives of rarity through communication and marketing are also effective in this sense.

However, in the luxury industry there is another issue in this respect, because if goods are not really scarce and are produced in large numbers they might become commonplace and lose their aura, which could in turn negatively affect brand image. But, at the same time, luxury fashion brands are also actively pursuing more sales and especially so for their more profitable items, further problematising the issue as sales and reputation have to balanced carefully to protect their value. This is theorised by Phau and Prendergast (2000) in terms of rarity principle, and framed by Dubois and Paternault (1995) in terms of luxury paradox.

Dubois and Paternault (1995) observe that luxury products are perceived as rare goods and examine the paradoxical nature of luxury consumption, as people need to be aware of a certain luxury fashion good (for example a Louis Vuitton monogram bag) in order for this awareness to feed into the desirability of the good, i.e. its dream value, but the more this product becomes visible as it's purchased by more and more people, the more this product also loses its desirability, as it is perceived as more commonplace and less appealing, gradually eroding its luxury character. Dubois and Paternault developed a 'dream formula' to describe this phenomenon that has complex implications for the luxury fashion industry. Too much awareness and over-diffusion of a product will cause the luxury good to be not seen as that desirable any more, but too little awareness and no one will buy it because people are not seeing it as an object of desire. In any other market segment apart from the luxury one more visibility and purchases are seen unproblematically as good things, but managing diffusion levels is essential in order to preserve the desirability of goods produced by luxury fashion brands and their brand equity. Dubois and Paternault suggest for example that luxury brands focus on supporting narratives of high quality and authenticity to seduce an elite clientele, in order to associate the goods in question, and the brand, with the legitimacy and status of this social group.

However, this rarity principle is not thought to be suitable to describe luxury consumption worldwide, because if it is applicable to the USA and more generally to Western and individualistic cultures, it seems not to resonate in the same way in collectivist cultures, as discussed by Phau and Prendergast (2000). By examining consumers in Singapore and Hong Kong, the authors discuss how increased purchase levels don't erode the desirability of goods in collectivist cultures, as the social acceptance and prestige associated with them is not tarnished, but actually supported, by increased brand awareness. In this sense they contradict the suggestions of Dubois and Paternault (1995), highlighting the need for luxury fashion brands to adapt their strategies to different countries, as to maintain a significant level of scarcity may be essential in Western markets in order to preserve the allure and desirability of the label, but such an approach would not be applicable everywhere.

Another characteristic trait of luxury goods is high quality, that can revolve around different elements, from the high quality of the raw materials employed to elements of good design and aesthetic value. A luxury fashion good, for example a haute couture dress, would be carefully designed by renowned designers with perfect fit and aesthetic appeal in mind, feature the highest quality materials and be meticulously sewn and decorated by highly skilled professionals. In this respect luxury products can be seen as works of art, and are characterised by attributes such as excellence, beauty, refinement and good taste.

However, high quality is also a problematic concept, because it's not a self-evident notion but implies a judgement of taste. In fact, the good quality or refined nature of an artefact, although based on some material characteristics of the object, are 'inactive' and remain implicit until people activate them by expressing judgements over them. Judgements of taste, according to Bourdieu (1984), derive from sociological criteria such as educational level or class, and differ in different strata of society. It is the elites, he claims, that naturalise their view and impose them as legitimate in opposition to the ones belonging to other classes (Bourdieu 1984: 56). It is this cultural capital (the knowledge that people acquire from education, both in terms of formal institutions and indirectly absorbed by the social background), that allows people to identify and recognize the high quality of luxury goods and assign them the status of work of art (Bourdieu 1984: 39).

Moreover, excellent craftsmanship is another trait that characterises luxury fashion brands and provides luxury status to the goods they produce. Luxury fashion goods are associated with ideas of artisans working in old-fashioned workshops and using traditional techniques, but this is not the case for all the products associated with luxury fashion brands. In fact, luxury fashion brands do not only produce unique pieces, but also mass-manufactured goods targeting a less affluent clientele, as, for example, in the case of perfumes, cosmetics or diffusion lines. The luxury fashion industry is characterised by a great variety in production methods ranging from the individual work of specialised artisans slowly creating masterpieces that are unique and expensive, to factory-made products that are far less exclusive. However, as argued by Chevalier and Mazzalovo (2008: xii), even if the goods associated with luxury brands are actually the result of mass-manufacture, people want to believe that they come directly from the designer's workshop.

Handmade craftsmanship is a trait that is pivotal for luxury fashion brands, and in fact is one that is greatly emphasised in their communication and marketing strategies. Dallabona (2014) examines how Italian luxury fashion brands showcase how their products are made to support connotations of craftsmanship and uniqueness in their products, and how they try to imbue such qualities even in products that are in fact mostly mass-manufactured. For example, Prada released a video showing how a special edition of their fragrance Amber Pour Homme featured a bottle that was encased in leather by hand, and highlighting how it took over a year to develop the flacon and pump, implying that all Prada goods are the product of such valuable skills and attention to detail even when, like in this case, goods are produced in automated factories. Special editions of mass-produced items often feature such elements of craftsmanship, heritage and uniqueness, as labels try to add value and support their aura and prestige (see also Chapter Six).

From this dimension of craftsmanship come other characterising traits of luxury goods, i.e., uniqueness and exclusivity. Uniqueness is seen as a function of hand-made production as it makes each product slightly different and distinctive, making it truly one-of-a-kind. However, exclusivity is also closely intertwined with issues of price, as examined in detail in the next section with regards to the different levels of luxury within the industry.

1.5 Different levels of luxury

For a long time, price has been seen as the most obvious characterising trait of luxury fashion goods, as fashion brands have a history of making products that are inaccessible to many. High prices were a function of material characteristics of the specific goods produced, as discussed in the previous section. In fact, the rarity and scarcity of materials used, the high quality, good design and sensory appeal of the end-products, in addition to the craftsmanship involved in their creation, which supported notions of uniqueness and exclusivity, also conveyed through restrictions in distribution, resulted in goods characterised by really high prices. In this sense only the very rich could access such products, whereas the masses could only dream of owning them.

However, during the 1980s, a revolution started taking place, as luxury fashion brands moved from a model that was focused on products to one that was centred around the extra value that the brands transferred to the goods they produced. As discussed by Mortelmans

(2005: 506), luxury brands are associated with a certain kind of magic that wraps their products in an aura of prestige and desirability that can justify high prices. This magic is so powerful that it enables luxury fashion brands to wrap any goods they produce in an aura of desirability and luxury, even when goods do not possess the characterising traits discussed above.

Potvin (2008: 247) argues that nowadays luxury fashion brands possess the kind of 'symbolic magic' theorised by Pierre Bourdieu, which allows them to transfer connotations of exclusivity and distinction to goods that have no real value but nonetheless elicit a 'fervent dedication' by consumers. This has meant that since the 1980s luxury fashion brands have expanded their brands more and more towards the mass market through products that are more accessible, increasing their profits by widening their customer base and expanding in areas where margins are higher. As discussed in more detail in section 2.5, those forms of downscale vertical extensions mean that cheaper goods are associated with luxury fashion brands, which is problematic in terms of the long-established association between price and exclusivity as it can negatively affect the brand in a variety of ways like for example through brand dilution. In fact, if a Valentino haute couture gown is only attainable by a few, a pair of Missoni socks featuring their distinctive zig-zag pattern that is priced at a few tens of Euros is accessible to more people, but it's a far less exclusive purchase than the former. Such a pair of Missoni socks are however still more expensive than other products in the same category, this follows from the fact that branded products can charge higher prices than unbranded ones (Rao and Monroe 1996: 518–9), and in this sense the reputation and desirability associated with luxury brands means they can charge even more.

Nowadays it's the most accessible level of luxury that is the most important for brands financially, which explains why luxury fashion brands face the risks associated with extending in the mass-market. Such goods feature a lower entry barrier and cater to the middle-classes, that are quickly growing in developing countries. In fact, as argued by Okonkwo (2007: 225), China had a very limited middle-class until recently, but now has a thriving and extremely fast-growing upper medium-class that is very interested in luxury products. However, this phenomenon has also meant that luxury fashion brands have at times associated their name to goods that can hardly compare, in terms of quality, to their more expensive and exclusive products (Thomas 2007).

In this sense, to claim *tout court* that luxury fashion goods are associated with high price is problematic nowadays, because even though it's still true that such brands produce goods that are very costly, it's also true that many people are able to afford the less expensive products they sell. The majority of the population may be unable to buy a Chanel bag, but they could afford to buy a lipstick or a nail varnish instead.

Scholars have created several conceptualisations to explain the different levels of luxury that can be found within the industry, and we examine those of:

- Okonkwo
- Alleres
- Silverstein and Fiske

Okonkwo (2007: 237) offers a classification of different luxury levels in the luxury fashion industry that is centred on the type of goods offered. The three categories theorised are lower-priced luxury products (like fragrances, beauty products and writing materials), medium-priced luxury products (like for example eyewear, restaurants, clubs and cafés) and expensive luxury products that are only accessible to few (like apparel, leather-goods, jewellery and time pieces, but also hotels and spas).

Danielle Alleres in her conceptualisation of luxury (Alleres 1990 in Chevalier and Mazzalovo 2008: xi) proposes three different levels of luxury goods based on their price and relative level of exclusivity. The first class of luxury goods is constituted by inaccessible luxury, that is characterised by very high prices and is represented for example by rare pieces and one-of-a-kind goods, whereas intermediate luxury comprises cheaper replicas of the goods in the previous category (i.e., inaccessible luxury). Chevalier and Mazzalovo (2008: xi) explain that, for luxury fashion brands, haute couture would be inaccessible luxury, while goods replicating all, or part, of couture models and that are produced more cheaply, such as diffusion lines, would fall into the intermediary category. The last level of luxury goods theorised by Alleres is accessible luxury, and is characterised by even cheaper prices than the ones associated with the other two levels, focusing on mass-manufactured products and less expensive products categories such as cosmetics or eyewear.

Like Alleres, Silverstein and Fiske (2005) argue that contemporary luxury goods are not always associated with premium prices, coining this phenomenon as 'new luxury', a type of luxury that is accessible to many. First there are accessible super-premium products, i.e., goods that come from low-priced ranges but that are considered to be at the top of their categories in terms of quality and that are sold at premium prices in comparison with other items in their class, but that remain nonetheless accessible to the majority of consumers. On the other hand, old luxury brand extensions are described as being lower-priced versions of products that are sold at premium prices, and in this sense this typology presents similarity to Alleres' conceptualisation of intermediate luxury. Last, Silvertein and Fiske describe the phenomenon of masstige goods as consisting of products that refer to established luxury brands but are sold at much cheaper prices and therefore are accessible to the majority of the population, despite being priced at an higher level than other items in the same product category. This conceptualisation of masstige products presents some similarities with the accessible luxury theorised by Alleres discussed above.

The term 'masstige' was first introduced by Silverstein and Fiske (2003) to describe a level of luxury accessible to many, but it's use is problematic as it is also commonly used to describe mass-market brands, such as Victoria's Secret or Starbucks, that are adopting strategies to imbue a sense of luxury into their products (Kumar, Paul and Unnithan 2020: 385).

It has been argued that extending luxury brands into cheaper goods implies a democratisation of luxury (for example Tungate 2005 and Thomas 2007) but it has been contended that the phenomenon only involves the democratisation of luxury brands (Dallabona 2017). By buying a Gucci fragrance, or a Moschino scarf, people are not really accessing the world of luxury but the one of the brand, and those are two different things. By broadening their customer base through cheaper goods, luxury fashion brands are only making their brand more accessible through certain products and lines, whereas the most luxurious aspect remains unattainable for the majority of the population. And it's those more high-end manifestations that are the ones actually creating the aura and prestige of luxury fashion brands and supporting their connotations of luxury, upon which they can subsequently cash-in through brand extensions.

After years of aggressive expansion downward, more and more luxury fashion brands are now focusing on elevating their brand to support narratives of prestige and exclusivity and to cater to the growing number of super-rich worldwide. In 2022, Chanel announced it was going to open private boutiques in Asia to cater to its most affluent clients. Many other luxury fashion brands in the last few years have already launched private spaces, within their boutiques, dedicated to their most expensive items and big-spenders. For example, in 2015, Ralph Lauren opened in Milan an exclusive space, by invitation only, where a select few could entertain, shop and access made-to measure services.

Moreover, luxury fashion brands are nowadays also raising prices. Bloomberg reported that Chanel raised the price of classic bags by two thirds in two years (Rascuet and Neumann 2021). The company claims that this is due to exchange-rate issues, rising production costs and in order to level prices worldwide but there have been claims that such a strategy also serves to compensate for the losses experienced during the pandemic, as Chanel only sells cosmetics and sunglasses online and was badly hit by lockdowns worldwide. Chanel is also enforcing limits on purchases, although not consistently everywhere, to make the brand more desirable. In 2022, many brands like Balenciaga have raised prices, globally or locally, in response to higher production and transport costs but some, like Louis Vuitton, are also exploring elevation strategies by entering new areas, as, for example the latter is acquiring large sought-after gems and looking into expanding into high quality jewellery, or by rethinking their brand structure, as seen in the case study of Armani examined in this chapter.

1.6 Case study: Armani

Giorgio Armani, born in Piacenza (Italy) in 1934, founded a brand that successfully operates worldwide and is emblematic for a variety of reasons, bust mostly so for its successful run in operating at different price levels through a variety of lines and sub-brands. Giorgio Armani has been able to establish and retain an independently owned label, even in a time where labels are being acquired more and more by luxury conglomerates to raise capital and remain relevant, by adopting carefully managed strategies of expansion and consolidation by restructuring the brand and focusing on elevation.

Giorgio Armani founded his eponymous brand in 1975 in partnership with Sergio Galeotti. The label was an immediate success, and gathered further recognition by establishing Hollywood collaborations, dressing celebrities for ceremonies like the Oscars and designing costumes for movies, with the first being *American Gigolo* (that was followed by many more such as *The Untouchables* or *The Wolf of Wall Street* to name but a few). Giorgio Armani immediately started to expand his brand, and in 1981 launched its first fragrance and the Emporio Armani and Armani Junior lines. A line of eyewear was first introduced in 1988, following three years later by a new sub-brand, Armani Exchange. The 2000s saw further expansion, with Armani/Nobu restaurants appearing around the world, and the launch of new lines Armani Casa offering furniture and home décor, the Armani Collezioni diffusion line, Armani Cosmetics for make-up and beauty products, followed by Armani Fiori and Armani Dolci offering, respectively, flower arrangements and confectionery products. In addition to the launch of Armani Hotels and Resorts, 2005 also saw the creation of the new Armani Privé haute couture line, and a new era of brand elevation.

In fact, for years the Armani empire had seen the label employ downward extension to create new brands that would cater to less affluent customers, as the founder understood, and aimed to make the most of, the socio-economical changes that drove demand of luxury products by the middle classes. In terms of segmentation, going from the most expensive brand to the cheaper, there was the main line, Giorgio Armani, the core and source of prestige and value of the sub-brands, followed by the diffusion line Armani Collezioni. Emporio Armani was aimed at younger and more trend-led consumers, similar in this sense to Armani Jeans, that specialised in denim products. Last there was Armani Exchange, more focused on casualwear and featuring even lower prices. When all those sub-brands were active, they were also associated to extension in the areas of fragrances, eyewear and accessories, further supplementing the brands' offering. This strategy was extremely profitable, and Giorgio Armani was able to achieve multibillion status.

By operating at different price levels, the different brands and sub-brands in the Armani universe were able to offer a myriad of products that targeted different market segments, and to remain unscathed by this strategy. In fact, brand extension involving producing cheaper products is associated with significant risks, especially the one of diluting the brand and decrease its value by associating it with lower quality of goods or a less prestigious clientele (as discussed in more detail in Chapter Two). Armani was able to minimise those risks by adopting a series of strategies.

First it adopted a differentiation strategy that involved creating an individual identity for each sub-brand whilst keeping them in line with the Armani universe. Stankeviciute and Hoffmann (2010) discuss how all the different Armani sub-brands operated in different market segments, with the distinctiveness of each reinforced through distribution strategies, as, for example, they were sold in different department stores and couldn't be found in the same outlets.

Moreover, goods associated with the sub-brands were priced at the top end of each market segment, retaining an expensive feel, whereas a focus on quality and innovation meant that the products were not perceived as significantly inferior or not in line with the values of Armani. Similarly, a coherent marketing strategy was also employed to further signal the belonging of the sub-brands to the Armani universe (Okonkwo: 2007: 282).

Another element that managed to avoid common pitfalls associated with extending into a less affluent clientele was represented by the fact that the Armani Group aimed to retain control over the ventures, which involved a strictly limited use of licensing and, where those were present, a strategic effort was made to re-acquire them, as seen in the case of Armani Exchange, whose full control was regained by Armani in 2014.

The Armani group is renowned for its vertical integration business, which is characterised by efforts to control all facets of the business. Moore and Wigley (2004) observe how Armani has been able to balance maximum segment coverage through a growing control over its manufacturing and distribution channels. They discuss how Armani has acquired a series of key manufacturers, allowing for a tight control over the whole production process that positively influenced the quality and consistency of goods. A similar strategy with regards to distribution was pursued, as Armani directly operates stores in key markets, whereas in other markets it operates consistently at wholesale to reduce risks and increase profits. This vertical integration strategy, coupled with the fact that the group is still fully owned by its founder Giorgio Armani, meant that key decisions could be taken swiftly when, in the aftermath of the 2008 global economic crisis, the Armani brand value decreased, leading many to question whether the consistent extensions in the lower market segment were also to blame.

Since then, the Armani group has changed its strategy, and adopted one that doesn't focus anymore on expanding into the lower market segments but on the consolidation towards the top end of the luxury segment, which is epitomised in the creation of the new Armani Privé haute couture line, in addition to the exclusive services of Armani Hotels and Resorts. It has to be noted that some services like Armani Dolci and Armani Fiori still offer more affordable services and products, within those settings, as do the brand's cafés and restaurants for example, but the fact that they are associated with the prestige and the high prices of the more expensive parts of the business enable them not alienate the affluent market whilst at the same time reinforcing the exclusivity and allure of the core brand. This strategy of elevation was further pursued through the reorganisation of the different sub-brands, as Armani Collezioni and Armani Jeans were axed to streamline the offering and signal a change of perspective.

Questions and activities

- How did Armani expand into the lower-market segment?
- What strategy of elevations did the brand adopt?
- Select a luxury fashion brand and compare and contrast the strategies it has adopted in this sense.

1.7 Conclusions

This chapter has explored definitions of luxury and discussed the characteristics of luxury goods. Moreover, a number of theories were explored to clarify the problematic issues concerning the presence of different levels of luxury within the industry. In fact, luxury fashion brands have been widening their customer base by expanding into lower-priced products that many can access. Moreover, the chapter also discussed recent strategies that on the opposite see luxury fashion brands elevating their offerings. Such issues were also explored in the case study focusing on Armani.

1.8 Revision questions

-   What does the notion of luxury entails?
-   What are the characterising traits of luxury goods?
-   What are the different levels of luxury within the luxury fashion industry?

1.9 References

Alleres, D. (1990) *Luxe: strategies-marketing*. Paris: Economica.

Appadurai, A. (1986) *The social life of things: commodities in cultural perspective*. Cambridge: Cambridge University Press.

Barthes, R. (1977) *Image-music-text*. London: Fontana.

Baudrillard, J. (1981) *For a critique of the political economy of the sign*. Candor: Telos.

Berry, C. J. (1994) *The idea of luxury: a conceptual and historical investigation*. Cambridge: Cambridge University Press.

Bourdieu, P. (1984) *Distinction: a social critique of the judgement of taste*. London: Routledge and Keegan Paul.

Calefato, P. (2014) *Luxury: fashion, lifestyle and excess*. London-New York: Bloomsbury.

Chevalier, M. and Mazzalovo, G. (2008) *Luxury brand management: a world of privilege*. Singapore: John Wiley and Sons.

Corbellini, E. and Saviolo, S. (2009) *Managing fashion and luxury companies*. Milan: ETAS.

Dallabona, A. (2014) 'Narratives of Italian craftsmanship and the luxury fashion industry: representations of Italianicity in discourses of production', in Hancock II, J. H., Muratovski, G., Manlow, V. and Pearson-Smith, A. (eds.), *Global fashion brands: style, luxury and history*. Chicago: Intellect.

Dallabona, A. (2017) 'Brand extension of Italian luxury fashion labels into the hospitality industry and conceptualisations of luxury: the cases of Armani Hotel Milano and Fendi Suites'. *International Journal of Management Cases*, 19(4), pp. 73–85.

Dallabona, A., and Giani, S. (2020) 'The Good, the Bad, and the Ugly: Dolce and Gabbana and Narratives of Heritage and National Identity', in Amanda Sikarskie (Eds.), *Storytelling in Luxury Fashion Brands, Visual Cultures, and Technologies*, New York: Routledge. pp. 38–50,

Danziger, P. N. (2005) *Let them eat cake: marketing luxury to the masses – as well as the classes*. Chicago: Dearborn Trade.

Dubois, B., Laurent, G. and Czellar, S. (2001) *Consumer rapport to luxury: analyzing complex and ambivalent attitudes* (No. 736). HEC Paris.

Dubois, B. and Paternault, C. (1995) 'Understanding the world of international luxury brand: the "dream formula"'. *Journal of Advertising Research*, 35(4), pp. 69–76.

Jennings, J. (2007) 'The debate about luxury in eighteenth- and nineteenth-century French political thought'. *Journal of the History of Ideas*, 68(1), pp. 79–105.

Kapferer, J.-N. (2014) 'The future of luxury: challenges and opportunities', *The Journal of Brand Management*, 21(9), pp. 716–726.

Kumar, A., Paul, J. and Unnithan, A. B. (2020) '"Masstige" marketing: a review, synthesis and research agenda'. *Journal of Business Research*, 113, pp. 384–398.

Okonkwo, U. (2007) *Luxury fashion branding: trends, tactics, techniques*. Basingstoke: Palgrave Macmillan.

Moore, C. M. and Wigley, S. M. (2004) 'The anatomy of an international fashion retailer – the Giorgio Armani Group', in *British Academy of Management (BAM)*, pp. 1–10.

Mortelmans, D. (2005) 'Sign values in processes of distinction: the concept of luxury'. *Semiotica*, 157(1/4), pp. 497–520.

Phau, I. and Prendergast, G. (2000) 'Consuming luxury brands: the relevance of the Rarity Principle'. *The Journal of Brand Management*, 8, pp. 122–138.

Potvin, J. (2008) *The places and spaces of fashion, 1800–2007*. London: Routledge.

Rao, A. R. and Monroe, K. B. (1996) 'Causes and consequences of price premiums'. *Journal of Business*, 4(69), pp. 511–535.

Rascuet, A. and Neumann, J. (2021) 'Chanel is aiming for Hermes status with handbag price hikes'. *Bloomberg*, 21 December 2021, available at: https://www.bloomberg.com/news/articles/2021-12-21/chanel-is-aiming-for-hermes-status-with-handbag-price-hikes

Silverstein, M., and Fiske, N. (2003) 'Luxury for the masses'. *Harvard Business Review*, 81(4), pp. 48–57.

Silverstein, M. and Fiske, N. (2005) *Trading up (Revised Edition): why consumers want new luxury goods… and how companies create them*. New York: Portfolio.

Stankeviciute, R. and Hoffmann, J. (2010) 'The impact of brand extension on the parent luxury fashion brand: the cases of Giorgio Armani, Calvin Klein and Jimmy Choo'. *Journal of Global Fashion Marketing*, 1(2), pp. 119–28.

Thomas, D. (2007) *Deluxe: how luxury lost its lustre*. London: Penguin.

Tungate, M. (2005) *Fashion brands: branding style from Armani to Zara*. London: Kogan Page.

Williams, R. H. (1991) *Dream worlds: mass consumption in late nineteenth-century France*. Berkeley; Oxford: University of California Press.

2 What is a Luxury Fashion Brand

Case study: Luxury Fashion Flagship Hotels

CHAPTER OBJECTIVES

This chapter:

- explores the history and evolution of luxury fashion brands
- discusses definitions of luxury fashion brands
- examines forms of brand extension

2.1 Chapter summary

This chapter considers the history and evolution of luxury fashion brands, addressing the leading role played by France and Italy in this sense. Moreover, the rise of luxury conglomerates is also explored. Then the chapter discusses the definition of luxury fashion brand. Several theories and models of luxury fashion brands are examined, in particular Moore and Birtwistle, Fionda and Moore and last Okonkwo, before proposing a novel model based on immaterial traits. Finally, the chapter explores notions of brand extension and the way such a strategy is implemented by luxury fashion brands, both in terms of expanding into the lower market segment and through elevation tactics that focus on a more affluent clientele and a sense of exclusivity. In particular, the practice of extending into the hospitality business is examined through a case study of hotels associated with luxury fashion brands, with a particular focus on luxury fashion flagship hotels.

2.2 Introduction

While luxury fashion has a millenary history, luxury fashion brands have a much more recent past. For centuries French fashion dominated, being considered the epitome of elegance and taste, and it was there that the first fashion label was born.

Charles Frederick Worth in 1858 founded his eponymous fashion house in Paris, entering a world that had so far be dominated by seamstresses, the most renowned being Rose Bertin,

DOI: 10.4324/9781003264811-4

who became the dressmaker for Queen Marie Antoinette. Worth is considered as a pioneer in the industry, effectively shaping it by introducing strategies still in use today. He is credited with the creation of fashion shows, as he no longer used wooden or wax mannequins to showcase his designs, but models in a carefully staged setting. Worth employed marketing techniques in an unprecedented way, and is mostly associated with the use of celebrities to promote his brand.

Some of the luxury fashion brands we know today were created in the late 19th century, but many of them did not originate in the clothing businesses. In fact, Lanvin started as a milliner, Loewe as leathermaker, Louis Vuitton as a luggage maker, Fendi as a fur specialist and Hermès as a harness maker. It is interesting to see, as examined in more detail in Chapter Six, how elements of craftsmanship and heritage are leveraged in contemporary luxury fashion marketing and communication practises, as myths of origin and tales of handmade productions are constantly employed to support the aura, prestige and credibility of labels, despite the growing use of mass-production.

2.3 History of luxury fashion

Many of the luxury fashion houses created in the late 19th and early 20th century have since closed down, unable to evolve with the times and to provide a lasting legacy to support growth, in this sense highlighting the difficulties that have intrinsically characterised the industry since its dawn. Examples of this are the House of Worth and the Schiaparelli brand, renowned for its imaginative and surrealist designs, that closed down in 1954 before being relaunched in 2013 by Diego Dalla Valle and the Tod's Group. Some, like Patou or Vionnet, are still operating but not at the same level as their golden age, when they were the main competitors of Chanel.

The late 20th century saw the launch of a number of luxury fashion brands still successfully operating, from Dior to Missoni, from Givenchy to Valentino, from Gucci to Ferragamo. Especially in the last quarter of the century we see the birth of many of the big names in the business, like Yves Saint Laurent, Armani, Versace and Dolce & Gabbana. More recent brands, like Alexaner McQueen, Stella McCartney or Tom Ford, created at the end of the 1990s and beginning of the 2000s, are still relatively new and are not immediately facing one of the major issues affecting older labels, the departure of their original founder. In fact many luxury fashion brands still leverage on the myth of the designer/founder, one of the most notable examples in this sense is represented by the case of Chanel, that was able to re-emerge as a power player under the aegis of another charismatic leader, Karl Lagerfeld (see section 6.5 and case study 6.6).

Okonkwo (2007) observes how marketing and branding practices have become increasingly important in the luxury fashion industry, and lists the trademark of the Burberry logo in the early 1900s, but also the renowned LV or GG logos for Louis Vuitton and Gucci as examples of how the focus has shifted from products to the symbolic dimension of the label. A growing focus on branding has also helped deal with major vulnerabilities of the sector, the losses involved in haute couture and first lines, the rising costs of operating flagship stores, and the difficulties in maintaining and growing brand equity in a sector where brand decline seems to be an unavoidable phase (as discussed in more detail in Chapter Three).

Djelic and Ainamo (1999) observe how French fashion labels, under the strict control of the Chambre Syndicale de la Haute Couture, were able to control access to the category and protect their interests, but later faced difficulties when rivals started to emerge in other countries. The first wave of competitors emerged from Italy after World War II and in those years, despite its insular organisation, the Italian luxury fashion industry started to go from strength to strength. Despite lacking the international reputation of French fashion, Italy nonetheless was quickly able to make its mark by capitalising on a millenary reputation in terms of craftsmanship (Steele 2003).

As discussed by White (2000) Italian craftsmanship had been employed by French fashion for centuries and was established in many fields, like embroidery and accessory production, and was able to revitalise and innovate its practices due to a wave of funding. White argues that the rise of Italian fashion was supported by the quality of Italian fabrics and colours coupled with innovative designs that appeared less formal than their French counterpart, which was appealing especially for the US market, that until that moment had relied primarily on French labels and designs. This, coupled with the competitive price of Italian fashion, contributed to the international success of Italian brands from the 1950s onward.

A two-axis system emerged, but, whereas Paris continued to focus on haute couture, Italian brands launched with a clear focus on ready-to-wear and were able to make the most of the emerging international middle-classes. Nowadays other countries have established a name for luxury fashion, especially Japan (e.g., Kenzo, Issey Miyake, Yoji Yamamoto) and the USA (e.g., Tom Ford, Ralph Lauren, Donna Karan) but they have so far been unable to dethrone France and Italy. Other luxury fashion brands have also been launched in a variety of other countries, such as Shang Xia in China, but they have so far not acquired the same status as French and Italian labels. Chevalier and Mazzalovo (2012: 45) observe how Italian fashion is leading in terms of turnover, as even the primacy of Louis Vuitton cannot compensate for the fact that Italian fashion has more high-performing labels among the top international brands.

Interestingly, many of those labels are now under conglomerates as they faced difficulties in trying to keep their labels relevant and profitable. Born as independent labels and driven by the creativity of a designer, sometimes with expert business partners (as in the case of Gianni Versace and Claudio Luti, Franco Moschino and Tiziano Gusti, or Yves Saint Laurent and Pierre Bergé), the ownership of many labels then exchanged hands like in the case of Valentino, Balenciaga or Dior. The birth of conglomerates is due to a variety of factors, discussed in section 3.4, as they can guarantee funds to support new strategic objectives aimed at preserving and growing iconic labels. Currently there are a variety of small groups, like Tod's (owner of Tod's, Roger Vivier, Hogan and Fay) or Prada (which owns other Prada, Miu Miu, Church's among the others) in Italy, or the Middle Eastern Mayhoola for Investments LLC, which owns Valentino and Balmain, but the industry is dominated by three groups listed in the stock exchange, LVMH, Richemont and Kering.

LVMH is the largest luxury conglomerate and owns a number of luxury fashion brands and leather companies. The group originates in the exponential growth of Louis Vuitton in the early 1980s due to increased sales in Asia. Profits were used to acquire Veuve Clicquot (a champagne brand), and later the group merged with the Moët Hennessy group, comprising champagne brand Moët & Chandon and cognac producer Hennessy (Donzé 2018). However,

Donzé (2018) adds, due to conflict among the CEOs of the two companies a minority share-holder, Bernard Arnault, was able to seize control of the group. At that time Arnault had already acquired Dior, Celine and Lacroix, and at first the group only targeted French companies, but moved towards internalisation in 1993 by acquiring Japanese brand Kenzo, followed by Spanish label Loewe and Italian shoemaker Berluti. LVHM currently owns also luxury fashion brands Patou, Fendi, Givenchy, Pucci, Celine and Marc Jacobs among the others.

The Compagnie Financière Richemont is the second major luxury conglomerate, and operates primarily in fashion, watches and jewellery. Created in 1988 by Anton Rupert, who at the time owned Yves Saint Laurent through Cartier in addition to Chloé, now also owns specialist jewellers Buccellati and Van Cleef & Arpels, eight watchmakers including Baume & Mercier and Vacheron Constantin, and luxury fashion brand Alaïa and Purdey. Richemont has unrivalled presence in luxury online retail, owning the majority of Net-a-Porter, which later merged with Italian luxury fashion online retailer Yoox creating the Yoox Net-a-Porter, but also The Outnet, which specialises in past-season fashion.

The Kering group started its life under the name of Pinault Group, before becoming Pinault Printemps Redoute in 1994, when its founder François Pinault acquired French department stores Le Printemps and an equity stake in French retailer La Redoute. In 2005 the group changed its name to PPR, but in 2013 adopted a new logo and name, Kering. The group started to operate in the luxury fashion sector in 1999 through the acquisition of a minority interest in Gucci, followed by the purchase of Yves Saint Laurent fashion and beauty, Bottega Veneta, and Balenciaga. The group now completely owns Gucci, after a long fight with LVMH. Donzé (2018) observes that LVMH had acquired a 34% stake of Gucci but PPR tried to contain its role by proposing Gucci an increase in capital and a 40% stake that would reduce LVHM capital to 20%, but after a long court case LVMH accepted to sell its shares to PPR. Chevalier and Mazzalovo (2012) observe how the group is one of the most active in terms of creating new brands, launching for example Alexander McQueen and Stella McCartney.

2.4 Defining luxury fashion brands

There are different models that aim to define what constitutes a luxury fashion label because there are a variety of elements to consider in view of the complexity of the industry. In this sense conceptualisations of luxury brands can also be useful to identify relevant elements and characterising traits.

For Chevalier and Mazzolovo (2012: viii), a luxury brand should offer goods characterised by strong artistic content and craftsmanship, and have an international presence. Ko, Costello and Taylor (2009) reviewed a large number of academic works to define what makes a luxury brand, and identified five characterising traits: they should offer high quality goods, provide authentic value to consumers (be that in functional or emotional terms), convey a prestigious image revolving around quality but also craftsmanship, command a premium price, and be capable of inspiring a profound connection with people. Moore and Birtwistle (2005) report how other elements that literature associates with luxury brands are desirability, status, exclusivity, but also excellent customer service, strong brand identity and high brand awareness. On the other hand, Beverland (2004) proposes that luxury brands are characterised by products integrity (related to attention to detail, product quality and credibility), value-driven emergence (related to the way the brand actively pursue a luxury positioning), culture/history (related to their unique background and the skills they showcase) and marketing/endorsements (essential sources of brand awareness, prestige and sales).

When it comes to luxury fashion brands, similarly, there are different definitions. Moore and Birtwistle (2005) supplement Beverland's model (2004) and propose six traits that characterise luxury fashion brands:

- product integrity and quality control over manufacturing
- culture and heritage
- premium pricing
- marketing (recognising pivotal activities such as fashion shows, window displays, PR activities and packaging)
- endorsements
- iconic products and designs
- flagship stores and store brand concepts (in association with controlled distribution)

Fionda and Moore (2009), on the other hand, developed a model with nine traits that characterise luxury fashion brands:

- clear brand identity (to provide differentiation and entice people, based on emotional and functional values or on elements such as fashionability and heritage)
- marketing communications (to increase brand awareness through fashion shows, advertising, PR, direct marketing and celebrity endorsements but also direct communication with customers)
- product integrity (related to issues of quality, craftsmanship, attention to detail but also innovation and creativity)
- brand signature (achieved through iconic products, but also attention to packaging and livery)
- premium price (seen as essential to retain luxury status, and enforced through strategies such as limited production and controlled distribution)
- exclusivity (supported by limited editions and exclusive ranges)
- heritage (revolving around the brand's history)
- luxury environment and experience (for example through grand flagship stores and excellent customer service)
- culture (the brand's expertise in managing internal and external relationships)

Okonkwo (2007) instead lists ten core characteristics of luxury fashion brands:

- innovative, creative, unique and appealing products
- consistent delivery of premium quality
- exclusivity in goods production
- tightly controlled distribution
- a heritage of craftsmanship
- a distinct brand identity
- a global reputation
- emotional appeal
- premium pricing
- high visibility

Okonkwo, however, also adds that a luxury fashion brand needs to possess a clearly recognisable style, to create an indelible impression and to focus on their country of origin, whilst also being emotionally enticing.

These models share some common elements, as they aim to make sense of a complex industry that is seeing many of its characterising traits also being appropriated by mass-retailers or premium brands. Elements like fashion shows are being consistently used by mass market brands, that are also using communication strategies that focus on similar aesthetics. For example, H&M has created campaigns characterised by a sophisticated aesthetic in collaboration with renowned film director Wes Anderson and many brands, from Victoria's Secret to Savage X Fenty, hold fashion shows and use the same celebrities used by luxury fashion labels. They also increasingly focus on complex storytelling to create value and emotional appeal and, in some cases, have even copied the flagship store model, although so far perhaps with less grandeur.

It seems that what makes luxury fashion brands stand out is the focus on quality and craftsmanship, a very tight controlled distribution and a sense of exclusivity and prestige that is built through PR, marketing and communication strategies. A common denominator in many models also seems to be represented by price, although as discussed in the previous chapter this is problematic. In fact, luxury fashion brands have launched different lines and products that can cater to less affluent market segments, for example a chocolate bar by Armani costs just over ten Euros. However, it is important to observe that no matter how low the prices of those products may seem in comparison with the high costs of the top lines, nonetheless all the prices associated with luxury fashion brands remain at the top of their product category. This is further counterbalanced by the fact that many luxury fashion brands are currently increasing the prices of their most high-end goods, as, for example, iconic bags by Louis Vuitton have been raised recently in order to further reinforce exclusivity.

These models demonstrate the multi-faced nature of the luxury fashion industry, that nowadays operates at different price levels and involves a myriad of services and products, as discussed in more detail in the next section. Moreover, as communication and technological development have changed the way luxury fashion brands operate and promote themselves, for example through dematerialisation (see Chapter Nine and in particular section 9.4) or social media (see Chapter Eight), to anchor a definition of luxury fashion brands to material traits becomes increasingly problematic. In a constantly-changing industry, luxury fashion brands have moved towards the immaterial, as they focus more and more on the branding elements to support their aura and reputation, which is why in this book we propose a definition of luxury fashion brand based on immaterial traits.

Following a semiotic perspective, we consider luxury fashion brands as signs consisting of a signifier and signified, with the latter being the meaning, concept, or idea expressed by the former, i.e., the physical manifestations of the brand. In this perspective, luxury fashion brands are characterised by a series of intangible traits that remain constant as their signifier, the material manifestations of such elements, can change due to socio-economical shifts, technological advancements but also communication developments or any other changes affecting the industry. Our model comprises four intangible concepts that characterise luxury fashion brands in all their manifestations:

- prestige
- excellence
- exclusivity
- desirability

The notion of prestige can be supported by a variety of elements such as extravagant fashion shows, lavish flagship stores in exclusive locations, but also through PR activities and advertising campaigns that employ international celebrities to make but a few examples. This dimension of prestige focuses on ideas of status and alludes to a desirable lifestyle that can be conjured up through any luxury fashion brand touchpoints, in this sense having the potential of being conveyed through any relevant novel technological elements or communication modalities that may arise and become salient in the future.

Similarly, also notions of excellence constitute a core value of luxury fashion branding that can be expressed through different manifestations, in this sense offering a flexible meaning that can easily be adapted to new situations, markets or uses in years to come. Ideas of excellence can be linked to the quality of products associated with luxury fashion brands, be that a real of supposed one (because, as discussed previously, not all goods produced by luxury fashion brands are unique hand-made pieces crafted from rare and exquisite materials), to the history and heritage of labels (which again can be the product of clever communication and management strategies), to iconic pieces and the creativity of renowned designers, but also to customer service and the many more facets that characterise luxury fashion brands and the way they express themselves.

Also, the exclusivity theme of luxury fashion brands can be conveyed through different signifiers, for example a tightly-controlled distribution strategy, releasing NFTs, dedicated services such as private shopping, special events but also high price, although this element is problematic, as discussed in Chapter One, and therefore this trait cannot be considered enough to express exclusivity in isolation. Exclusivity can be supported through marketing and PR in a variety of different ways that can evolve over time, as for example certain communication and promotion methods are becoming less effective and more commonplace when they are appropriated by less prestigious brands, or when new media, platforms or technological tools arise.

Desirability is also a key dimension for luxury fashion brands that can be showcased in a myriad of ways through different touchpoints. It can be supported through communication and marketing strategies, for example by focusing on aspirational narratives or a covetable lifestyle, or conveyed through different means such as the characteristics of the goods produced by luxury fashion brands and the status of those who are associated with the label, be that brand ambassadors, celebrities or more broadly a wealthy clientele in the higher market segment. Again, desirability can also be expressed through other signifiers as its immaterial nature as a concept allows it to be conveyed through different methods and modalities that may emerge in the future.

Moreover, in this model we add to those four elements a fifth trait: international dimension. In fact, one characterising trait of luxury fashion brands is the fact that the four elements discussed above are recognised not only where the brand originates but also in the global market. This dimension of internalisation is a function of, and is supported by, different strategies concerning how luxury fashion brands operate, for example through different distribution channels in foreign markets, or through international PR teams, marketing and communication tactics.

The main benefit of this model is that is not tied up to the specific material traits that characterise the industry today, making it a flexible tool that can change with the times, as the luxury fashion industry evolves and responds to macro and micro changes worldwide. The model focuses on identifying defining traits that have so far remained constant in the face of such changes, as they focus on the essence of luxury fashion brands and on not their current physical manifestations and brand touchpoints.

2.5 Extending the brand

One of the main characterising elements of luxury fashion brands nowadays is represented by the fact that they do not solely sell luxury nor fashion. In fact, as discussed in section 1.5, luxury fashion brands are now associating their names to cheaper products that are accessible to many, but they are also launching new products and services in different categories that feature very high prices and are therefore only accessible by few people.

Through brand extension, luxury fashion brands expanded and created diffusion lines, sub-brands and accessories that are cheaper than the mainline products, whilst also launching fragrances, make-up, skin-care lines and eyewear collections that are accessible to many. At the same time, however, luxury fashion brands have also extended into the higher market segment by launching more collections, such as menswear and childrenswear, by offering made-to-measure services but also by creating homeware lines comprising furniture and home décor, by launching lines for pets or designing high-end sport equipment, but also by creating new spaces such as residences, restaurants, clubs, spas and hotels where an affluent clientele can live the brand (the last element is examined in more detail in section 2.6, the case study within this chapter).

Virtually all luxury fashion brands have expanded their brands in a variety of products and services, and now offer a range of options at different price points. As discussed in the case study of Chapter One, Armani has launched childrenswear, accessories, fragrances, make-up and eyewear lines, and created a number of sub-brands such as Emporio Armani and Armani Exchange that have similarly extended in those product categories. Moreover, the Armani brand has extended into home décor, restaurants, clubs, spas and even launched a flower and confectionery line. Nowadays luxury fashion brands have expanded to include almost any product one might want, and, in this sense, they can provide a complete lifestyle offering. For example, people can now buy goods that range from Yves Saint Laurent make-up and perfumes to Louis Vuitton dog carriers, from Chanel skis to Fendi bicycles, from Missoni furniture to Versace strollers, from Bulgari hotels and restaurants to Gucci Xbox game consoles, from Givenchy glasses to Dolce & Gabbana pasta. Bulgari and Versace have opened residences in London and similarly Armani residences are available in Dubai, whereas Fendi Château and Missoni Baia residences can be found in Miami.

Although brand extension has been employed more and more often in the last few years, this phenomenon has a long history. Brand extension has been pioneered in the luxury industry by French couturier Poiret, who in 1911 launched his first fragrance. Early cases are also represented by Coco Chanel, who in the 1920s created a series of fragrances, a make-up and skin-care line and also a jewellery line.

Aaker and Keller (1990: 27) observe that brand extension is appealing for brands because it offers them a way to capitalise on their recognition and reputation to enter new areas. Luxury fashion brands invest heavily in communication and marketing, and to amortise the expense on more products makes sense (Chevalier and Mazzalovo 2012). Moreover, the luxury fashion industry is characterised by high running costs, due to extravagant fashion shows, grand flagship stores in prestigious locations, not to mention the high production costs of haute couture and main lines. However, despite the outrageous expenses, those elements cannot easily be reduced, as they contribute to create the prestige and aura of the brand in the first place.

Therefore, luxury fashion brands have to amortise such costs on a larger number of products, and especially on more profitable ones. In fact, the luxury fashion industry is characterised by a great variety of margins. As claimed by Bottelli (2008), Merrill Lynch's report states that leather and shoes can reach margins of over 35% whereas watches and jewellery stand at over 29% and 21%, respectively, which dwarfs the meagre 10% margin for clothing. This explains why luxury fashion brands have expanded greatly in those areas, offering more and more accessories and leather products to boost their profits. Bottelli for example reports that Prada saw accessories' importance steadily increase, as in 2007 they represented almost 40% of profits, whereas for Gucci they represent more than half of total profits.

Brand extension, however, can be a costly business, as to launch new ventures in an area that is completely new for the brand, like cosmetics, involves acquiring new relevant expertise and new manufacturing capability. For this reason, luxury fashion brands tend to employ a specific strategy, called licensing, that allows them to reap the benefits at virtually no financial cost. Chevalier and Mazzalovo (2012) observe that licensing greatly contributes to the income luxury brands, as, for example, Balmain gets over 50% of its revenues from it, and some brands, like Calvin Klein, are mainly developed through such a strategy.

Licensing involves allowing other companies the right to use a brand name on products for a period of time in exchange of royalties, which can vary greatly and can involve one-off payments and percentages on sales. The companies acquiring the license, i.e., the licensee, manufacture goods and also usually cover advertising and marketing costs for the extensions, which is extremely convenient for the licensor. In this sense the licensor benefits as it can expand in distant categories that require specific know-how and profit financially from the extension through very limited efforts, and for this reason such a strategy is employed even by companies that otherwise focus on vertical integration like Armani (Moore and Wigley 2004: 3–4).

For the licensee the benefits are represented by lower developing costs (Keller 2008) and lower risk of failure of the new ventures, coupled with instant recognition and positive reputation deriving from the parent brand's identity (Milewicz and Herbig 1994: 39). In particular Italian luxury fashion labels have been the most active in this respect launching a large number of lines and products under the umbrella of the parent brand, capitalising on their brand image (Dallabona 2017). However, despite being profitable, such strategy can also be quite risky, especially when brands are extending into lower market segments.

There are different conceptualisations of brand extension. First, the distance from the core category where the brand originates can be considered. Category extension takes place when a brand creates a product in a distant area from the one it operates in, as seen for example when Chanel launched an eyewear line. On the other hand, line extension is created when a brand expands in the same product category, for example when a luxury fashion brand launches a second line, like in the case of Cheap and Chic for Moschino. Luxury fashion brands have extended widely and have associated their names to a broad range of products, so much so that the term brand stretching also applies. This term is used to describe extreme forms of extension where the new venture operates in a very distant category.

Moreover, issues of pricing in the extension can be considered. In fact, extensions can involve operating at a higher price level than the parent brand through upscale vertical extension, as for example in the case of Armani with the creation of the Armani Privé haute couture line. However, the most common case in the luxury fashion industry is constituted by downscale (or step-down) vertical extension, that sees the extension targeting a lower market segment to widen the brand's appeal among the middle classes and increase sales and profits. This is, for example, the case for second lines and fragrances or cosmetics ranges associated with luxury fashion brands. In literature, the riskiest form of brand extension for a luxury fashion brand is considered to be the downscale (or step-down) vertical extension, with the most emblematic case being represented by Pierre Cardin, who ended up eroding the prestige of his eponymous label by employing such strategy widely and consistently.

Pierre Cardin was a pioneer in many ways, he was the first luxury designer to collaborate with a mass-market retailer in the 1960s, was at the forefront of global expansion, and also started to adopt brand extension consistently, especially through licensing, to diversify its empire and to extend into the profitable lower market segment (Okonkwo 2007: 296–303). Pierre Cardin launched his brand in 1950, after a few years at Dior. He built a strong reputation for his artistic vision, making record profits which he invested back into his Pierre Cardin brand, that he fully owned. He created a very financially successful empire by offering a plethora of cheaper products that became available through many different outlets, but financial success came at a price, as the constant association with less exclusive goods and uses ended up eroding the prestige of his eponymous label. Okownkwo observes how the brand Pierre Cardin signed a large number of licensing agreement, allowing for the use of the brand name on different products like bags, tableware but also tiles and even toilet seats. She observed how the company had more than 900 licensing agreements in over 140 countries involving different market segments, including low and discount pricing. The constant association with cheaper and lower-quality goods affected the luxury aura and prestige of the Pierre Cardin brand, but the designer nonetheless continued with this strategy even when others, like Gucci for example, started to question its role in luxury fashion and started buying back licenses to protect their brand equity and value, as he declared that he wanted to create a brand that was not only for the ultra-rich but could be afforded by ordinary people. However, the constant downscale extension caused a loss of brand positioning, and the use of licensing also caused a loss of control over products and affected their fit within the brand universe, creating confusion over the positioning and status expectations for the brand.

Another good example of how the profitability of brand extension venture can damage the parent brand is represented by the case of the second line D&G by Dolce & Gabbana. In 1994 Dolce & Gabbana launched a diffusion line called D&G, which became very successful, Zargani (2011) reports that the line was worth approximately 400 million Euros a year and was particularly popular in Asia and Eastern Europe, where it was actually stronger than the main line. In 2009 the line was moved upscale and started to compete with the main line, cannibalising its sales. So much so that in 2011 Dolce & Gabbana closed down the D&G line, despite the investments in the second brand and the profits it made, in order to protect their core line.

However, the biggest risk in adopting brand extension is the possibility that undesirable association will weaken the brand and dilute it (Aaker 1990), which appears to be more topical for luxury brands (Lye, Venkateswarlu and Barrett 2001). Downscale extensions are particularly risky for luxury fashion brands because they could reduce perceptions of prestige and exclusivity (Phau and Prendergast 2000) and even alienate previous customer by broadening the target market (Keller 1993: 15). Truong, McColl and Kitchen (2009) state that for luxury fashion brands dilution tend to occur when less affluent market segments make frequent purchases, as this affects perceived exclusivity of labels. There are some strategies that can be adopted to mitigate the negative impact of brand extension, for example introducing a certain distance between the parent brand and the new venture (Milberg, Park and McCarthy 1997) through a slightly different brand name, like for example in the case of the Valentino RED diffusion line by Valentino.

However, any new venture created through brand extension contributes to reshaping the reputation and prestige of its parent brand, and could risk spoiling the latter through unfavourable associations or the failure of the extension (Milewicz and Herbig 1994: 39). Low congruence between the new venture and the parent brand can also be problematic (Keller 1993: 15). In fact, people might hold less positive opinions if they believe that brands are stretching too much beyond their area of expertise (Aaker and Keller 1990: 30). However, this concern is primarily associated with mass market brands, as brand extension works particularly well for brands that are widely known and appreciated by the public, as their positive traits can be more easily transferred to the new venture (Barone and Miniard 2002). Keller and Aaker (1992: 44) also note that high-quality brands can be extended further and to a more diverse range of products because their identity revolves less on material benefits and more on symbolic meanings. By evoking ideas of quality, simplicity and good taste, one can easily imagine how those values could translate the world of Armani from clothes to accessories, and then to furniture, cosmetics, confectionery and flowers but also restaurants, clubs and hotels. The latter phenomenon, the extension of luxury fashion brands into the hospitality industry, defined as luxury fashion flagship hotels (Dallabona 2015), is examined in the case study of this chapter.

2.6 Case study: luxury fashion flagship hotels

To create places where people can experience the brand in a coherent and carefully staged environment is something that many luxury fashion brands have explored. A number of cafés and restaurants have been opened by luxury fashion brands, as, for example, there are many Armani/Nobu restaurants around the world, and Gucci Osteria are currently open in Seoul, Tokyo, Los Angeles and Florence, whereas Louis Vuitton has opened cafés and restaurants in France, China and Japan. However, the epitome of this phenomenon is represented by the creation of hotels where people can actually live, in its literal sense, the brand, through what is defined by Dallabona (2015) as 'luxury fashion flagship hotels'.

Luxury fashion flagship hotels present similarities with flagship stores because they follow the same logic as they are located in prestigious locations in key cities and offer media coverage and PR opportunities to raise the profile and desirability of the brand through a place where the brand completely controls every detail. In luxury fashion flagship hotels people can explore a branded lifestyle through the five senses, as those places include at least one outlet providing food and drinks, to create a fully immersive experience that speak of the brand and its values.

The relationship between luxury fashion brands and hotels can take different forms, from occasional collaborations through curating special suites or whole hotels to business opportunities that respond to the logic of differentiating investments and that do not see the label creating a true brand extension. Many designers or labels have invested into the hospitality businesses to diversify their portfolios, as for example in Italy the Ferragamo family owns the brand Lungarno hotels whereas Alberta Ferretti launched two independent hotels, whilst in Miami Diesel's founder Renzo Rosso launched the Pelican Hotel.

Examples of occasional collaborations are the designer suites at St. Regis hotels, such as the ones curated by Dior in New York City and those designed by Bottega Veneta in Florence and Rome, but also the Vera Wang bridal suite at Hotel Halekulani in Honolulu, or the suites curated by Diane von Fürstenberg for Claridge's in London. Some collaborations involve the complete design of new or established hotels, as for example designer Karl Lagerfeld curated the Schlosshotel Vier Jahreszeiten in Berlin, the Hotel Metropole in Monaco and the Sofitel So Singapore, whereas in Paris Martin Margiela refurbished the Maison Champs Élysées hotel and Christian Lacroix the Hotel le Bellechasse and Hotel le Petit Moulin. Through these occasional collaborations hotels can gain media coverage and support their aura of prestige, luxury and sophistication whilst similar benefits, in addition to financial gain, are also experienced by the designers or labels involved.

However, only Italian luxury fashion brands have so far created true hotel brands and launched luxury fashion flagship hotels, as they were already particularly active in terms of brand extensions.

The trailblazer in this sense is thought to be Krizia, with the K Club in Bermuda which opened in the 1990s. The phenomenon of brand extension grew as Bulgari launched their own branded Hotels and Resorts, as did Versace and later on Armani, Missoni, Moschino and Fendi. As discussed by Dallabona (2017), the phenomenon reached its apex between 2004 and 2012, when eight hotels were launched. In fact, in those years Bulgari opened hotels in Milan, Bali and London, Missoni opened one hotel in Edinburgh and a resort in Kuwait whilst Moschino launched their one-off Maison Moschino in Milan and Armani opened their first hotel in Dubai, followed by the one in Milan. These hotels quickly became established, hosting celebrities and wealthy individuals from around the world, responding to the growing consumers' need for experiences whist at the same time providing attractive backdrops for social media post through their striking and distinctive design. For example, at Missoni hotels and resorts the label's signature colourful patterns, such as zig-zags and stripes, featured heavily whereas at Palazzo Versace Medusas and mosaics inspired by Ancient Greece dominated.

However, as discussed by Dallabona (2017), luxury fashion flagship hotels entered a critical phase following the financial crisis of 2008. As the market slowed down and the luxury sector suffered, many of the new hotels and resorts announced by luxury fashion brands never materialised, and some branded hotels even closed down due to vulnerabilities concerning the specific way that such brand extensions were carried.

Luxury fashion flagship hotels can be the result of different strategies, such as joint ventures like in the case of Bulgari, which developed its hotels and resorts with the Marriot International group, or partnership like in the case of Armani, that collaborated with Emaar Properties for its foray in the hotel business. But others like Missoni and Moschino employed a much riskier strategy, i.e. licensing. We have discussed in section 2.5 how licensing offers significant benefits, as for example in this case all the expenses incurred to build and manage the hotels would be covered by the licensee, with the licensor further benefitting from royalties and the provision of specific products such as linens for example. However, licensing is often associated with limited control over the new venture and can leave the licensor vulnerable to opportunistic behaviour from the licensee, that is not as committed as the licensor to grow and develop the brand.

This was for example the case for the Missoni hotel in Kuwait, as brand founder Rosita Missoni accused the management of the hotel of giving out their patterns to copy, which contributed to the decision to terminate the agreement with the Rezidor Group (now Radisson Hotel Group) in 2014. Sometimes the lack of control can have even more serious consequences. This was the case for Maison Moschino in Milan, that abruptly closed down in 2014 when the licensee went bankrupt, resulting in a very unpleasant experience for staff and guests, who were escorted out by bailiffs.

Nowadays the expansion has slowed down, the only new luxury fashion flagship hotel brand created after the golden years of 2004–2012 is represented by Fendi with its Fendi Suites in Rome. Moreover, with the closure of Missoni and Moschino hotels, licensing now has a limited role. In 2023 Versace chose not renew the agreement for Palazzo Versace in Australia, build in collaboration with development company Sunland Group, but the Dubai one, developed in collaboration with Enshaa Group, is still operating. Another shift is represented by the fact that Milan has been replaced by Dubai as the city offering more luxury fashion flagship hotels (with brands Armani, Versace and Bulgari operating hotels there). Similarly, a new focus on the Middle East and Asia has emerged, as luxury fashion brands target those rapidly growing and profitable markets. They currently feature more hotels than Europe, as in addition to Armani and Versace hotels in Dubai, Bulgari Hotels are currently available in Dubai, Bali, Beijing, Shanghai, and Tokyo. Moreover, new hotels have been announced by Versace in Macau and by Bulgari in the Maldives.

Questions and activities

- What are luxury fashion flagship hotels?
- What strategies have luxury fashion brands adopted to extend into hotels and resorts?
- Monitor the practices of luxury fashion brands and identify more forms of extension into the hospitality industry

2.7 Conclusions

Chapter Two offered an historical overview of luxury fashion brands, focusing in particular on France and Italy, and addressed the development of luxury conglomerates. Then, the chapter explored different definition of luxury fashion brands and offered a novel model that focuses on immaterial traits. Then the notion of brand extension and the way it is implemented by luxury fashion brands were discussed, identifying different contractual agreements and the advantages and downsides involved in such a strategy. The latter issue was also discussed through the case study of hotels associated with luxury fashion brands.

2.8 Revision questions

- What is the origin of luxury fashion brands?
- How can luxury fashion brands be defined?
- How have luxury fashion brands been extending their brands?

2.9 References

Aaker, D. (1990) 'Brand extensions: the good, the bad, and the ugly', *Sloan Management Review*, 31(June), pp. 47–56.

Aaker, D. A. and Keller, K. L. (1990) 'Consumer evaluations of brand extensions', *Journal of Marketing*, 54(1), p. 27.

Barone, M. J. and Miniard, P. W. (2002) 'Mood and brand extension judgments: asymmetric effects for desirable versus undesirable brands', *Journal of Consumer Psychology*, 12(4), pp. 283–90.

Beverland, M. (2004) 'Uncovering "theories-in-use": building luxury wine brands', *European Journal of Marketing*, 38(3/4), pp. 446–66.

Bottelli, P. (2008) 'Only energy beats luxury in profitability' *Il Sole 24 Ore*. Available at: http://www.luxury24.ilsole24ore.com/ModaStili/2008/02/analisi-lusso-energia-english_1.php?

Chevalier, M. and Mazzalovo, G. (2012) *Luxury brand management: a world of privilege*. Hoboken, NJ; Chichester: John Wiley and Sons.

Dallabona, A. (2015) 'Luxury fashion flagship hotels and cultural opportunism: the cases of Hotel Missoni Edinburgh and Maison Moschino', *Hospitality and Society*, 5(2–3), pp. 117–43.

Dallabona, A. (2017) 'The challenges of luxury fashion flagship hotels: the case of Maison Moschino', *Critical Studies in Fashion and Beauty*, 8(2), pp. 219–37.

https://doi.org/10.1386/csfb.8.2.219_1

Djelic, M. L. and Ainamo, A. (1999) 'The coevolution of new organizational forms in the fashion industry: a historical and comparative study of France, Italy, and the United States' *Organization Science*, 10(5), pp. 622–37.

Donzé, P-Y. (2018) 'The birth of luxury big business: LVMH, Richemont and Kering', in Donzé, P-Y. and Fujioka, R. (eds.) *Global luxury*. Singapore: Palgrave.

Fionda, A. M. and Moore, C. M. (2009) 'The anatomy of the luxury fashion brand', *Journal of Brand Management*, 16(5–6), pp. 347–63.

Keller, K. L. (1993) 'Conceptualizing, measuring, and managing customer-based brand equity', *Journal of Marketing*, 57(January), pp. 1–22.

Keller, K. L. (2008) *The new strategic brand management: building, measuring, and managing brand equity*. London: Kogan Page.

Keller, K. L. and Aaker, D. A. (1992) 'The effects of sequential introduction of brand extensions', *Journal of Marketing Research*, 29(1), pp. 35–50.

Ko, E., Costello, J. P. and Taylor, C. R. (2019) 'What is a luxury brand? A new definition and review of the literature', *Journal of Business Research*, 99, pp. 405–13.

Lye, A., Venkateswarlu, P. and Barrett, J. (2001) 'Brand extensions: prestige brand effects', *Australasian Marketing Journal (AMJ)*, 9(2), pp. 53–65.

Milberg, S. J., Park, C. W. and McCarthy, M. S. (1997) 'Managing negative feedback effects associated with brand extensions: the impact of alternative branding strategies', *Journal of Consumer Psychology*, 6(2), pp. 119–40.

Milewicz, J. and Herbig, P. (1994) 'Evaluating the brand extension decision using a model of reputation building', *Journal of Product and Brand Management*, 3(1), pp. 39–47.

Moore, C. M. and Birtwistle, G. (2005) 'The nature of parenting advantage in luxury fashion retailing–the case of Gucci group NV', *International Journal of Retail and Distribution Management*, 33(4), pp. 256–70.

Moore, C. M. and Wigley, S. M. (2004) 'The anatomy of an international fashion retailer–the Giorgio Armani Group', in *British Academy of Management (BAM)*. St. Andrews, UK.

Okonkwo, U. (2007) *Luxury fashion branding: trends, tactics, techniques*. Basingstoke: Palgrave Macmillan.

Phau, I. and Prendergast, G. (2000) 'Consuming luxury brands: the relevance of the Rarity Principle', *The Journal of Brand Management*, 8, pp. 122–38.

Steele, V. (2003) *Fashion, Italian style*. New Haven-London: Yale University Press.

Truong, Y., McColl, R. and Kitchen, P. J. (2009) 'New luxury brand positioning and the emergence of Masstige brands', *Journal of Brand Management*, 16(5–6), pp. 375–82.

White, N. (2000) *Reconstructing Italian fashion: America and the development of the Italian fashion industry*. Oxford: Berg.

Zargani, L. (2011) 'Dolce and Gabbana said mulling D&G options', *WWD: Women's Wear Daily*, 201(44).

3 Strategic Challenges for Luxury Fashion Brands

Case study: Burberry

Alice Dallabona

CHAPTER OBJECTIVES

This chapter:

- explores how brand equity is managed
- examines how luxury fashion brands respond to change
- discusses brand rejuvenation, repositioning and rebranding

3.1 Chapter summary

The chapter investigates the strategic challenges faced by luxury fashion brands with regards to creating and maintaining brand equity and value. In this sense, different definitions of brand equity are discussed, and the models of Aaker, Keller and Kapferer are examined in detail. Moreover, the chapter investigates the strategies that luxury fashion brands have adopted in order to respond to changes in business and society. With regards to this, the chapter examines how luxury fashion brands have evolved, identifying different management models emerging in France, Italy and the USA, and also addressing how conglomerates are reshaping the industry in a variety of ways. Moreover, the chapter further examines the many challenges luxury fashion labels have to navigate due to the ever-changing global scenario. Finally, the chapter addresses what happens when luxury fashion brands don't respond effectively to change, leading to a decline in brand equity. In this sense different strategies such as brand rejuvenation, repositioning and rebranding are explored. These issues are further examined through the case study of Burberry.

3.2 Introduction

This chapter focuses on the challenges involved in maintaining brand equity and brand value in the luxury fashion industry. Despite initial financial success and worldwide recognition, a number of luxury fashion brands have been unable to respond to challenges and have

DOI: 10.4324/9781003264811-5

disappeared, as in the case of the House of Worth, or remained active but no longer among the top players, like in the case of Patou, whereas some, like Gucci, have been able to overcome difficulties and recover. Others, like in the case of Pierre Cardin, faced serious question about what their brand value is as their positioning had changed. Pierre Cardin notoriously declared that he was willing to sell his company for a Billion Euros, claiming that his wide empire was actually worth much more due to his aggressive and financially profitable licensing strategy, but the claims were met with scepticism, as some observed that the luxury aura of the Cardin brand had been diluted and therefore was not as valuable.

3.3 Managing brand equity

To calculate the value of a brand is a complex task, which is why, in the case of acquisitions, specialist firms are employed and lengthy negotiations take place behind the scenes. Brand equity can ultimately be considered as the value of a brand, and is both a function of its financial success and of the way in which it is perceived by consumers or the general public. Several theorisations have emerged in this sense, and in the following section the key brand equity models by Aaker (1991), Keller (2003), and Kapferer (2004) are examined.

Aaker's model (1991)

Aaker (1991) defines brand equity as the function of the assets and liabilities associated with a brand, that he divides into five categories: brand loyalty, name awareness, perceived quality, brand associations and other proprietary brand assets. They all contribute to create value for customers, as they influence the information people hold about the brand and the way it's processed, and affect both confidence in purchasing and customer satisfaction. This means that, for example, people who hold in high regards the brand Chanel are more likely to be satisfied with their purchase.

To maintain brand equity requires efforts and investments, but it's essential to retain customers and attracting new ones, for example through promotion as people are more willing to try something new if it's from a brand they know and trust. Positive brand equity supports premium pricing, which is a pivotal issue in luxury fashion, and can help reduce the marketing and communication costs aimed at supporting brand positioning. Positive brand equity can be also used by brands to support brand extension, provide leverage in distribution channels, and to gain competitive advantage, especially when they have a strong association with a specific product and sector, like, for example, in the case of Hermès for scarves and foulards.

Aaker considers brand loyalty both as a contributing factor and the result of brand equity, and also states that all brand equity dimensions are interrelated. Brand loyalty is a very valuable asset because it's costly to attract new customers, but relatively inexpensive to retain current ones, provided they are satisfied with their experience with the brand. Loyal customers are less willing to switch to competitors and provides sales, and this can also offer leverage in retailing as people expect certain brands to be available. Name awareness is another important factor, as positive brand equity is associated with a place in consumers' mind.

Perceived quality also positively affects brand equity, and can support extension in other sectors. Positive brand associations can offer competitive advantage and even provide a barrier for competitors, as, for example, the association between Louis Vuitton and luggage contributes to the brand's leading position in the field. Other proprietary assets, such as patents, trademarks or channel relationships also contribute to create brand equity. Last, Aaker proposes that to estimate the value of brand equity one needs to consider the price premium that the brand can command, the impact of the brand name over consumer preference, the replacement value of the brand, its stock price and its earning power.

Aaker's 1996 model

In a later model, Aaker (1996) identifies ten key measures, in addition to financial information such as sales, margins and profits, that can support the assessment of brand equity. Those are divided into five categories, loyalty measures, perceived quality/leadership measures, associations/different measures, awareness measures and market behaviour measures.

Aaker considers brand loyalty to be closely intertwined with premium price, as devoted customers are prepared to spend more to purchase products from their preferred brands. In this sense, customer satisfaction also plays a role. Perceived quality can influence return of investment (ROI) and stock returns, and is associated with not only functional benefits but also with issues of leadership and popularity, as people tend to assume that a leading brand has merit and tend to value popular brands.

Associations and differentiation measures relate to the value people attribute to the brand, the brand personality and the relationship it creates with customers but also to organisational associations. On the other hand, awareness measures focus on the knowledge people have about a brand and the importance they place on it, whereas market behaviour measures focus on the market share that characterises a brand, its market price and distribution coverage.

Keller's model (2003)

Another pivotal model of brand equity was developed by Keller. Keller (2003) observes that brand equity is affected by brand architecture, requires long-term vision, and can be difficult to maintain in different geographic areas, cultures or market segments. Keller proposes different steps, or building blocks, that brands need to undertake to reach significant brand equity.

For Keller the bottom of the pyramid is represented by salience, that measures brand awareness and the ability to recall the brand in different circumstances, creating associations with the brand name, its logo, symbols, etc. Salience helps people to associate a brand to a specific product, category or need. The second step in building brand equity concerns the creation of brand meaning, and involves a more rational side, i.e., performance, and a more emotional side, i.e., imagery, that are created through people's experiences or indirect contact with the brand.

Performance relates to customer experience and is informed by brand communication and marketing, and comprises five traits:

- primary ingredients and supplementary features (the level that the products operate in)
- product reliability involving consistency of performance over time, durability of product and serviceability (how easy it is to repair the good)

- service effectiveness (how well a brand satisfies consumer needs), efficiency (how quick and responsive the service is) and empathy (concerning how a brand is seen as caring and trustworthy)
- style and design, which influence performance
- price, as people create a hierarchy of brands in their own mind based on pricing and discount policies.

On the more emotional side, brand imagery considers intangible brand aspects such as:

- user profiles (imagery related to the real or idealised users of a brand)
- purchase and usage situations (based on how and when people use the brand)
- brand personality and values (based on the traits people attribute to a brand)
- brand history, heritage and experiences (associations based on a brand's past and people's specific interactions with it).

The next step of the pyramid comprises a more rational side, brand judgements, and a more emotional side, brand feelings. Brand judgement represents customers' evaluations of a brand and, among the many possible options, Keller considers four to be particularly important:

- brand quality (usually based on the products and benefits of a brand in terms of perceived quality and customer value)
- brand credibility (how credible people consider the brand in terms of brand expertise, trustworthiness, and likeability)
- brand consideration (whether people would actually consider buying a brand's products)
- brand superiority (how people consider the brand to be unique and better than other brands).

Brand feelings are the emotions evoked by a brand, which can also involve people's feelings about themselves and others. Emotional responses can be very powerful in creating a relationship with customers, and represent a valuable tool to create brand equity.

At the top of Keller's pyramid, we find brand resonance, representing the maximum possible identification with a brand. It comprises two dimensions, the intensity of the bond and the level of activity stimulated by this loyalty, that are articulated into four categories. First, behavioural loyalty (translating in repeat purchases and how substantial and frequent they are), second, attitudinal attachment (representing how the intensity of the bond translates into loving the brand), third, a sense of community (people's identification with a brand can create a sense of community, that can also be experienced online) and last active engagement, representing the ultimate affirmation of brand loyalty, which sees people actively pursuing different ways to engage with a brand in a way that may influence others too.

Kapferer's model (2004)

The last model of brand equity we consider was developed by Kapferer. Kapferer (2004) highlights how consumer and financial issues are interrelated in creating brand equity, as financial value is built upon a series of elements and starts with brand awareness. Kapferer theorises brand equity in terms of progressing from brand assets, to brand strength and brand value.

Brand assets are the sources of influence a brand can use, and comprise brand awareness, brand reputation (that can be based on benefits or attributes such as the know-how associated with a brand), perceived brand personality, perceived brand values, reflected customer imagery, brand preference or attachment and, last, patents and rights. Brand assets are created in time through consumer's mental associations, interactions and experiences with the brand in question.

Kapferer considers brand strength as originating in the brand assets discussed above, but this can change at different times or in specific markets. Brand strength can be seen in a series of indicators such as market share, market leadership, market penetration, share of requirements, growth rate, loyalty rate, price premium and the percentage of product the trade cannot delist. Last, brand value is conceptualised by Kapferer as the ability of a brand to drive profits, based on its assets and mediated by its specific market strengths, and the economic value added (EVA) that a brand can deliver in the future.

3.4 Responding to changes in business and society

What all the previous models have in common is the fact that they outline how brands need to develop strategies and actively work not only to grow brand equity, but simply to sustain it, whilst navigating the challenges and opportunities deriving from changes in business and society worldwide. As luxury fashion brands now operate in a number of sectors, market segments and in different countries, to adapt to change can be problematic as it now involves a myriad of elements and practices that need to be adapted. In this sense, the luxury fashion industry has been shaped by a variety of events that have influenced product development, marketing, promotion and communication, management and distribution strategies, ultimately causing seismic shifts that have disrupted established associations and practices.

For example, during and right after World War II a series of challenges in terms of design and productive capabilities emerged. Many materials became scarce or unavailable, forcing brands such as Ferragamo to explore the use of previously overlooked elements such as raffia to satisfy demand. Moreover, the war also disrupted exports, and the primacy of French fashion started to be challenged by brands that developed in main markets like the USA but also Italy. The latter, in particular, gained status quickly thanks to attractive pricing, less formal designs and investment in modernising production methods.

Corbellini and Saviolo (2009: 106-7) observe how ready-to-wear took off in the 1970s due to the partnership of Italian luxury fashion brands, like Armani, and manufacturing companies, resulting in high-quality products that costed a fraction of haute couture pieces. The authors also discuss how a new middle segment, demi-couture, has emerged to bridge the gap between a declining haute couture, associated with extremely high costs and long production times, and a rising ready-to-wear that is more readily available, cheaper (costing one tenth of haute couture) and nonetheless able to retain uniqueness and sensory appeal.

Chevalier and Mazzalovo (2012: 56) also observe how the scarcity of French manufacturers that could produce ready-to-wear further stimulated the rise of Italian luxury brands, which focused greatly on that segment and capitalised on the rise of the middle-class. Chevalier and Mazzalovo however state that nowadays even ready-to-wear is rarely profitable, as, for example, it involves expensive prototypes and significant production costs that are not amortised through enough sales, so that luxury fashion brands have to rely on other products where margins are higher, like accessories. Despite generating limited profits, however haute couture and ready-to-wear are still essential in terms of retaining an aura of creativity and providing prestige that can be capitalised on in different products categories. In fact, Corbellini and Saviolo (2009: 106) report the words of Perre Bergé (the co-founder of Yves Saint Laurent), who declared that luxury fashion houses like Chanel or Dior will abandon haute couture altogether if they could still sell the same amount of cheaper products without their first lines.

As the context changed, luxury fashion brands developed different strategies to support their brand equity. Djelic and Ainamo (1999) claim that luxury fashion brands from different countries (France, Italy and the USA), developed three different network types in their move towards greater flexibility and modularity. The authors discuss how France had been able to create a stable and predictable environment through the formalisation of the Chambre Syndicale de la Haute Couture, that prevented competitors to join the sector but also hindered innovation, as fashion houses remained small businesses focusing on handmade production that relied on a small, homogeneous and mostly loyal group of customers mainly consisting of aristocracy and upper-middle classes.

The opportunities associated with the rise of the middle classes were seized by Italy and the USA, that developed successful brands focusing on ready-to-wear. French labels reacted to this either by creating umbrella holdings (developing different lines and products to create different and relatively autonomous entities, paving the way for the conglomerate groups like LVHM or Kering) or by focusing on outsourcing production and licensing (especially for fragrances, accessories and ready-to-wear), facing the risk of diluting their brands.

Djelic and Ainamo state that the Italian model was substantially different, originating in industrial districts of small and medium enterprises that worked in synergy in specific areas. This manufacturing capacity was a significant contributing factor in the success of Italian luxury fashion brands, as they could easily deal with variations in consumer demand without affecting quality. This was for example the case for Gucci, that in the 1990s under designer Tom Ford was able to become successful again by focusing on quality products from reliable partners, and by adopting a coherent restructuring of all lines and products. The US model is, on the other hand, rooted in mass production, with brands like Ralph Lauren and Donna Karan being able to scale up their image through a focus on branding and by enforcing strict quality control, as they keep minimal activities in-house and outsource in a variety of areas from design to advertising.

Corbellini and Saviolo (2009: 132–6) observe that luxury fashion brands that are part of conglomerates can benefit from access to the capital market and expedite listing on the stock market, can access top quality management, whilst also gaining leverage with suppliers and distributors and better supporting international growth through monobrand retail. Donzé (2018) observes that independent luxury fashion brands may struggle to compete with luxury conglomerates in this sense, as, for example, LVHM went from 1280 to 3708 directly owned stores between 2000 and 2014, whilst Kering went from 196 to 1186 in the same years.

Conglomerates also have the means to sustain the significant costs involved in marketing and communication, for example extravagant fashion shows, grand marketing campaigns with sought-after celebrities, or lavish flagship stores. Conglomerates can segment demand

and target similar customers with different products while retaining the integrity of their brands, and can better support brand growth as the losses of a label can be compensated by the strong performance of others.

However, this seem to be the case only if the conglomerates are strongly invested in a brand as, for example, in 2021, after operating for just two years, LVMH closed down the Fenty fashion house, which they created in collaboration with Barbadian superstar Rihanna, as it didn't perform as well as expected. The costs of creating new luxury fashion brands are very onerous, and conglomerates are more capable of sustaining them, for example Stella McCartney was created in 2001 as a joint venture with Kering. It is however generally believed that independent luxury fashion companies can react more quickly when challenges arise, although they may need to seek external funding to support and expand their brands.

With the development of the oil industry in the Middle East, the economic growth of Asia and the fall of the Berlin Wall, luxury fashion brands started to develop a global presence, resulting in increased sales and profits. Many European luxury fashion brands are now operating more stores in emerging markets than in their home countries. However, Djelic and Ainamo (1999) observe that this strategy also involves some challenges as demand becomes less homogeneous and brands have to adapt to local practices and situations. For example, the flagship model and customer services can differ in some countries due to customer expectations (see also Chapters Five and Eight), local distribution issues can provide a barrier to online sales, whereas difficulties navigating cultural sensibilities can also damage brands (see section 10.5).

As luxury fashion brands developed a global presence, they had to satisfy the needs of customers living in warmer climates, and therefore cruise collections (also known as resort collections) increased in number and became more popular. Initially launched in the 1920s as a way to provide appropriate clothing to wealthy customers from the northern hemisphere that were travelling to warmer destinations during winter, now cruise collections provide an important stream of revenues for luxury fashion brands. They are presented through lavish fashion shows that usually don't take place where the main lines are showcased, as, for example, Chanel debuted its lines in Cuba and Dubai, and not in Paris like usual.

Moreover, technological developments like the internet changed the mediascape, disseminating new trends to an international public quicker than ever before and making people crave novelty at a much higher rate. This, coupled with developments in manufacturing processes, made it easier for mass-retailers to copy luxury fashion designs and to deliver their products before the originals became available. This forced luxury fashion labels to engage more and more with lines that are available immediately (such as cruise, capsule and flash collections) to renew their offerings and retain people's interest.

In turn, this changed the way luxury fashion brands operate, moving away from two seasonal shows towards regular drops of new lines, with wide repercussions on production processes but also marketing and communication strategies. Corbellini and Saviolo (2009: 108) highlight how luxury fashion brands now have to balance a number of novel lines and products whilst retaining a clearly identifiable individual style, for example for Prada that would be minimalism and research on materials, or for Armani simplicity and neutral colours such as greige. They also observe that luxury fashion brands are also focusing more and more on their heritage, typical patterns and iconic products to reassert their identity and support their recognisability in different markets. A generational shift also occurred, as luxury fashion brands started to focus more and more on younger consumers with ad hoc strategies, for example embracing digital communication and marketing (see Chapter Eight), but also dematerialisation and a more extensive use of technology to engage consumers (see Chapter Nine).

Moreover, as luxury fashion brands have lowered their entry level in order to capitalise on the less affluent market segments and associated their names to a variety of cheaper goods, from beauty lines to eyewear, they have started to compete with premium brands. Corbellini and Saviolo (2009: 127-8) define premium brands as a heterogeneous group of companies that operate in the medium to high price segment and that adopt strategies usually associated with luxury fashion brands in terms of distribution, marketing and communication, for example by producing fashion shows or using controlled distribution. They observe how many premium brands originate in industrial know-how and expanded from wholesale, in some cases even building a portfolio of brands as, for example, the Aeffe Group owns Alberta Ferretti, Moschino, Pollini and also licenses Jean Paul Gautier and Bluegirl among the others, similarly in this sense to Diesel that though Staff Internationals owns or license brands like Dsquared, Maison Martin Margiela and Vivienne Westwood.

As a result of the competition with premium brands, luxury fashion brands had to evolve their strategies in order to retain distinctiveness and support prestige and desirability, for example by focusing on grander flagship stores and PR events, launching interactive exhibitions but also through a new focus on experiences. In fact, the shift towards experiential marketing has caused luxury fashion brands to look at different ways to engage and entertain their public, for example by creating pop-up shops and bars but also developing the flagship format into a place where customers can stay all day. For example, at the Armani flagship in Milan people can shop all collections and products, have coffee, buy a book at Armani/Libri (that specialises in fashion and design books), purchase a flower arrangement at Armani/Fiori or a box of chocolates at Armani/Dolci, before moving on to the Armani/Privé club and rest at the Armani hotel.

Moreover, in order to further differentiate themselves from prestige brands, luxury fashion brands have engaged with personalisation and customisation. For example, Louis Vuitton offer customers the possibility to feature monograms on their leather goods, but also the opportunity to personalise them with travel sticker-style designs (in line with the heritage of the brand as a luggage maker). The label also offers the chance to engrave initials on perfume bottles and perfume travel cases. Burberry, on the other hand, offers the opportunity to customise its iconic trench coat by choosing style, fabric, lining, buttons and embroidery, whereas Gucci offers engraving on a wide selection of goods, from bags, to belts, and from stationary to pet collections. By offering personalisation and customisation, luxury fashion brands can convey a more personal caring approach to their customers, and satisfy people's need for differentiation in a globalised world where offerings are becoming more and more similar.

Furthermore, the need to elevate the status of luxury fashion brands to cater to the higher market segment whilst at the same time supporting differentiation from premium brands has also seen luxury fashion labels engage more and more with their heritage, but also art. For example, Ferragamo and Zegna have company museums where people can learn about the labels, and a number of brands such as Chanel and Dior have launched museums exhibitions around the world. In addition, luxury fashion brands like Louis Vuitton have collaborated with artists on special products or projects, and even launched their own art foundations, such as the Fondazione Prada in Milan, or the Fondation Louis Vuitton in Paris (Grassi, Swindells and Wigley 2019).

Moreover, as society becomes more aware of certain ethical issues (in terms of providing social standing) luxury fashion brands have engaged more with charitable causes. For example, a number of brands support breast cancer awareness month and the Elton John AIDS foundation. Giorgio Armani has supported a variety of causes, as, for example, in 1992 it raised funds for the Italian AIDS foundation. In 2002, Giorgio was named Goodwill Ambassador by the United Nations High Commissioner for Refugees (UNHCR) for his support in the Afghanistan crisis, and in 2010 the brand collaborated with Green Cross International and UNICEF to support a clean drinking water initiative, whilst also participating and launching a number of initiatives with regards to sustainability (see Chapter Eleven).

These initiatives aim to support the prominent role of brands in society and to reinforce their aura and prestige through patronages, although by associating to charitable causes and goodwill brands can also deflect criticism. In this sense, luxury fashion brands have progressively engaged with other issues that have become topical, like diversity and inclusivity (see Chapter Ten), and have been particularly active with donations and through diverting production during the COVID-19 pandemic.

The COVID-19 pandemic caused a drastic contraction in sales, and accelerated some shifts within the luxury fashion industry. First, lockdowns and restrictions forced physical stores to limit capacity or close, leading to a growing interest in online shopping, although challenges were also experienced in this sense as the pandemic also disrupted distribution, supply chain and production. Moreover, the restrictions also shaped product design, as the fact that millions of people were confined at home led to a decline in occasion wear and forced luxury fashion brands to engage more with casualwear, loungewear, and more generally with the notion of insperiences.

In this sense, luxury fashion brands focused on goods people may need to have a cosy and comfortable experience at home, with products ranging from Hermès throw blankets, to Prada candles or Louis Vuitton cashmere loungewear trousers. At the same time, luxury brands also focused on developing a more personal relationship with customers, as, for example, the Fondation Louis Vuitton launched a series of online events to engage the public through art and music.

3.5 Brand rejuvenation, repositioning and rebranding

As discussed in the previous section, there are many changes and challenges with regards to business and society that luxury fashion brands have to navigate, and it can be difficult to retain positioning, thrive and expand in this sense. Moreover, inevitable events such as the death, or retirement, of the designer-founder can be challenging for luxury fashion brands. This was, for example, the case for Chanel that, before being led to new heights under Karl Lagerfeld, had faced some troublesome years, leading many to lose hope that the brand could have a comeback. Lagerfeld strengthened the legacy of Coco, reinterpreting the brand's symbols and motifs in a way that resonated with new audiences, and introduced new lines that performed extremely well.

However, luxury fashion brands have to constantly put in significant effort even to simply remain at the same level. If luxury fashion labels do not change with the times, evolving their marketing and communication practices, adapting their designs and strategies to accommodate new trends and markets, their brand equity will be affected, with the worst possible outcome in this sense being represented by the complete demise of the brand.

It has been claimed in literature that brands are like living organisms, characterised by birth, growth and maturity, before reaching decline. Brands are very costly to launch and establish, and even when declining they usually still feature some equity, which is why companies prefer to focus on sustaining and relaunching labels instead of closing them down and start afresh with a new brand.

There are a number of signs that a brand is facing decline, for example a diminished brand awareness, poor performance, loss of market share, and loss of competitive advantage and distinctiveness. In this phase, more and more customers are switching to competitor brands as their bond with the brand has weakened, leading to a sustained decline in sales. During decline, luxury fashion brands may be tempted to resort to licensing and create cheaper lines in order to increase turnover and profits, however this strategy is generally considered risky if not associated with a strong strategic focus, because it can improve the situation temporarily but does not solve the underlying problems.

When declining, brands may lose their positioning and need significant effort to return to their former glory. A declining brand is not able to successfully attract new market segments, and relies primarily on loyal clients, leading to vulnerability as numbers can dwindle further, for example due to customer age or if core clients decide to abandon the brand in favour of more appealing competitors.

Kapferer (2004: 451-3) identifies many signs that a brand is declining, which are grouped in seven categories:

- insufficient preparation for the future (a brand lacks planning and is not actively focusing on maintaining brand equity, for example by failing to register trademarks for new products and services, by not investing enough to support the brand development, or by not thinking about how societal changes might provide opportunities and challenges)
- insufficient dual management (a brand sees most sales originating from a limited number of individuals, and focuses more on existing customers, of increasing age, and not enough on reaching new segments)
- insufficient capacity to capture growth pockets as they emerge (meaning that a brand retreats into itself, focusing on its heritage and current offerings in an excessive brand coherence, without innovating its products or following consumer trends and demands)
- insufficient relevance (labels can lose their relevance by not having clear brand values that are expressed effectively through different touchpoints, and by having clients that are only moderately satisfied and therefore may not make repeat purchases)
- insufficient vitality at contact (that happens if brands don't refresh and keep relevant their logos, visuals, packaging or store environments, and don't offer good customer

services, in addition to not engaging effectively in terms of merchandising, marketing and communication)
- insufficient self-stimulation (brands don't try to entice or surprise the general public or the media, don't stage events or engage with opinion leaders and celebrities)
- insufficient staffing (with a significant presence of older managers and a marked lack of diversity).

Luxury fashion brands have to constantly move on with the times to be successful, and to try gain new customers without alienating the current ones, which can be challenging. For example, Chevalier and Mazzalovo (2012: 151) observe how the new direction of Louis Vuitton, launched in 1997 with designer Marc Jacobs, was not initially well received as many struggled to see how the brand's values could be retained. However, the new collections were successful and guaranteed valuable media coverage (which was also supported by the opening of many new stores around the world) by reinterpreting key values of tradition and nostalgia, excellence and the art of travel (further enhanced by the launch of a series of books on the subject) in a way that resonated with a younger audience without alienating core customers.

In literature, brand rejuvenation and revitalisation are often used as synonyms, and refer to a phase in the life of a brand that is focused on increasing brand equity after having experienced poor performance for some time. At this stage the focus is on revamping the brand and breathing new life into it. Scholars identify a range of strategies that can be effective in this phase, ranging from refreshing visual elements to the complete rethink of brand identity.

Kapferer (2004: 438–50) considers revitalisation as the complete update of a brand's offerings to support new growth and relevance, and highlights how a challenging element is constituted by identifying what part of brand identity (such as iconic products for example) are to be reinforced to reach the objective.

Kapferer (2004) also suggests a series of strategies to rejuvenate a brand:

- redefining the brand essence (in fact if the brand has declined it means that it has lost relevance to consumers, in addition to positive associations or elements for differentiation, a situation that can be overcome by focusing on identifying brand values that are more aligned with the target market)
- revitalising through new uses (because to target a new market segment a brand needs to do things differently, for example by supporting new user occasions or adopting new marketing strategies)
- revitalising through distribution change
- revitalising through innovation (for example by creating new products that are specifically designed to be appealing to the new market segment)
- revitalising through segmentation (for example different sub-brands and lines can be created to attract new segments whilst not alienating their current clientele)
- revitalising by contact with opinion leadership
- revitalising through 360° communications (a brand makes the most of a variety of tools and strategies to increase brand awareness, for example through global advertising and PR events or through celebrity endorsement)
- changing the business model (as, for example, to rely too much on limited numbers of products can prove challenging if there is a drop in sales).

Some brands can be more vulnerable to brand decline, as they may be too closely associated with an aesthetics that is no longer considered fashionable. As discussed by Corbellini and Saviolo (2009), this was the case for Italian brand Missoni. Missoni gained recognition in the 1960s thanks to distinctive colourful knitwear featuring patterns like stripes and zigzags, and thrived for years but struggled in the 1990s as fashion embraced minimalism. Missoni had to rethink its product ranges, introduced solid colour pieces and monochrome zigzags to fit in with the new aesthetics, but also had to invest heavily in directly operated shops to support sales and profits.

To fight decline, many luxury fashion brands resort to restructuring their company and try to improve their internal processes, but this may not be enough and a relaunch may be necessary to try to save the brand, as in the case of Gucci. Chevalier and Mazzalovo (2012: 156) observe that Gucci in 1992 hired designer Tom Ford, who created a new identity for the brand based on core values of quality and craftsmanship that were revitalised with a focus on seduction and Hollywood glamour, successfully renewing the brand's customers, that had dwindled significantly in the 1980s.

In those years, the brand had undermined its credibility and prestige by adopting licensing in product development and distribution, leaving Gucci with little control over the products bearing its name. However, since the 1990s, Gucci changed its method and focused on regaining control in a variety of areas, from manufacturing to real estate management. Chevalier and Mazzalovo (2012: 156) discuss how the relaunch was so successful that the business volume went from around 140 million Euros in 1992 to over 1.5 billion in 2001 and over 2.5 billion in 2010, which made it possible for the company to acquire other brands and to develop its own conglomerate (now operating under the Kering name). The brand reinvented itself again in 2015 when designer Alessandro Michele became creative director and created a new whimsical identity for Gucci, making the ready-to-wear line extremely successful again through eclectic pieces that took inspiration from a variety of sources.

Brand rejuvenation and revitalisation can overlap with the notions of rebranding, as the term is not only used in cases where the name of a brand has changed or its logo completely overhauled, but also in cases where those elements have been tweaked and the connection with the old brand has not been lost. In the luxury fashion industry, slight changes are not rare and introduced at pivotal moments such as mergers and acquisitions, changes in business model or organisational structures, as seen, for example, in the case of Ferragamo and Dior as they lost the first name of their founders.

Sometimes logos are refreshed to respond to new visual trends, as, for example, many elaborate visuals have been recently changed into more simple designs, leading to a situation labelled as 'blanding' and characterised by the adoption of less distinctive but more modern fonts which simplified logos, such as in the case of Balmain and Burberry. Some have even lost their special characters, as, for example, Celine lost its accent. However, people can have strong opinions and develop significant attachments to the luxury fashion brands they favour along with their symbols, as seen, for example, in the uproar and social media backlash following changes.

In this sense the case of Yves Saint Laurent is emblematic, as when, in 2012, the brand was renamed Saint Laurent Paris under Hedi Slimane, many were not aware that it was supposed to be a return to the label's roots by adopting the same Helvetica font and a more similar name to the one used for the brand's very first fashion show, presented as Saint Laurent Rive Gauche (see also section 7.6 for a discussion of the PR scandal that followed the relaunch of the brand). Despite the backlash, the rebranding was successful and sales increased significantly.

By adding the city of origin to the label's name it was possible to capitalise on the interest for traditional European luxury fashion brands in emerging markets, despite the fact that the Saint Laurent brand actually moved its headquarters to Los Angeles. The new logo also symbolised the move towards a more quiet luxury, and the brand introduced a permanent collection featuring iconic pieces like the motorcycle jacket, further referencing and capitalising on the past. However, there is still some confusion as the brand is now associated with different names, as the full name Yves Saint Laurent is still used in the beauty sector, and the Yves Saint Laurent beauty brand is owned by L'Oréal.

Another case of rebranding is constituted by Hugo Boss, that has recently split into two labels, Hugo and Boss, and aims to target younger consumers by completely overhauling brand touchpoints and collaborating with Senegalese-Italian social media sensation Khaby Lame, who featured in campaigns and co-designed special collections.

3.6 Case study: Burberry

A good example of a luxury fashion brand that has worked hard to regain its brand equity is represented by Burberry, that has changed products and practices to overcome difficult moments and has demonstrated a continued commitment to explore novel strategies in order to create value.

The brand Burberry was founded in Basingstoke (UK) in 1856 and was soon renamed Burberry's. It gained notoriety thanks to the invention of gabardine, a durable waterproof fabric that was adopted by the British Army and became popular with explorers and adventurers alike, contributing to the reputation of the iconic trench coat. In the early 1900s, Burberry started to operate internationally, and gained further notoriety and status when its trench coat featured in iconic Hollywood films like *Casablanca* and *Breakfast at Tiffany's*.

Burberry's retail network greatly increased after the acquisition of the company by Great Universal Stores in 1955, that also licensed the brand widely, especially in Asia. This led to a series of setbacks, as licensing facilitated the creation of counterfeits, causing the brand's characteristic check pattern to become overexposed and leading to brand dilution. In the United Kingdom the brand became ubiquitous among football fans and the 'chav' subculture, eroding the prestige and status of the brand. Asia came to represent a primary market, with dramatic consequences when economic crisis hit Japan in the 1990s (Moore and Birtwistle 2004). Burberry was a brand in decline, but in the late 1990s and early 2000s underwent a major revitalisation, as examined by Moore and Birtwistle (2004).

Moore and Birtwistle (2004) discuss how Burberry in the late 1990s faced significant challenges. At the time, Burberry relied on a small base of core products, owned a

retail network based within non-strategic locations, had an inconsistent wholesale distribution strategy that saw the brand being sold in a variety of retail environments of
varying quality, experienced parallel trading to non-approved distributors and stockists,
did not effectively control its licensees creating issues with regards to inconsistencies
in prices, design and quality, whilst also under-investing in corporate infrastructure.
The brand had lost its lustre, so much so that at the time Burberry was available from
over 60 different stores in central London but not in any luxury department stores
such as Harrods or Selfridges.

In 1997, Rose Marie Bravo became the CEO and was tasked with repositioning the
brand in the luxury segment. This started by changing the name back to Burberry and
introducing a more contemporary logo and packaging, opening a flagship store on New
Bond Street (an exclusive retail location where leading luxury brands like Chanel and
Dior are also present) and launching advertising campaigns featuring leading models
and shot by famed photographers. Second, Burberry focused on extending their offerings to compete with the ranges offered by leading luxury brands and aimed at moving
the brand upwards by introducing the high-end fashion line Burberry Prorsum under
designer Christopher Bailey.

Burberry also started to regain control over their licensees, acquiring their Spanish
one and securing greater control over its Japanese ones. In terms of brand distribution,
Burberry closed down unprofitable stores and terminated relationships with a number
of wholesalers and stockists that were deemed not in line with the new upscale brand
identity pursued. This, Moore and Birtwistle (2004) further observe, caused Burberry
to increase turnover and profits by 263 and 630%, respectively.

Burberry in this sense adopted a new successful business model. With regards to products, Burberry worked on extending their range and focused in particular on continuity
items that are not seasonal, like the trench, to minimise exposure to changes in consumer
preferences. At the time, the Burberry universe comprised six brands at different levels:
Burberry Prorsum as the first line, with a renewed focus on spring/summer collections
to adapt to warmer climates, two further Burberry London lines created especially for
Spain and Japan, in addition to three diffusion lines, the Thomas Burberry range targeting young adults (initially launched only in Spain but then made available also in Europe),
plus Burberry Blue and Burberry Black, sold exclusively in Japan. The aim was to offer
maximum market coverage and flexibility to adapt in their stronger markets.

With regards to manufacturing and sourcing, Burberry focused on maintaining control of the different collections that were designed by the London team or overseen by
them if designed by teams in Spain and Japan. Moreover, Burberry also worked with a
select number of suppliers, but retained control of all materials bearing its trademarks
(the brand also owns fabric weaving capabilities). Quality control was the key to coor-
dinate internal and external manufacturing, and licensing was used only in categories
where specific expertise is needed such as perfumes, eyewear or watches (although
in Japan licensing was used for designing, manufacturing and distribution). Logistics
were also mainly managed in-house.

With regards to distribution channels, Burberry developed four retail formats: flagship stores in London, New York, Barcelona and Tokyo (owned by licensee), owned retail stores, department store concessions and a series of designer outlets and factory stores around the world. The focus was to maximise control over brand experience and profits and to minimise risks by having the full offering only available in a handful of flagship stores and devising a strategy to manage excess stock. A strong network of international wholesalers and licensees in Japan further provided market coverage at minimal costs. All marketing and communications were managed by Burberry at their London headquarters, with a focus on international prestigious publications, lavish events and advertising, and proactive PR to increase media coverage and brand awareness.

The new approach worked, and Burberry increased brand equity, elevating their brand and increasing market share. However, as discussed by Robinson and Hsieh (2016), in the mid-2000s Angela Ahrendts was appointed as the new CEO as new challenges emerged, leading to a new strategy. A difficult trading environment and a global recession were cited by Burberry as the reasons for restructuring its supply chain, which led to the closure of some plants in the UK that had become unsustainable.

In fact, costs and market pressures led Burberry to pursue single product manufacturing to maximise production economies of scale, but this also created vulnerabilities. Controversy ensued, the closure of a plant in Wales saw celebrities burn their trench coats in protest, and a similarly star-studded campaign to 'keep Burberry British' was launched. Nonetheless, Burberry moved production abroad and delegated more responsibilities to overseas manufacturers, leading to a loss of operational control.

Ahrendts, however, reassured that the iconic trench coat would continue to be made in the UK (alongside another core product, i.e., cashmere scarves), and the brand continued to focus on their heritage and Britishness in their communication. For example, in 2015 the Queen's First Battalion Grenadier Guards took part in an event in Los Angeles. When Christopher Bailey became CEO, he pioneered the see-now-buy-now model, which had an impact on the company's supply chain strategy. He also aimed at regaining control of the brand's global image by terminating licensing agreements in Japan, and brought children's lines back in-house.

In the 2010s, to further raise the profile of the brand and rejuvenate it, Burberry pioneered the use of digital communication in response to a loss of net profits, the expansion of lines and an incoherent global marketing strategy (Straker and Wrigley 2016). As examined by Phan, Thomas and Heine (2011), Burberry was the first luxury fashion brand to broadcast a show live and in 3D on social media and, with the aim to attract younger customers, spent over 40% of its overall advertising budget on digital media.

Burberry was the first luxury fashion brand to offer shoppable Tweets, and also launched two platforms not focused on selling, Burberry Acoustic offered people the opportunity to listen to upcoming musicians (discreetly wearing some Burberry items) whereas 'the Art of the Trench' is a company-owned social media platform where people can upload their photo wearing their Burberry trench coat and join the community.

As observed by Straker and Wrigley (2016), Burberry aimed to make the most of different touchpoints to convey a coherent brand identity, and launched digital campaigns focusing on eliciting an emotional response in consumers to reinforce the relationship with its public and support loyalty.

As discussed by Mastropetrou and Bithas (2021), technology was a pivotal part of Burberry's rebrand. The company redesigned its website, introduced labels with radio frequency identification (RFID) and even created an internal platform that facilitated communication between staff, suppliers and other stakeholders. Burberry devised a digital strategy centred on storytelling, the use of new technology such as augmented reality and, more generally, on consumer-facing content and digital partnerships. For example, in this sense Burberry integrated the Farfetch operating system and made all inventory available there, enhancing its global distribution.

More recently, Burberry further updated its image; in 2019 a new logo and monogram pattern was devised, changing the name to Burberry London and dropping the equestrian knight, whilst using the initials of the founder to develop a design meant to substitute the traditional Burberry check one, which had been used more and more sparingly (at times even being eliminated from collections due to unfavourable associations).

However, this change of direction was not met with unwavering support, and in 2023 Burberry changed its logo again, modifying the font and re-adopting the equestrian knight logo containing the word Porsum (that had been first registered as a trademark by Burberry in 1901) to support differentiation and emphasise the heritage and history of the label, alongside its Britishness, in this sense recognising the value of such intangible traits to provide differentiation and prestige, and their ability to drive sales.

Questions and activities

- What issued caused Burberry to decline?
- What strategy did the company adopt to rejuvenate the brand?
- Select a luxury fashion brand and compare and contrast the strategies it has adopted in this sense.

3.7 Conclusions

The chapter considered different strategies to manage brand equity and addressed the challenges that luxury fashion brands have to navigate in terms of business practices and societal changes. Moreover, the chapter examined how extensions into the lower market segments and the rise of premium labels have changed the face of competition, whilst also addressing the importance of adapting to changes in society in order to remain relevant and attract customers. The last section of the chapter focused on what happens when things go wrong, exploring different strategies such as brand rejuvenation, repositioning and rebranding and their role in fighting brand decline. The theoretical concepts outlined with regards to the latter were illustrated through the case study of Burberry.

3.8 Revision questions

- What is brand equity?
- What are the challenges luxury fashion brands have to face?
- What is brand rejuvenation, repositioning and rebranding?

3.9 References

Aaker, D. A. (1991) *Managing brand equity: capitalizing on the value of a brand name*. New York: Free Press.

Aaker, D. A. (1996). *Building strong brands*. New York: Free Press.

Chevalier, M. and Mazzalovo, G. (2012) *Luxury brand management: a world of privilege*. Hoboken, NJ; Chicester: John Wiley and Sons.

Corbellini, E. and Saviolo, S. (2009) *Managing fashion and luxury companies*. Milan: Rizzoli Etas.

Djelic, M. L. and Ainamo, A. (1999) 'The coevolution of new organizational forms in the fashion industry: a historical and comparative study of France, Italy, and the United States', *Organization Science*, 10(5), pp. 622–37.

Donzé, P-Y. (2018) 'The birth of luxury big business: LVMH, Richemont and Kering', in Donzé, P-Y. and Fujioka, R. (eds.) *Global luxury*. Singapore: Palgrave.

Grassi, A., Swindells, S. and Wigley, S. (2019) 'The art foundations of luxury fashion brands: an exploratory investigation', in Carlotto, F. and McCreesh, N. (eds.) *Engaging with fashion*. Amsterdam: Brill Rodopi.

Kapferer, J. N. (2004) *The new strategic brand management: creating and sustaining brand equity long term*. Kogan Page Publishers.

Keller, K. L. (2003) *Strategic brand management: building, measuring, and managing brand equity*, 2nd edn. Boston, MA: Pearson Education.

Mastropetrou, M. and Bithas, G. (2021) 'Digital transformation in the luxury industry', in Saksas, D. P., Nasiopulos, D. K. and Taratuhina, Y. (eds.) *Business intelligence and modelling: unified approach with simulation and strategic modelling in entrepreneurship*. New York: Springer.

Moore, C. M. and Birtwistle, G. (2004) 'The Burberry business model: creating an international luxury fashion brand'. *International Journal of Retail and Distribution Management*, 32(8), pp. 412–22.

Okonkwo, U. (2007) *Luxury fashion branding: trends, tactics, techniques*. Basingstoke: Palgrave Macmillan.

Phan, M., Thomas, R. and Heine, K. (2011) 'Social media and luxury brand management: the case of Burberry', *Journal of Global Fashion Marketing*, 2(4), pp. 213–22.

Robinson, P. K. and Hsieh, L. (2016) 'Reshoring: a strategic renewal of luxury clothing supply chains', *Operations Management Research*, 9, pp. 89–101.

Straker, K. and Wrigley, C. (2016) 'Emotionally engaging customers in the digital age: the case study of "Burberry love"', *Journal of Fashion Marketing and Management*, 20(3), pp. 276–99.

Part II

Luxury Fashion Retail and Consumer Behaviour

4 Luxury Fashion Consumer Behaviour

Case study: The Millennials market

CHAPTER OBJECTIVES

This chapter:

- examines who are the consumers of luxury fashion brands
- considers the drivers of luxury fashion consumption
- explores the differences between mature and emerging markets in terms of luxury fashion consumption

---

4.1 Chapter summary

Chapter Four examines issues related the consumers of luxury fashion brands, a multifaceted group resulting from a variety of factors. The chapter examines the first models that were created to make sense of luxury consumption, focusing on notions of class and status. In this sense the seminal work of Veblen is considered, before moving on to Bourdieu and Leibenstein. Then the chapter examines how notions of class have been challenged by the concept of lifestyle. Moreover, contemporary drivers of luxury fashion consumption are explored, discussing their features and roles in supporting the purchase of luxury fashion goods and their desirability. Furthermore, differences between mature and emerging markets, in particular China and India, are also examined. Finally, a case study is proposed, investigating the characteristic traits of millennial consumers.

4.2 Introduction

Luxury fashion has long been used by those at the top of the social hierarchy to convey power and status. For example, in Roman times only the Emperor was allowed to wear a particular shade of red, and in Indonesia certain Batik patterns were reserved solely for the royal family. Sumptuary laws have been introduced in the past to protect the distinction of

DOI: 10.4324/9781003264811-7

the elites by preventing other classes from acquiring the same goods, for example limiting the type of fabrics or trimming allowed. The issues at play here originate from the fact that luxury consumption means so much more that what luxury goods are made of, as it's not only their material characteristics that make them desirable, but the fact that they are symbols that represent something else and are capable of conveying complex social messages (Appadurai 1986: 38).

For a long time, to identify and devise strategies to attract and retain luxury fashion consumers was a relatively straightforward exercise, as people accessing those goods were a relatively homogenous group, namely the very rich. However, as we have seen in previous chapters, nowadays luxury fashion brands are associating their names to less expensive goods and widening their target market so much that the luxury fashion consumer could be almost everyone.

Of course not every person can have access, as even the cheaper facets of luxury fashion brands are out of reach for a high percentage of the world's population, but, nonetheless, the number of luxury fashion consumers has increased massively in comparison to 50 years ago. Chevalier and Mazzalovo (2012: 119) observed that half the population of developed countries are now luxury consumers. In developing countries middle classes have emerged as a new source of potential clients whilst a rapid economic growth is also leading to increasing numbers of very affluent consumers.

4.3 From class to lifestyle

Many theories have been developed to make sense of the consumption patterns of luxury goods. They have evolved as societies have changed in view of new opportunities and challenges in the market. The first models to emerge with regards to consumption of luxury consider socio-economical factors, and originate from a conceptualisation of society as a stratified entity characterised by a one-way legitimacy pattern. In this sense, we examine here the pivotal role of Veblen and consider its influence over the theories on consumption developed by Leibenstein and Bourdieu.

Veblen, in his seminal 1899 work, developed a model to make sense of the luxury consumption patterns seen in a stratified society where those at the top of the social hierarchy, i.e., the leisure classes, were using different ways to display their wealth and social standing. Veblen observed the specific behaviour of individuals who showed their wealth and prestige by emphasising their leisure practices, in opposition to those who had to work in order to sustain themselves.

They employed a specific consumption pattern that involved significant displays of wealth, that he termed conspicuous consumption, involving the constant and substantial purchase of luxury goods that were out of reach for the majority of the population. Those luxury goods in this sense were signs that showcased and cemented their place in society, as by purchasing luxury goods such as expensive garments they were signalling their status to others.

Moreover, the leisure class was also employing another practice, termed conspicuous waste, which saw them showcasing a nonchalant attitude towards the very same goods that signalled their social standing. In this sense, by displaying a less than caring attitude towards extremely expensive goods, that can go as far as their destruction, people demonstrate their high purchase power as they showcase how luxury consumption is commonplace and unremarkable for them, reinforcing the difference with those for whom such purchases are exceptional.

For Veblen, luxury consumption is used to demonstrate exclusivity and status by the higher classes, and their consumption pattern is adopted as a model by the lower classes, that yearn to be able to achieve social distinction by emulating their consumption practices. In this sense, the model only works in one direction as the lower classes emulate the higher classes and desire the goods that they purchase, but as they achieve that then such luxury goods lose their ability to convey status and prestige, leading those at the top of the social hierarchy to look towards new goods that can convey prestige and exclusivity. This leads to a constant cycle, because as the lower classes catch up and acquire goods that were the exclusive domain of the higher classes, the higher classes move on to other luxury goods as they strive to maintain status and distinction.

Veblen's model is still applicable in the luxury segment nowadays, and is especially important in countries characterised by a stratified society, but later theories have also developed to make sense of other elements that have emerged in society. Veblen theorises that consumption of luxury is driven by invidious comparison and pecuniary emulation, as people aim to distinguish themselves from the lower classes and their visible symbols by emulating the consumption patterns of the higher classes to demonstrate social standing. This means that social legitimacy is associated only to the higher classes, which demonstrate control over matters of taste, and implies that the lower classes simply adopt the taste of those at the top of the social hierarchy.

However, Bourdieu (1984) rejects this one-way model and argues that different classes don't necessarily share the same taste. Different classes look at different things when purchasing goods because they don't possess the same cultural capital. Bourdieu defines cultural capital as something that can be acquired not only from educational institutions, as it is the product of the specific circumstances of individuals, and can be acquired indirectly through one's social upbringing and the knowledge one is exposed to through life experience.

Bourdieu (1984: 278) observes that luxury goods are selected and selective, as they are selected by the higher classes as signs to convey distinction and social standing, but at the same time those luxury goods select their own audience in the sense that only those who possess a specific cultural capital would showcase the capacity to properly appreciate and consume them (Bourdieu 1984: 281). This is, for example, the case for luxury fashion brands like Bottega Veneta, that has based its recognisability on specific elements such as the intrecciato pattern, but also for other brands, like Louis Vuitton, that have recently launched more discrete products and embraced the quiet luxury trend, removing big logos and visible signs to create goods that would be recognised only by connoisseurs.

In this sense, luxury fashion goods require knowledge and competence in order to be recognised as such and provide social distinction. Veblen's trickle-down model argues that the lower classes always try to emulate the higher ones by copying their consumption patterns and implies that different classes share the same taste, but Bourdieu argues that each class has its own particular taste and a cultural capital that results in a different display of social stratification. According to Bourdieu's theory, consumers from different classes would showcase preferences for certain goods and brands and not necessarily adopt the taste of the higher classes, and in this sense wouldn't follow their consumption patterns. However, Bourdieu also recognises that not every taste and consumption pattern possesses the same social legitimacy, as it's often those at the top of the socio-economical hierarchy who are associated with power and status and whose cultural capital is considered to be more desirable by others.

Leibenstein (1950), recognises the impact of Veblen's theory when identifying a series of different patterns of consumption. He states that a Veblen effect occurs when consumer demand is driven by the high price of goods, as, for example, one would be driven to purchase a Chanel handbag over a Moschino one based on the fact that the former is more expensive, in order to signal wealth and status. However, Leibenstein also argues that there are other drivers and theorises two other consumption patterns, that are influenced by other people's consumption patterns. A bandwagon effect occurs when people buy goods because others are already buying them, whereas the snob effect on the contrary occurs when people avoid certain goods precisely because they are purchased by, and are associated with, others. At play here are the psychological needs to conform and the one to stand out.

In the models discussed above, the main factors considered were of socio-economical nature, and a strong focus was placed on notions of status and class when addressing why people consume luxury. However, it has been claimed that recently a disaggregation of social structure into lifestyles has been taking place, and in this respect the relationship between social class and consumption has become more complex. In this sense it is claimed that distinction from, and belonging to, a group is no longer seen primarily as a function of elements like social class or education, but of lifestyles that cut across the social hierarchy, especially in Western countries (Trigg 2001). This has caused a seismic shift in advertising and communication strategies, as the notion of lifestyle becomes the culturally dominating paradigm in public discourse (Kress and Leeuwen 2001).

Moreover, new salient characteristics have been identified as contributing to luxury fashion consumption, as the impact of social constructs and also psychological elements and individual differences drive contemporary practices, as examined in the following section.

4.4 Drivers of luxury fashion consumption

The widening of the luxury market to include not only the most affluent segments of society, and the sharp increase in global wealth driven by Asia, has resulted in a complex scenario, where different, and at times conflicting, elements are driving consumption. Contemporary luxury fashion consumers differ greatly in terms of spending power, knowledge and motivation, but there are some common elements.

First, frequency of purchase and the kind of goods acquired can be considered. High-net-worth individuals buy often and can access the most expensive facets of luxury fashion brands but can also afford to buy everyday items like plain T-shirts or socks made by luxury brands, whereas consumers in the lower segments display different consumption patterns.

Chevalier and Mazzalovo (2012) identify two different types of luxury consumers that emerged from the downward expansion of luxury brands, namely excursionists, and new consumers. Excursionists belong to the lower-middle-class, they are generally careful about their spending but would purchase luxury goods occasionally. Excursionists value goods that are expensive, scarce or difficult to obtain, they expect high-quality products and services, as they want their shopping experience to be pleasurable and memorable, hence supporting the need for impeccable customer service in the luxury fashion industry. New customers are defined as those who purchase goods based on their individual situation, focusing on a mix and match approach that would see them consume luxury and mass-market brands at the same time. They are driven by hedonic values and expect goods that provide a multisensory experience, and are attracted by the sophisticated shop atmosphere of luxury retailers, their exclusive locations and affluent clientele. They favour brands that align with their own values, and don't display strong brand loyalty.

Gifting is also a major driver of luxury fashion consumption, as luxury fashion goods are often considered as an appropriate way to celebrate special occasions or the achievement of personal milestones. Moreover, contemporary luxury fashion consumers display a series of traits revolving around socio-cultural changes and macro trends.

Okonkwo (2007) theorises that, first, luxury fashion consumers nowadays have access to an abundance of information on brands, their values, their products and performance, and are able to assess and compare offerings in a very knowledgeable manner. Second, luxury consumers are now aware of their role, as a power-shift saw them become the authority in the field, as a saturated market with myriad of brands coupled with a variety of offerings, and also shopping channels, means that switching costs are lower. Moreover, luxury consumers are becoming more individualistic and demanding, expecting excellent customer care, individual attention and customisation.

Furthermore, luxury consumers also have high expectations when it comes to the products they buy, for example in terms of quality of materials or their origin. Besides, luxury fashion consumers nowadays have a disposable attitude, they are used to a flow of new products and trends, and no longer display strong loyalty to a single brand. Last, nowadays luxury consumers are characterised by strong values and principles, and prefer to associate with brands that align with their views.

For example, sustainability has recently emerged as a driver of luxury fashion consumption. As discourses of sustainability (see Chapter 11 for a more detailed discussion) are becoming increasingly widespread, more consumers are exposed to the reality of what their consumption means in terms of environmental and social impact and expect brands to adopt less harmful practices, forcing luxury brands to engage with the issue. Initially, luxury fashion brands were not very active nor particularly open in declaring what their sustainability practices entailed, as they were wary of accusations of greenwashing and of potentially alienating clients, as sustainable materials, and especially recycled ones, were initially perceived negatively, in terms of not possessing the attributes of high quality and desirability that people expected from luxury goods.

However, because sustainability concerns became more common and the market share for sustainable goods rose, and because some consumers buy sustainable goods to achieve status and to enhance social standing, more and more luxury fashion brands are associating their names to virtuous products and practices. Other values that are becoming more and more important drivers of consumption concern ethical elements such as diversity, inclusivity and charitable causes. In a new mediascape where social media can make scandals go viral in a matter of hours, luxury fashion brands have to adopt a series of strategies to showcase their ethical credentials, supporting charitable initiatives and good causes, and act swiftly to avoid scandals (see also Chapter Seven).

At the same time, luxury fashion brands have to deal with lower levels of brand loyalty among consumers, supported by lower switching costs, and the constant need to entice people with new products and engaging content. In the luxury fashion industry we are seeing increasing competition for market share between luxury fashion brands, but now labels also have to contend with premium brands, that often mimic their communication and marketing tactics. This is forcing luxury fashion brands to create more costly and flamboyant campaigns and events, for example lavish store openings and opulent events with a plethora of celebrities.

Looking at contemporary drivers of luxury consumption, it seems that four variables are at play. Dhaliwal, Singh and Paul (2020), theorise in their review of luxury consumption research that consumption is initially driven by personal factors, such as income, knowledge and personality. Moreover, psychological factors such as beliefs, perceptions and attitudes, in addition to socio-cultural factors such as living in an individualistic or collectivist culture, play a significant part in the way people consume luxury. Last, they argue that people buy luxury because of specific traits related to luxury products and brands, such as heritage, country of origin, prestige and brand image.

In this sense, as luxury fashion brands try to widen their consumer base to boost profits, they have at the same time to reinforce their desirability by projecting narratives emphasising their uniqueness and exclusivity through their products (for example in terms of rare materials and excellent craftsmanship), and practices (for example through extravagant fashion shows and celebrity ambassadors). Luxury fashion brands have to convey a sense of belonging to a world of privilege by adopting the practices that consumers expect from those labels, but, at the same time, they need to provide differentiation and a sense of identity based on values such as tradition and history, like for example in the case of Hermès, but also country of origin like in the case of Dolce & Gabbana.

Luxury fashion brand consumption has also been associated in literature with the desire to create or maintain one's self-identity, following the seminal work of Belk (1988), who argued that possessions both contribute to, and are a reflection of, one's identity. In this sense, luxury fashion goods can be considered as an extension of one's personality, a way to send a message to others about who a person is or who it aspires to be. In this sense, services like personalisation and customisation services offered by the likes of Louis Vuitton and Gucci can satisfy people's desire for individuality, meet their preferences and create a stronger brand relationship.

It has been observed that in Western countries luxury consumption is driven mainly by individualism, as the socio-cultural focus is on people's uniqueness and needs, whereas in collectivist countries there is a greater focus on the social self. Another element to take into consideration is the level of materialism of specific consumers, which revolves around the importance people attribute to possessions. It has been claimed that materialism is becoming less important in Western countries and more prevalent in developing countries, but nonetheless individual attitudes can vary greatly, and materialism can contribute both to create and enhance self-identity and to project group identity.

Hedonism is another important driver of luxury fashion consumption, as people pursue the pleasure of buying desirable goods characterised by material traits (such as quality) and immaterial ones (for example those related to heritage), to treat themselves. More generally, the emotional dimension of luxury consumption is seen as pivotal. Luxury labels fuel attachment and emotional responses through their marketing and communication campaigns, fostering a dimension of closeness and desirability to create a bond with consumers. At the same time, hedonism is also reshaping the luxury fashion industry, because as people move on to experiences to satisfy their needs for pleasure, fun, excitement and beauty, brands need to provide people with spaces like restaurants or hotels where they can live special moments. At the same time, we see a shift towards insperiences as consumers also use luxury fashion more and more at home, both online and in real life. For example, in order to attract consumers' attention, luxury fashion brands are experimenting with gaming (see 9.5 for a more detailed discussion), developing products and spaces where people, in particular younger demographics, can engage with the brand.

Moreover, luxury fashion consumption has also been theorised in terms of being spontaneous and unplanned, related to treating oneself, and often occurs abroad or whilst on holidays. In particular, purchases by tourists represent a big share of sales in European luxury stores, and were severely affected by travel restrictions during the COVID-19 pandemic. At the same time, however, luxury consumption has also been associated with more pondering, as consumers tend to seek more information and think longer before purchasing a luxury item in opposition to non-luxury items (Bughin 2010).

Furthermore, although there are similarities, consumer behaviour and motivation for luxury consumption can vary in different geographical areas for a number of reasons. For example, in Europe the population is getting older, whereas the median age of the luxury fashion consumer in Asia is significantly lower, and this has an impact on shopping patterns and marketing preferences, shaping luxury fashion brands' strategies. At the same time, individualist and collectivist countries are characterised by opposite values, as the main drivers of luxury consumption revolve, respectively, around individual gratification and the need to stand out, in opposition to the will to conform and showcase status for the relevant groups. The characteristics of emerging Asian markets are examined in more detail in the following section. Moreover, the Millennials market segment is analysed in more depth through a case study.

4.5 Emerging markets

For a number of years the primary market for luxury fashion brands has been represented by Europe and the US, but also by the international elites, until rising economies and ease of travel led to an internalisation drive which saw brands reach unprecedented numbers of consumers, and boost sales and profits.

The first emerging market for luxury fashion was Japan. The country saw a sharp economic rise in the 1970s that opened up new possibilities for luxury fashion brands, and Japan became a primary driver of internationalisation for luxury fashion brands. Japan is now a mature market for luxury fashion, sharing some common characteristics with Western countries such as an ageing population. Nonetheless, Japan is still one of the largest markets of luxury fashion brands, Chadha and Husband (2006) note that Japan used to account for at least 40% of worldwide sales for most luxury fashion labels, at one point representing almost 90% of the sales of Louis Vuitton, the majority of which were made by tourists abroad. The Japanese market is characterised by specific traits that luxury fashion brands have to indulge to make the most of the country's potential.

Chevalier and Mazzalovo (2012) for example observe how the Japanese purchase more leather goods than North-American customers, and favour ready-to-wear, so much so that they represented 30–40% of worldwide sales for French and Italian luxury fashion brands. Whereas in Japan womenswear is the most popular category, China is still more oriented towards menswear, as it was the main driver when luxury brands started to operate in that market (although womenswear is quickly rising in importance). Luxury fashion brands often focus on sensuality in their communication and products, but in markets such as Japan, and more generally in Asian countries, their most provocative goods and campaigns do not fit in with societal values, shaping what merchandise is made available there and the labels' marketing and communication strategies.

Chadha and Husband (2006) consider Japan as belonging to the last stage of a luxury consumption model, one that sees luxury become a way of life. They theorise that in Asia a five-stage model sets the trajectory for the next emerging markets. They argue that the massive wealth growth in Asia resulted in an increasing number of extremely affluent clients, but also a growing middle class that can afford the less expensive facets of luxury fashion brands. For example, throughout Asia the majority of luxury fashion consumers may not be able to buy the most exclusive bags, but would be able to purchase small and less expensive items such as wallets or belts, and other entry-level goods.

Asia is characterised by strong collectivist sentiments, which means that brands are mostly purchased because everybody buys them, and individual preferences are considered less important drivers. In Western countries, luxury fashion consumers are primarily driven by individualistic values, but in collectivist cultures other elements are more relevant. This is supported by the importance of the concept of 'face', which means that conforming to social norms, also in consumption terms, is considered important to support not only one's status and prestige but also the one of their family or group.

Wong and Ahuvia (1998) argue that in collectivist societies consumption is influenced by a more interdependent self-concept that focuses on relationships with others, for example in terms of family, culture or profession. Moreover, collectivist societies see a bigger focus on group needs, resulting in a desire to conform, which is further reinforced by the higher legitimacy of group affiliation and a stronger sense of hierarchy than in Western countries.

In this sense, if in Western countries the over-diffusion of a luxury brand or product has a negative effect over its desirability, on the opposite in collectivist countries consumption of luxury is driven by popularity of goods and brands, as the rarity principle does not seem to apply in the same way (Phau and Prendergast 2000). For example, the fact that the Louis Vuitton Monogram Bag appeared to be ubiquitous in the early 2000s (also through the significant proliferation of fakes) made it lose desirability and status in Western markets, as people saw it as commonplace and no more associated to ideas of exclusivity and prestige, whereas in Asian markets the bag's popularity drove further sales.

At the moment China is the main emerging market for luxury fashion brands, but when labels started to enter the market there were considerable difficulties and costs, initially due to high taxes and the need to employ agents. Moreover, due to the high costs involved in opening stores and establishing the brands in a country where there was little to no brand awareness, the first luxury fashion brands to expand in China didn't see much profit or were initially even operating at a loss. Pioneers in creating lavish events to promote their brands in China were Pierre Cardin with a fashion show at the Temple of Heaven and Laura Biagiotti with a show in the Forbidden City in Beijing.

Of course now the situation is very different, Bonetti, Perry and Fernie (2017) observe that by 2011 China became the second largest market for luxury brands after the USA, dethroning Japan, but, as observed by Chadha and Husband (2006), there is still major potential for this market. In fact, as the country moves from stage 3 (the show-off stage), to one where luxury becomes more and more widespread within society and can reach the majority of the population, luxury fashion brands can expect even more growth and bigger profits.

Chadha and Husband (2006) observe how Zegna was one of the first luxury fashion brands to enter China in 1991, and is nowadays one the most popular menswear labels there. Louis Vuitton followed in 1992, but the potential of the market was recognised by a number of brands, which advertised there even before their products were available in China. Chinese nationals are drawn to Western luxury fashion brands because they are recognised internationally as symbols of status and power, and are in this sense particularly sensitive to the provenance of the goods they buy, which can be problematic for luxury fashion brands.

Chadha and Husband (2006) report that many luxury fashion brands have moved their production abroad to cut costs, for example to places like Western Europe (Armani makes 18% of the Armani Collezioni there, whereas Prada has shoes manufactured in the area), Egypt and also China (for example there Celine produces its Macadam handbag line and Hugo Boss makes some suits). Nonetheless luxury fashion brands tend to send to Asia products that are made in Europe, as those made elsewhere do not possess the same aura of desirability within that market. Ironically, however, Chinese nationals may still end up purchasing goods that are made abroad when buying luxury fashion goods while travelling in Western countries (as a significant percentage of sales there is represented by Asian tourists).

Corbellini and Saviolo (2009) observe that China represents over 50% of total sales for LVMH and 45% of foreign sales for Gucci, and that the 'Made in the West' appeal is a strong driver of consumption. Chinese nationals want to buy European luxury fashion precisely because of its difference, as Armani learned in 2001 when the brand opened a store in Beijing featuring a red lacquer door as a tribute to China. This door was not perceived positively and the brand later opted to replace it with the same door style it used in stores elsewhere. In a country where brand awareness is still low, and people are not always familiar with the history of brands their country of origin, it's the fact that labels are recognisable as being from the West that convey status. For example, Louis Vuitton made a wise move in associating itself with Western luxury since entering China by launching, in 1997, a touring exhibition focusing on the history and heritage of European luxury that created a positive association in consumers' mind. This association was further cemented the following year through the Louis Vuitton Classic China Run, a rally taking a number of vintage cars throughout rural China that helped spread the message within the country.

Bonetti, Perry and Fernie (2017) observe that, despite some recent challenges, China remains a key market. In fact, the country was affected by the stock market crash of 2014, leading to the depreciation of the Yuan and to a financial crisis that greatly affected the population. Moreover, luxury fashion sales were also affected by the growing crackdown on corruption. However, a third of worldwide luxury purchases are still made by Chinese consumers, either directly or through Daigou. Daigou sales are purchases made abroad on behalf of consumers in China, and are popular as a way to avoid hefty taxation and benefit from more product choice, but is a grey market that luxury brands are trying to fight by lowering prices to align them with prices in Europe.

The country is also experiencing a rapid rise in brand awareness, as brands reap the rewards of years of costly communication and marketing campaigns. Conglomerates are also heavily promoting their smaller portfolio brands, such as Loewe and Saint Laurent, in China to boost sales and profits. Chinese consumers are also displaying new consumption patterns, as some people abandon conspicuous consumption and become interested in more subtle and less showy goods, like for example the Louis Vuitton bag with no logo created in 2013.

To engage and connect with such a profitable market has become a priority for luxury fashion brands, that upon entering the country had to invest heavily in marketing and communication, and especially through lavish flagship stores and events, in order to make an impression and convey an aura of desirability and prestige. Moreover, luxury fashion brands have engaged with Chinese traditions and festivals in order to create a connection with consumers, trying to retain their identity whilst creating a rapport and showcasing understanding and appreciation for Chinese culture (although some brands have been less successful in this sense, as examined in Chapter Ten, where the case study examines the controversy created by Dolce & Gabbana).

As the median age of the wealthy is significantly lower in China than in Western countries, and social media use became increasingly commonplace, luxury fashion labels have also rapidly adopted the most popular digital tools there. This was pivotal, as in a collectivist society where luxury consumption is significantly influenced by other people's consumption patterns and by recommendations among peers, social media marketing plays an important role.

If China was characterised by low brand awareness and luxury fashion brands had to invest heavily to establish their brand and capture people's imagination, on the other hand, in India, brand awareness for luxury fashion brands was already high, as links to the West and ease of travel resulted in consumers being familiar with labels long before they became available in the country.

Chadha and Husband (2006) observe how the rapid growth of China's sales led luxury fashion brands to enter the Indian market despite many difficulties. One key obstacle was represented by restrictions on imported goods, for example leather, that severely impacted the ability of brands such as Louis Vuitton to enter the market. But even now that restrictions on imports have been lifted, rigorous checks on materials and especially colours mean that operating in the country can still be challenging. For example, Corbellini and Saviolo (2009) report how bureaucracy and checks on textile colours means that for a brand like Missoni, that is known for its very colourful pieces, to get products into shops at the right time could be problematic, as a piece with over 16 shades could remain in customs for up to four months.

Another barrier to luxury fashion brand expansion in India is represented by high taxation, as hefty duties on imported goods leave labels facing the dilemma of either maintaining the same price featured abroad, hence affecting profits, or passing the burden and the costs on to the consumer, increasing prices but risking alienating customers, especially as many Indian people are used to shopping abroad. Moreover, another challenge for luxury fashion brands entering India is to find a suitable retail location because, as examined in Chapter Five, the structure of Indian cities does not allow for the flagship model to be implemented, so that luxury fashion brands had to open stores inside prestigious hotels in key cities instead. However, lack of space and increased competition have proved to be barriers to expansion and market growth in India.

Moreover, restrictions on foreign investments and the need to find local partners to enter the market proved to be similarly problematic. Louis Vuitton opened its first flagship store in 2003 in Delhi, and a few year later became the first label to own a majority stake in its Indian distributor when the Indian government allowed for an increased level of direct investment by foreign companies.

However, for those who entered the Indian market early, the rewards were significant. In this sense the case of Tommy Hilfiger is emblematic, as the brand was one of the first to enter the Indian market in the early 2000s, and for that reason was able to develop a strong reputation, achieve visibility and prestige and capture a significant market share while simultaneously positioning itself as a more luxurious label. In fact, in Western markets Tommy Hilfiger is not considered to be as exclusive as it is perceived to be in India, where sales and profits are substantial.

In line with the tactics adopted to conquer the Chinese market, luxury fashion brands have similarly pursued lavish events and raced to secure the most sough-after celebrities as brand ambassadors. Corbellini and Saviolo (2009) observe that Indian consumers are demanding and expect luxury fashion brands to convey a sense of prestige and exclusivity in all touchpoints and through impeccable customer service. In terms of the areas with most potential, menswear seems to play a pivotal role, as traditional womenswear fashion styles are preferred for special occasions, but accessories are extremely popular. Fabrics and materials are extremely important in this market, so that luxury fashion brands need to think of the wearability of their pieces and to adapt designs to the specific climate (spring, summer and monsoon) of the country, and to offer a continuous supply of goods to satisfy the market. Indian consumers have high expectations and are very demanding in terms of the quality of the materials and colours used by luxury fashion brands, forcing labels to develop suitable designs and products to entice a knowledgeable and demanding market.

4.6 Case study: the millennials market

Luxury fashion is a competitive business where brands try to outdo each other in order to boost sales and reach their target market. Due to changes in society and the structure of luxury fashion brands, which now offer a variety of cheaper products and services, companies are no longer looking at younger consumers primarily in terms of captivating them in view of possible sales in the future, but put them at the very core of their business strategies. Bain & Company and Farfetch (2017), estimate that by 2025 millennials will represent 40% of the global personal luxury goods market. In some countries, for example the Middle East, millennials already represent the biggest market segment. In China, millennials are around 25% of the population but represent over 50% of luxury purchases (Kim, Hsu and Yuen 2020). In the last quarter of the 2010s Gucci sold half of its goods to millennials, whereas for Saint Laurent it was over 65% of sales (Kusumasondjaja 2020).

The meaning of the term millennials can differ in literature, but is most commonly associated to those who were born between the early 1980s and the early 2000s, in this sense at times overlapping with other labels such as generation Y. Consumer markets can be segmented in a number of ways, and the one established on age is often used, based on the assumption that people of a similar age share some common characteristics as they have lived through similar historical experiences and have been influenced by the same changes in society and the economy. However, the millennial market is a vast segment that can also features significant differences, especially from country to country.

For example, it has been argued that millennials predominantly buy luxury fashion for self-gratification, but although this might be the case in Western countries, in countries like India and the UAE many consumers are still at the show-off stage and acquire such brands to achieve social status (Mishra, Jain and Jham 2021). Moreover, even in the same country one can find significant differences and luxury fashion brands need to take this into account to be successful, as, for example, in China high-income millennials value uniqueness and pursue extravagant and rare luxury fashion products, whereas low-income ones aim to be associated with high-status consumers by opting for less ubiquitous affordable products offered by popular luxury fashion brands (Kim, Hsu and Yuen 2020).

Millennials have been attributed a number of traits, from being more sophisticated and savvy, as they are more informed about products and brands, to being more disenchanted with traditional advertising and marketing strategies. Some have claimed that millennials are more hedonic in their consumption of luxury fashion goods, more demanding in their brand interactions, and more prone to impulse buying.

Jones and Kang (2020) observe that millennials also have a strong intergenerational influence. Millennials focus on actively seeking information (especially through media with a strong visual element) and value instant gratification, and their behaviour affects not only the older generation but younger people too. At the same time, millennials also tend to be more influenced by their peers and to discuss potential purchases more than any other cohort. To cater to this market segment, luxury fashion brands have adopted a series of strategies with regards to communication, distribution and merchandise, shaping the way businesses operate.

Millennials differ greatly from other cohorts because they are digital natives. They grew up around digital technology and consider it a key part of their life, using it for communication and entertainment but also for gathering information and to shop. Millennials tend to use technology throughout the customer journey, use social media to learn about brands and products, shop online and share their experience with others both privately and publicly, which is both an opportunity and a challenge for brands, as they need to find ways to keep people's attention and convert it into sales. Millennials have disrupted traditional marketing and communication strategies and forced luxury fashion brands to engage more with the online world, initially by reluctantly developing websites and engaging in social media, and then supporting e-tail. Nowadays, younger consumers are driving luxury fashion brands to engage more with digital fashion, dematerialisation and gaming both as a form of promotion and an opportunity to boost sales through new products. In this sense, initiatives like Burberry's 'The Art of the Trench', a company-owned social media created to boost emotional attachment whilst putting customers at the centre of communication, or the game B-Bounce, contribute to increase connection and sales.

Solomon (2014) observes that millennials are more willing to adopt new technologies but are less understanding then previous generations if that is not working properly or if it's not user friendly, in this sense putting pressure on brands to provide a seamless experience. This means that millennials are more likely to switch to competitors, and can be affected by the negative experience of others. However, millennials are also more willing to engage with companies than previous cohorts, for example through social media interaction, by co-creation of products and participating in brands' activities, like joining online challenges.

Millennials drive online sales and are especially important for luxury fashion brands, as several studies have found that this cohort buys such goods more often than older customers. However, they showcase less loyalty and use different platforms to make purchases. Kim (2019) observes that millennials in the USA buy from a variety of retailers as they pursue bargains due to limited disposable income, despite demonstrating more emotional attachment to the chosen brand. Furthermore, it has been claimed that millennials are also more open to different forms of ownership when it comes to luxury fashion, and are the driving factor for the sharing economy, as demonstrated by the development of rental platforms featuring luxury fashion goods. Moreover, millennials are also more likely to engage with pre-loved luxury fashion than older cohorts. However, the growing focus on millennials has also been associated to shorter product life cycles, as overexposure on social media and the constant need to catch people's attention and entice consumers has led to an increasing number of products being launched by luxury fashion brands.

Moreover, focusing on millennials meant that luxury fashion brands had to change their physical spaces and develop more engaging events, as Solomon (2014) observes that millennials are more receptive to experiential retail. In this sense, luxury fashion brands have developed opportunities for people to live the brand. This can be achieved by creating places like restaurants, for example in 2019 Paris saw the opening of the Saint Laurent Rive Droite Café, whereas Louis Vuitton in 2020 opened its first café and restaurant, Le Café V and Sugalabo V, in their new Osaka flagship, and later added a restaurant (The Hall) next to its Chengdu flagship store. Moreover, luxury fashion flagship hotels (see also 2.6) also allow people to explore branded lifestyles through comprehensive offerings. Furthermore, luxury fashion brands are also launching events and exhibitions, and even creating foundations and museums to spread the brand message and engage consumers.

Last, millennials are more values-driven in their consumption practices, as they tend to support and engage more with brands that align with what they care about, and this is pushing the luxury fashion industry to engage more with charity and issues of sustainability, circularity, human and animal rights, but also ethics, inclusivity and diversity. Among the many initiatives, luxury fashion brands have, for example, contributed millions of Euros to the restoration of historical landmarks, often in their place of origin to reinforce their distinctive national character, as Chanel did for the Grand Palais in Paris, and Fendi for the Trevi fountain in Rome, whereas in Milan, Versace and Prada teamed up for the restoration of the Galleria Vittorio Emanuele II. At the same time, millennials' sensibilities also make them more prone to abandon brands when they are involved in scandals and controversies concerning issues they care about, which is forcing labels to respond quickly to consumers' outcry, through apologies and remedial actions, to avoid being 'cancelled'.

Questions and activities

- Who are millennials?
- What are the characterising traits of millennials?
- Identify the strategies that luxury fashion brands have launched to entice millennials.

4.7 Conclusions

Chapter Four focused on the luxury fashion brand consumer, arguing that the peculiarities of the industry, with its extensive offerings and different levels of luxury, alongside the international presence of labels and the socio-economical disparities between established and emerging markets, contribute to problematise the notion. The chapter examined the seminal works of Veblen, Bourdieu and Leibenstein in this sense, but also addressed how notions of class have been challenged by notions of lifestyle. Moreover, other contemporary drivers of luxury fashion consumption were explored, Furthermore, differences between geographical areas, and in particular the divide between mature markets and emerging markets such as China and India was discussed. Last, the chapter featured a case study investigating the characteristic traits of millennial consumers.

4.8 Revision questions

- Who are the consumers of luxury fashion brands?
- What are the drivers of luxury fashion consumption?
- What are the differences between mature and emerging markets in this sense?

4.9 References

Appadurai, A. (1986) *The social life of things: commodities in cultural perspective*. Cambridge: Cambridge University Press.

Bain & Company and Farfetch. (2017) *The millennial state of mind*. Available at https://www.bain.com/contentassets/0b0b0e19099a448e83af2fb53a5630aa/bain20media20pack_the_millennial_state_of_mind2.pdf

Belk, R. W. (1988) 'Possessions and the extended self', *Journal of Consumer Research*, 15(2), pp.139–68.

Bonetti, F., Perry, P., Fernie, J. (2017) 'The evolution of luxury fashion retailing in China', in Choi, T. M. and Shen, B. (eds.) *Luxury fashion retail management* (pp.49–67). Springer Series in Fashion Business. Singapore: Springer.

Bourdieu, P. (1984) *Distinction: a social critique of the judgement of taste*. London: Routledge & Keegan Paul.

Bughin, J., Doogan, J. and Vetvik, O. J. (2010) 'A new way to measure word-of-mouth marketing', *McKinsey Quarterly*, 2(1), pp.113–16.

Chadha, R. and Husband, P. (2006) *The cult of the luxury brand: inside Asia's love affair with luxury*. London; Boston: Nicholas Brealey International.

Chevalier, M. and Mazzalovo, G. (2012) *Luxury brand management: a world of privilege*. Hoboken, NJ; Chichester: John Wiley and Sons.

Corbellini, E. and Saviolo, S. (2009) *Managing fashion and luxury companies*. Milan: Rizzoli Etas.

Dhaliwal, A., Singh, D. P. and Paul, J. (2020) 'The consumer behavior of luxury goods: a review and research agenda', *Journal of Strategic Marketing*, pp.1–27.

Jones, A. and Kang, J. (2020) 'Media technology shifts: exploring millennial consumers' fashion-information-seeking behaviors and motivations', *Canadian Journal of Administrative Sciences/Revue Canadienne des Sciences de l'Administration*, 37(1), pp.13–29.

Kim, J. (2019) 'Luxury fashion goods ownership and collecting behavior in an omni-channel retail environment: empirical findings from affluent consumers in the US', *Research Journal of Textile and Apparel*, 23(3), pp.212–31.

Kim, J. H., Hsu, M. M. and Yuen, C. L. A. (2020) 'Individual and social factors impacting Chinese millennials' luxury consumption', *International Journal of Costume and Fashion*, 20(1), pp.27–43.

Kress, G. and Leeuwen, T. V. (2001) *Multimodal discourse*. London: Arnold.

Kusumasondjaja, S. (2020) 'Exploring the role of visual aesthetics and presentation modality in luxury fashion brand communication on Instagram', *Journal of Fashion Marketing and Management: An International Journal*, 24(1), pp.15–31.

Leibenstein, H. (1950) 'Bandwagon, snob, and Veblen effects in the theory of consumers' demand', *The Quarterly Journal of Economics*, 64(2), pp.183–207.

Mishra, S., Jain, S. and Jham, V. (2021) 'Luxury rental purchase intention among millennials – a cross-national study', *Thunderbird International Business Review*, 63(4), pp.503–16.

Okonkwo, U. (2007) *Luxury fashion branding: trends, tactics, techniques*. Basingstoke: Palgrave Macmillan.

Phau, I. and Prendergast, G. (2000) 'Consuming luxury brands: the relevance of the "rarity principle"', *Journal of Brand Management*, 8, pp.122–38.

Solomon, M. (2014) Forbes Entrepreneurs. 2015 is the year of the millennial customer: 5 key traits these 80 million consumers share. Retrieved 6 November 2015 from http://www.forbes.com/sites/micahsolomon/2014/12/29/5-traits-that-define-the-80-million-millennial-customers-coming-your-way/

Trigg, A. B. (2001) 'Veblen, Bourdieu, and conspicuous consumption', *Journal of Economic Issues*, 35(1), pp.99–115.

Veblen, T. (1899) *The theory of the leisure class* (reprinted 1994). Toronto: Courier Dover.

Wong, N. Y. and Ahuvia, A. C. (1998) 'Personal taste and family face: luxury consumption in Confucian and western societies', *Psychology & Marketing*, 15, pp.423–41.

5 Luxury Fashion Retail

Case study: Off-White and luxury fashion collaborations with mass-market retailers

---

CHAPTER OBJECTIVES

This chapter:

- examines luxury fashion retail
- considers the luxury fashion consumer experience
- discusses online retail and omnichannel strategy for luxury fashion brands

---

5.1 Chapter summary

Chapter Five focuses on luxury fashion retail. First it examines strategies of controlled distribution and the different channels luxury fashion brands use to reach their customers, i.e., flagship and monobrand stores, department stores, independent boutiques, duty-free, pop-up stores and designer outlets. Moreover, the chapter examines strategies of collaborations with mass-retailers through the case study of Off-White. Furthermore, the chapter considers the different elements that characterise luxury fashion retail. In particular issues concerning location and typology of stores adopted, and the various elements used in retailing to provide a pleasurable and exclusive experience for customers are examined. Finally, the chapter explains the reluctance of luxury fashion brands in selling online, and explores the strategies they employed when they finally adopted such method of distribution in order to overcome issues and problematic elements. In this sense, the challenges concerning omnichannel strategies are also considered.

5.2 Introduction

Luxury fashion retail differs from mass-retail both in terms of time frame and distribution practices. Luxury fashion products are characterised by a specific retail schedule, with goods traditionally becoming available long after their fashion show debut, which happens

DOI: 10.4324/9781003264811-8

off-season. However, this time frame allows mass-retailers to copy designs off the catwalks and have them ready for purchase before the originals are available.

This can impact demand by making designs feel obsolete, through overexposure, before they even hit the shops, leading luxury fashion brands to explore different strategies. For example, many luxury fashion brands now launch capsule or cruise collections that are immediately available, on the other hand the practice of having the full fashion show collections available through see-now-buy-now (a strategy first adopted by Burberry in 2016) is still not widespread.

See-now-buy-now involves a shift from the traditional six months' time-to-market as products become available for purchase right after the fashion show, and this can cause issues for retailers. In fact, buyers, who still have to finalise sales months in advance and without knowing the public reaction to the collection, also have to navigate through extra collections that are launched at different times by different luxury fashion labels (Boardman et al. 2020).

5.3 Controlled distribution and retail marketing

Luxury fashion brands sell their products through a variety of outlets. In fact, the vast and luxurious flagship stores are only one facet of a much more complex structure that is governed by controlled distribution. Even though selling merchandise and making a profit is obviously a primary concern for luxury fashion brands, those goals have to be achieved whilst avoiding over-diffusion, brand dilution and, more generally, any potential negative impact over brand identity and brand image, and in this sense distribution channels are pivotal.

Luxury fashion brands need to retain an aura of exclusivity, mystique and prestige through their retail environment and therefore cannot allow their pieces to be sold in non-luxurious shops or at a very discounted price, which can be problematic if shops are not run in-house. To maintain control over their distribution, luxury fashion brands are very careful in selecting which outlets to use, and enter strict agreements that offer third parties limited freedom when it comes to presentation and pricing, as they aim to convey a coherent brand identity. Controlled distribution can be controversial in terms of being anti-competitive, which is illegal in a number of countries, but it's usually allowed as long as it's not applied in a discriminatory fashion and employs objective criteria.

Chevalier and Mazzalovo (2012: 256) discuss how a parallel grey market, where merchandise is sold by retailers that are not authorised do so, can damage luxury brands through association with a less then exclusive experience. For luxury fashion brands the grey market consists primarily of fragrances and cosmetics, that are usually acquired by non-authorised retailers from foreign markets where prices are lower, infringing defined policies set by labels that forbid parallel distribution and that only allow their products to be presented through displays created by luxury fashion brands themselves, which is the norm in the beauty sector.

However, controlled distribution doesn't only aim to prevent authentic luxury fashion goods being available through unauthorised retailers of dubious quality, but also to protect the labels, and their clients, from fakes and counterfeits, which are rife in the sector. Another form of grey market that luxury fashion brands are trying to eradicate is represented by Daigu sales, which entail Chinese nationals being commissioned to purchase specific luxury goods overseas on behalf of customers in the country. In the past this practice was associated with significant savings, as prices in China have traditionally been higher than in mature markets, but nowadays a number of luxury fashion brands are aligning their Chinese prices to those in Europe, aiming to cut off such parallel forms of distribution, that has also been associated with spreading fakes.

In order to fight parallel markets and counterfeits, some have advised that for luxury fashion brands an ideal retailing model would consist solely of directly operated monobrand stores, but this strategy is only attainable for established brands that have the necessary resources, like, for example, those that are part of luxury conglomerates or groups, and out of reach for many independent labels. Moreover, this is a tactic that is difficult to achieve in the current retail environment.

In fact, certain goods such as eyewear needs to be sold by specialist retailers or, as in the case of cosmetics, require an extended presence to meet demand. It has to be noted that generally beauty and skincare lines by luxury fashion brands are not available to purchase in stores directly operated by the labels, this is due to the fact that brands want to avoid the risks of selling products at a higher price and disappoint loyal customers, as other retailers usually run promotions that labels don't allow in their stores. Moreover, to operate through some distribution channels, like duty-frees and department stores, is almost a necessity in certain markets for luxury fashion brands (Chevalier Mazzalovo 2012: 282-3).

There are a number of types of retailing formats associated with luxury fashion brands. In fact, in addition to flagship stores and monobrand shops, luxury fashion brands are distributed through a complex network of retailers. Luxury fashion products can be found in department stores, independent luxury boutiques, designer outlets, duty-free, pop-up stores and also online, being sold either directly from luxury fashion labels or through the online version of the channels listed above.

When it comes to discussing flagship stores and monobrand stores, it has to be observed that there is some confusion about terminology. In fact, sometimes the term flagship store is used indiscriminately to identify any monobrand store associated with luxury fashion brands, whereas terms such as mega-flagship or uber-flagship are sometimes used to differentiate between the many smaller monobrand stores worldwide, and the handful of grand flagship stores where labels showcase all (or the majority) of their collections. For example, Burberry operates a number of monobrand stores worldwide, but only has flagships in London, New York, Barcelona and Tokyo, whereas Prada currently has Epicenters in New York, Los Angeles and Tokyo in addition to several stores around the world.

Flagship stores are usually owned by the brands, but this is not always the case as, for example, Louis Vuitton in Japan operates through a joint venture (Nobbs, Moore and Sheridan 2012), and the Burberry flagship in Tokyo is owned by a licensee. However, luxury fashion brands are generally moving towards a more tightly controlled distribution, as, for example, Gucci and Burberry have strengthened their brands by buying back licenses that saw them operating through multiple manufacturers and distributors (Okonkwo 2007: 142).

For flagship stores the rule seems to be that bigger is better, as luxury fashion brands aim to showcase more products but also to convey power, exclusivity and prestige through a lavish display. However, the high costs involved in creating and operating flagship stores means that they often represent a loss-making display (Moore and Doherty 2007: 278), although a necessary one to support the prestige and status of the brand.

Flagship stores need to be located in strategic areas, and in this sense there are different formats in Western countries and in key markets like China and India, as examined in more detail in section 5.5. Flagship stores employ a series of strategies to entice customers and build loyalty, for example by offering attentive service and exquisite facilities, but can also offer multiple opportunities to strengthen the relationship between luxury fashion brands, distribution partners and the media.

Moore, Doherty and Doyle (2010) examine how flagship stores can be pivotal to enhance the profile and credibility of luxury fashion brands in foreign markets, which in turn can have a positive impact on wholesale sales, can attract new and affluent customers, and positively affect the way a brand is perceived by the media. The authors observe that when one luxury fashion brand closed its flagship store in London due to the high operating costs then it completely lost media coverage, causing sales in other outlets to decline and forcing the brand to reverse its decision and reopen the flagship.

Moreover, luxury fashion goods are also available through pop-up stores. They are usually launched by luxury fashion brands to celebrate specific collections or ranges, a strategy that has been employed for example by Prada, Balengiaga and Chanel to name but a few. Pop-up shops can foster media attention and consumer engagement, and can vary greatly in terms of design and dimensions. In fact, for example, Jaquemus launched a pop-up shop that consisted of a vending machine selling handbags near the flagships in Paris and London in 2021 and 2022, respectively, whereas Dior in 2022 created a 7,500-square-foot structure that comprised a boutique, gardens and a restaurant in Seoul. Luxury fashion brands also retail in exclusive independent boutiques, such as Joice in Hong Kong or 10 Corso Como in Milan.

Luxury fashion brands are also available from luxury department stores like Macy's, Bloomingdale and Saks Fifth Avenue in New York, or Galeries Lafayette, Printemps and La Samaritaine in Paris. Those department stores offer luxury fashion brands a way to reach consumers, meet demand and boost profits in a prestigious setting that contributes to reinforce the status of the label. However, it has been observed that this dimension of exclusivity has been affected by the fact that luxury department stores have been expanding their ranges to include more premium brands that don't share the same aura of prestige and exclusivity of luxury fashion labels.

Similar concerns about potential dilution risks have also been raised with regards to the practice of selling luxury fashion goods through designer outlets. Designer outlets are shopping centres dedicated primarily to luxury goods, which are offered there at a discounted price. Designer outlets have mushroomed in recent years and they offer price-conscious consumers the opportunity to evaluate a variety of brands.

There are many companies and groups operating such outlets, for example the McArthur-Glen Group, Intrend or the Bicester Collection, and some of them were even created by luxury fashion brands themselves, like in the case of Prada with the Space and Gucci with The Mall in Tuscany (Italy). In the past, such outlets were not actively advertised by luxury fashion brands and both their very existence and the relationship they held with labels were kept private, but now this is no longer the case.

For example, Gucci even mentions The Mall outlet on its website, as more and more labels try to attract price-conscious consumers. If outlets are managed in-house by labels, then the risk of losing prestige through sub-par presentation and association with brands that are not quite as exclusive can be mitigated, as more control is retained, but nowadays the majority of designer outlets also sell less exclusive brands, including mass-market ones, which can negatively affect the prestige and reputation of luxury fashion brands.

5.4 Case study: Off-White and luxury fashion collaborations with mass-market retailers

Luxury fashion brands have recently engaged more and more in collaboration with other brands, using a strategy defined as co-branding. This entails the use of two distinct brand names on one product, a phenomenon that is also sometimes known, when luxury fashion brands are involved, as fashion collaboration (Ahn et al. 2010), inter-brand collaboration or strategic alliance (Wigley and Provelengiou 2011).

Usually in the luxury fashion business co-branding entails associating with a company operating in a different sector (for example a technology company as seen in the case of Versace, Prada and Dolce & Gabbana as they launched limited edition mobile phones in the early 2000s, creating the Nokia 7270, the Prada-LG and Motorola V3i Gold, respectively, or, more recently, for the Apple Watch Hermès) or with a mass-retailer.

Pierre Cardin was a pioneer in this sense, as he created a special collection for a department store in the late 1950s, at the time such strategy was deemed so unacceptable and damaging to the reputation of French Haute Couture that he was temporarily suspended by La Chambre Syndicale. For a long time, this strategy was deemed too risky in terms of brand dilution but as more and more brands started to capitalise on the rise of the middle-classes and to widen their customer base through less expensive items, collaborations have become increasingly popular, and this tactic is now employed by many luxury fashion labels.

For example, sportswear giant Adidas launched a co-brand (Y-3) with Japanese designer Yohji Yamamoto in 2003. However, since the groundbreaking collaboration between Karl Lagerfeld (creative director of Chanel, Fendi and of his eponymous brand) and mass-retailer H&M in 2004, this phenomenon has intensified. Since then, H&M launched a number of collaborations with luxury fashion brands such as Stella McCartney, Viktor&Rolf, Lanvin, Versace, Balmain, Simone Rocha, Comme des Garçons, Balmain, Maison Martin Margiela, and Moschino. North-American retailer Target also launched a series of capsule collections, for example with Anna Sui, Zac Posen, Missoni, Jean Paul Gautier and Alexander McQueen.

Mass-retailers benefit in terms of generating media interest, increasing brand awareness and driving sales, also beyond the specific designer collaborations. The success of those collaborations has led to more and more being launched, as, for example, in terms of footwear, Adidas teamed up with Stella McCartney, whereas Puma with Alexander McQueen and Balmain, Missoni with Converse and Burberry with Dr. Sholl.

This phenomenon was considered in detail by Luck, Muratovski and Hedley (2014), who list the benefits of engaging in mass-market collaboration for luxury fashion brands in terms of expanding customer base, achieving financial benefits, responding to expressed and latent needs of customers, strengthening competitive position, introducing new products with a strong image, creating new customer perceived value, gaining operational benefits, achieving marketplace exposure, sharing expenses, gaining access to new markets and enhancing reputation. However, disadvantages of this strategy are represented by giving competitive advantage to co-branding partners in terms of creating potential competition, limiting potential market reach of cheaper brand extension goods and causing customer confusion.

This was, for example, the case for the Missoni for Target 400-pieces capsule collection, as it maintained the main aesthetics of the label with its signature colourful patterns, which were featured on a wide range of goods, from bicycles to garden furniture and accessories. The quality of those goods was different to that of regular Missoni products, the collaboration was a mass-market adaptation that looked like the real thing, which was potentially confusing for consumers. In this respect differentiation was pursued by Missoni by avoiding mentioning the collaboration through their own channels and by conveying a sense of prestige and exclusivity by producing only a limited number of pieces. This suggests that co-branding with mass-market retailers should not become the norm but should be seen as a way to go beyond the target market through a carefully selected partner whilst maintaining exclusivity, status and differentiation.

Sometimes luxury brands also launch special collections with other entities belonging to the realm of luxury, such as luxury retailers or other luxury brands. For example, the renowned 10 Corso Como boutique in Milan launched collaborations with Armani, Borsalino, Diesel, Fiorucci, Maison Margiela, and Moncler to name but a few. However, co-branding can also happen between luxury fashion companies, as, for example, Wolford, a brand mostly associated with hoisery, has collaborated with Karl Lagerfeld, Emilio Pucci, Missoni, Zac Posen and Valentino.

The most renowned co-branding between luxury fashion labels, however, is represented by Fendace, that in 2022 saw Kim Jones from Fendi design a collection for Versace, and Donatella Versace designing one for Fendi. Fendace products were also available to purchase from dedicated pop-up stores around the world. Moreover, co-branding between artists and luxury fashion brands are also a way to boost media attention, desirability and sales, for example Louis Vuitton collaborated in this sense with artists Takashi Murukami and, most recently, with Yayoi Kusama.

Co-branding has become a popular and profitable strategy for luxury fashion brands, with the most emblematic case being represented by its use by Virgil Abloh. Virgil Abloh, an iconic US designer of Ghanian origin, successfully operated in a variety of fields and became renowned for his creative use of streetwear in luxury fashion. He created his own brand in 2013, Milan-based Off-White, with menswear and womenswear lines showcased at Paris Fashion Week. Abloh was also creative director for menswear at Louis Vuitton, a role he held from 2018 until his death in 2021.

Abloh employed co-branding as a strategic tool in a consistent and productive manner to support prestige and to cement his iconic status through collaborations with luxury brands, to boost sales through imaginative partnerships with mass-retailers but also through other prestigious collaborations. Abloh collaborated, for example, with artist Takashi Murakami for a gallery exhibition in 2018, and acted as art director for the joint album of Jay-Z and Kanye West in 2011. Virgil Abloh created a long list of collaborations, mostly for Off-White or under his own name, but also some for Louis Vuitton during his time there. At times, like in the case of its collaboration with Nike, the partnership involved the many brands linked to him.

Abloh launched a large number of co-branding projects for Off-White. In 2016, he collaborated with outwear luxury brand Moncler for the Moncler O collection, but also with denim brand Levi's to create a capsule collection for their main line, Made & Crafted.

In 2017, the Off-White x Nike long-standing collaboration started with The Ten project, which saw Virgil Abloh reinvent ten iconic sneakers including the Air Jordan, whereas 2018 saw the release of the studded Mercurial Vapor 360 boot. In 2017, Off-White collaborated with mass-market sportswear brand Champion for a 16 pieces capsule collection and with New York concept store Kith for two different capsule collections, whilst also partnering with Swedish furniture giant IKEA for a series of rugs and a special take on their iconic blue bag (more products were released later).

In 2018, the Off-White collaboration with luxury show brand Jimmy Choo was launched, followed by a unisex collection of eyewear for Sunglass Hut, a collaboration with footwear brand Timberland to renew its iconic boots and a collaboration with perfume house Byredo to create fragrances, apparel and beauty products. The year also saw the beginning of Off-White's partnership with luxury luggage brand Rimowa and a collaboration with Parisian department store Le Bon Marché for a pop-up café.

Under his name, Virgil Abloh collaborated with Moët & Chandon to create a signature champagne bottle in 2018. In 2020, Virgil Abloh started his collaboration with German car manufacturer Mercedes-Benz (Virgil Abloh x Mercedes Benz) first with Project Geländewagen, creating a new version of the G-Class SUV and then in 2022 for Project Maybach, working on a limited edition of the Maybach S-Class S680 consisting of just 150 units (available for purchase also through Off-White channels). The launch was coupled with a special capsule collection.

Also in 2020, Virgil Abloh collaborated with jeweller Jacob & Co. to create the 'Office Supplies' line, where paperclips acted as inspiration for fine jewellery (Virgil Abloh x Jacob & Co.). In 2021, the Virgil Abloh x Braun project involved the redesign of the BC02 alarm clock and of the Wandanlage hi-fi stereo system, and was accompanied by an explanatory short film and a music remix by Abloh.

Moreover, Abloh also introduced collaborations with Louis Vuitton. In 2020, Virgil Abloh masterminded the brand's collaboration with Japanese designer NIGO to create a capsule collection named LV2, which continued with a second collection in 2022. Abloh also established a collaboration between Louis Vuitton and the National Basketball Association (NBA) to create a first capsule collection in 2020, followed by a second in 2022. Moreover, in 2022, a collaboration with Nike saw the launch of 47 LV Nike Air Force 1 sneakers.

Questions and activities

-   Why are luxury fashion brands launching collaborations with mass-retailers?
-   What strategy did Virgil Abloh adopt for fashion collaborations?
-   Select two luxury fashion brands and compare and contrast the strategies of co-branding they adopted

5.5 The luxury fashion customer experience

Luxury fashion brands focus on creating an effective retail environment where customers can experience attentive service, impeccable presentation, and an aura of prestige and exclusivity throughout their touchpoints. Many brands develop a concept for their flagship stores that is then filtered through and adapted to their stand-alone stores, department stores, point-of-sales and so on.

Service is also considered a key aspect for enhancing customer experience, and includes a variety of figures from doormen to sales assistants in physical environments, to customer-service staff working on-line or over the phone. In this sense uniforms, staff performance, store atmospherics and luxurious surroundings are functional to create an aura of prestige and desirability. Moreover, stores can also become the backdrop for extravagant PR events and showcase the brands' heritage and craftsmanship in an effort to achieve brand awareness and loyalty.

First, luxury fashion brands can convey their status through strategic retail location, as they need to attract, and be accessible to, the right clientele. This means, for example, that monobrand stores and flagships are located in important cities where tourists are also present, for example in established destinations like Paris but also upcoming ones like Dubai.

Moreover, they are also located in the most prestigious part of such cities as exclusive locations reinforce the brand's aura and reputation. For example, in Milan luxury fashion stores are located within Via Della Spiga and Via Monte Napoleone in the Quadrilatero D'Oro, in Paris on the Champs Elysées and Avenue Montaigne, whereas Ginza and Omotesando are the most sought-after locations in Tokyo. The proximity of other luxury stores also contributes to reinforcing a sense of prestige and exclusivity, and in this sense Bond Street in London is emblematic as the average distance between luxury stores in this retail agglomeration is only 230 metres (Arrigo 2015). If in Europe this format is established, in other countries the situation is different.

Bonetti et al. (2017) observe how distribution in China differs from other markets. Initially, luxury fashion brands entered the market through boutiques located in five-star hotels like the Peninsula Palace in Beijing, as they experienced difficulties in obtaining a retail license. Then wholesale arrangements were made with local distributors in order to achieve a number of benefits, from being able to better comply with regulations, navigate cultural and business differences, and to penetrate the market better by using the knowledge and infrastructure of local distributors. When restrictions were eased luxury fashion brands then introduced monobrand stores in China either by running them directly or through franchisees and local partners required to follow strict guidelines set by the labels' headquarters. Last, luxury malls have emerged.

In this sense the luxury fashion consumer experience has been more dynamic in China, as it had to be adapted to a rapidly changing environment, closing down underperforming stores and moving to more desirable locations, and adopting a hybrid model that sees luxury fashion brands deciding to use agents to increase distribution in certain areas whilst retaining full control of outlets elsewhere. It has to be observed that Chinese nationals also tend to make large purchases while travelling, especially when visiting the country of origin of luxury fashion brands as that is considered a more authentic experience.

Also, in another emerging market, India, the luxury consumer experience is shaped by differences in legislation and cultural elements, and has evolved differently than in Western markets. In fact, in Indian cities the independent flagship format is difficult to adopt due to socio-economical issues, and problematised by legislation. As examined by Chadha and Husband (2006), governmental restrictions on foreign investments and the lack of clear luxury districts that would be suitable to convey notions of status and exclusivity led luxury fashion brands to enter the market through prestigious five-star hotels like the Taj, the Oberoi, the Imperial or the Sheraton.

However, this practice has some implications. First, as such hotels don't have enough retail spaces, luxury fashion brands face a very competitive environment in trying to secure prime locations. Despite the fact that many hotels are trying their best to carve out as much space as possible, as for example in 2004 the Taj moved its cake shop and beauty salon to allow the creation of a Louis Vuitton store, demand outstrips supply. Second, luxury fashion brands have had to adapt their distribution formats as the space available simply doesn't allow for the development of the vast flagship store model. Furthermore, by being located in different hotels, customers experience significant fragmentation.

For years, luxury fashion brands have experienced issues in controlling their distribution in India, as legislation limited the role they could play. However, as the Indian government eased restrictions and allowed more foreign investments, luxury fashion brands have now been able to increase their stake in monobrand stores and establish more involvement and control over their distribution, being better able to provide a coherent and engaging shopping experience for customers.

Flagship stores represent a place where brands can channel their brand identity, creating a brandscape (Riewoldt 2002). As mentioned earlier, flagship stores are bigger, more lavish, and offer more products than other monobrand stores, showcasing their primacy through original designs by leading architects and artists, hosting special events and offering customers a place where they can engage with, and fully live, the brand through a variety of extra spaces like bars and restaurants, clubs and hotels. In this sense the Armani flagship in Milan is emblematic, as it hosts collections from the many sub-brands in the Armani universe, an Armani/hotel with Spa and Armani/restaurant, the Armani/Bamboo Bar, a bookshop, a flower and confectionary shop, and an Emporio Armani café.

In retailing, a number of dimensions can be manipulated to create and support the aura of exclusivity and distinction that luxury fashion brands aim to achieve. They range from interior design through playing with colour schemes, lighting and decorations to atmospherics as music, sound and olfactory elements are employed by luxury fashion brands as they try to engage all senses and provide a memorable experience for customers. For example, the Paris flagship of Luis Vuitton features a lift where people are left in total darkness and experience sensory deprivation, so that when the doors open the impact of the retail environment in all of its facets would be enhanced. Moreover, many luxury fashion brands employ museum techniques such as placing objects on pedestals, or using display cases, to convey an aura of prestige and exclusivity, but also a sense of authority and timelessness.

Another dimension that has been used by luxury fashion brands to convey their status and desirability is represented by a focus on visual elements and packaging, as refined and high-quality materials are used to enhance the sensory appeal for the customer. The importance of those ancillary elements as markers of exclusivity and prestige has been further enhanced through digital means, as, for example, on social media unpacking videos allow the wider public to catch a glimpse of the elaborate way luxury fashion brands present their products and reinforce notions of prestige through a coherent strategy.

Window displays are also used by luxury fashion brands to support and disseminate brand identity, to convey notions of power and status, but also distinctiveness and uniqueness through engaging and appealing displays. For example, Italian brand Moschino is known for its imaginative window displays that often incorporate the use of irony, in line with the brand's values. Moreover, window displays can also mobilise elements of cultural capital and legitimacy, as leading artists are sometimes used, for example by Louis Vuitton, not only to create buzz and media attention but to entice people and to refer, once again, to a dimension of legitimacy and authority.

Technology in store is also used by luxury fashion brands to reinforce their trailblazing role and set them apart from their mass-market counterparts. Prada is in this sense emblematic as it was among the first brands to leverage on this dimension extensively to enhance consumer experience and increase engagement.

Prada Epicentres, and especially the first one opened in New York and designed by renowned architect Rem Koolhaas, pioneered a variety of elements including a digital wall covering a whole block in length, dressing rooms where customers could control lighting and settings (for example making the glass become opaque for privacy), whilst allowing customers to obtain more information on products by using radio-frequency identification and electronic tags on products (Masè and Silchenko 2017).

Moore and Doherty (2007: 294) observe how much of the technology installed in the early 2000s has now been removed either because of negative feedback from staff and customers or for failure to integrate with the brand's IT system, but nonetheless luxury fashion brands have continued to explore the use of technology to engage and entertain customers (see section 9.3 for more details). For example, in 2020 Burberry created its first social retail store in Shenzhen (China), developing a series of unique spaces that people could explore in person and online through social media, unlocking rewards such as menu items at the Thomas Cafe (named after the brand's founder). Moreover, customers there can even book their favourite fitting rooms and select which playlist to listen to, whilst earning rewards by scanning the QR code of goods to unlock additional information and exclusive content.

Luxury fashion consumer experience needs to be memorable, and brands use a variety of elements to convey their philosophy and provide an attentive, enticing and pleasurable encounter to increase consumer satisfaction, support brand loyalty and the development of an emotional bond. However, expectations may differ as luxury fashion brands now cater to a large number of individuals that come from different socio-economic backgrounds, which has pushed labels to adopt strategies aimed specifically at their most affluent clientele.

Okonkwo (2007: 95-6) observes how elite clients are pursued through private shopping experiences like trunk shows, pre-season shows, post-season sales and shopping lunches. Trunk shows are private fashion shows to showcase new collections to carefully selected clients and offer the opportunity to pre-order products and cut long waiting lists, whereas pre-season shows focus on cruise collections only. Okonkwo observes that post-season sales were traditionally limited to selected customers but nowadays more and more brands are holding them for the general public too. Shopping lunches, similarly, offer a chance for a select audience to purchase products privately whilst also enjoying a relaxed environment.

Moreover, to provide a more enticing and engaging customer experience for top clients, luxury fashion brands have also been focusing on made-to-measure and personalisation services, access to private lounges and exclusive events where a select audience can socialise under the aegis of the label. For example, Fendi has a whole private floor in its flagship in Rome dedicated to its most valuable customers, and those staying at the Fendi Private Suites above are also offered a private tour of the store.

However, differences in luxury fashion experience are not necessarily only based on wealth, as, for example, brands have to adapt their retail practices to local customs and sensibilities. In fact, Bonetti et al. (2017) observe how in China, a market notorious for low brand loyalty, flagship stores represent a tool for luxury fashion brands to engage consumers through spectacular displays, exhibitions and offering full ranges and rare products, as seen for example in the Hermès Maison in Shanghai. Competition among brands is fierce, as luxury fashion labels make large investments to maintain consumer attention, as, for example, in 2012 Louis Vuitton celebrated their 20 years in China by launching their first grand Maison in Shanghai.

It is also observed that in China brand loyalty can be supported by offering a discount, which is not common practice in more mature markets but is something that resonates with Chinese sensibilities. Chevalier and Mazzalovo (2012: 272) however observe that even if in Western markets luxury fashion brands don't usually offer discounts they may, for example, offer price reductions to fashion journalists and celebrities or supply loyalty cards providing some benefits to their best customers.

Moreover, Sresnewsky et al. (2020) highlight how pivotal the interactions with salespeople are to achieve customer satisfaction and loyalty, and how rapport-building behaviour in this respect varies greatly from country to country, as cultural differences and different expectations are at play. If sales assistants at every luxury fashion store worldwide have to be able to showcase knowledge concerning their brands, such as their values and history, and to provide detailed information on their products and practices, on the other hand to create and support a relationship with customers, staff operating in different countries would need to adopt different tactics. For example, in Brazil flexible payment options, home delivery, gifts and extra discounts are considered essential.

Last, it has to be observed that nowadays customers expect a pleasant and seamless experience with regards to online shopping and in an omnichannel perspective, as discussed in the following section.

5.6 Omnichannel and the evolution of e-commerce and mobile-commerce

For a long time, luxury fashion brands focused solely on physical retail, from flagship stores to concessions, and labels were initially reluctant to abandon the traditional model of selling their products and embrace the opportunities afforded by the Internet. This was the result of different concerns.

Initial reluctance to sell online was motivated by fear that the exclusivity and prestige of luxury fashion brands could be affected. Also, this retail method was perceived as inferior by luxury brands due to limits in replicating the multisensory experience that characterises physical retail. Moreover, brands may have also wanted to protect their wholesale distribution networks (Chevalier and Mazzalovo 2012: 283). Furthermore, concerns were raised about the fact that online distribution would be more difficult to control and could leave consumers more vulnerable to counterfeits.

Okonkwo (2007: 183) observes that other factors which prevented luxury fashion brands to embrace e-tail at first were concerns about the high capital investments and high running costs of launching a new platform, the complex logistics involved in global distribution, challenging post-sales interactions, legal complications, coupled with low impact sales and fewer impulse purchases. Moreover, still in the early 2000s, consumers were cautious in buying online due to concerns about secure payment, delivery, lack of human contact, and difficulties in after-sale services, barriers that didn't encourage luxury fashion brands to prioritise online retail.

Pioneers in this sense were Louis Vuitton and Christan Dior. Gucci was also one of the early adopters, within the luxury fashion industry, in the field of e-commerce, having first launched a platform in 2002. The brand then launched its Digital Flagship store in 2010, showcasing the integration of e-commerce, m-commerce and digital marketing in an immersive experience designed to be as close as possible to the one customers might experience in Gucci physical stores, for example through the consistent use of display techniques and brand imagery whilst also offering extra content and reinforcing the brand myth through a number of resources.

The few luxury fashion brands engaging with e-commerce initially sold online only a few products in a few destinations and did do using different platforms. In fact, they operated in limited capacity through their own e-commerce, but were primarily making their products available online through the new platforms of established department stores such as Macy's and Neiman Markus or through new independent e-malls such as Net-a-porter and Yoox.com. The latter was quickly adopted by many luxury fashion brands, enticed by the fact that Yoox. com bought overstock or unsold items from previous seasons directly from labels so that discounts didn't undermine the brands or cannibalise sales from current collections.

Also department stores were sometimes limited to only selling past collections online as luxury fashion brands sought to avoid customer confusion and brand dilution. However, another form of dilution was more difficult to avoid, as even though agreements concerning discounting strategy were stipulated between luxury fashion brands and department stores, the latter were also selling more and more mass-market fashion brands and this created undesirable associations with less prestigious entities. For years luxury fashion products were primarily sold online through those channels as, still in the mid-2010s, a number of labels didn't have their own e-commerce platform, showcasing a clear lack of commitment.

Even when luxury fashion brands, or the luxury conglomerates that control many of them, finally entered into e-tail directly and launched their own platforms things didn't necessarily progress smoothly, as sometimes sudden changes of strategic direction were observed. This is, for example, the case for LVMH, that employed contrasting strategies and ended up back to where it started. The group was one of the first luxury fashion players to engage with e-commerce by launching eLuxury, a platform selling goods from a number of the luxury brands it controlled, in 2000. However, the platform was closed by LVMH in 2009 and substituted, in many cases, by new e-shops for each brand (Chevalier and Mazzalovo 2012). However, in 2017 a new common platform, 24 Sèvres, was launched, selling goods by the likes of Luis Vuitton and Dior in over 100 countries, whilst the LVMH group later also developed an app following the development of m-commerce.

To this day, some luxury fashion brands use their digital channels mainly to provide information and direct users in stores, as only limited goods are sold online, like accessories or beauty products. In this sense Chanel is notorious for being among the brands that showcase the more extensive restrictions on online sales, which is motivated by the desire to maintain an aura of prestige through a memorable physical shopping experience. However, this choice of limiting the number of products available online caused issues during the COVID-19 pandemic, as lockdowns saw the closure of shops around the world.

Saviolo and Corbellini (2014: 210–11) observe how the limited range of products that luxury fashion brands sell online is also a function of the difficulties faced in terms of logistics, as significant investments are needed when transitioning from bricks-and-mortar only to ensure seamless distribution. Luxury fashion brands may also want to avoid conflict with traditional distribution. Moreover, the high-return rate that characterises online shopping also provides a barrier to extending the number of goods sold online by luxury fashion brands.

However, Internet technology has revolutionised retail and created shifts in consumer behaviour that cannot be ignored by luxury fashion labels if they want to retain market share. Bain & Company (2016) estimated that by 2025 luxury goods will primarily be purchased through online and monobrand stores, and observe how over 70% of purchases are already influenced by interactions online. Technology has enabled consumers to have quick access to more information than ever before, it allows people to compare products and brands more effectively, and it has reshaped expectations and affected loyalty due to lower switching costs.

Online shopping is appealing for the growing time-poor and convenience-driven consumer segment, and is something that consumers are nowadays expecting. Online distribution allows brands to reach customers who might be unable or don't want to travel to physical stores stocking luxury fashion goods, offering a convenient service especially appealing in areas where distribution is limited, whilst offering brands a platform to support international expansion.

For luxury fashion brands, to sell online involves trying to make sure that the experience is impeccable in a variety of areas, such as payment, insurance, customer service but also logistics and shipping, which has proved problematic at times as global distribution is now expected by customers but local infrastructure and policies can differ greatly from country to country. Luxury fashion brands have often been extremely cautious and only entered the e-commerce and m-commerce sphere after long deliberation and significant investments behind the scenes.

In this sense to collaborate with more established companies may be beneficial in terms of accessing expertise and infrastructure, but luxury fashion brands are also extremely wary of choosing partners that may be perceived as less exclusive and dilute the brand, leading for example to the extremely limited number of labels which have so far paired with Amazon to support their online distribution. The e-commerce giant in 2020 launched a 'Luxury Store' that now features Oscar de la Renta, Altuzarra, La Perla, Elie Saab, Missoni and Rodarte, but a number of labels have publicly criticised the move, arguing that, despite the obvious convenience of the platform in terms of fast shipping, the lack of prestige that characterises Amazon was too big an obstacle as unfavourable associations would be created in the consumer's mind, cheapening the brand image and affecting brand equity in the long term.

Moreover, luxury fashion brands also have to deal with controlled distribution issues when selling online, as it's not only where products are available from that can prove problematic, but also how many products are available. In this sense, Holmqvist, Wirtz and Fritze (2021) observe that luxury fashion brands support notions of rarity and scarcity, especially for their most iconic products, by monitoring how much they sell online so that if too large numbers are sold then the item is taken off the platform. This strategy is adopted, for example, by Hermès and Dior, and is in line with similar strategies employed in physical stores, as limits of how many products can be sold each month are also sometimes enforced.

Channel integration was a challenge for luxury fashion brands, in fact as they were initially reluctant to join the e-tail revolution, and used online channels primarily to only provide information, they had to catch up to provide the standard that consumers had grown accustomed to by mass-retailer brands. In fact, mass-retailers had been at the forefront of e-commerce, and later on m-commerce, and had engaged with more varied selling methods and platforms for years so that they were more advanced in terms of omnichannel strategy, providing a level of service that luxury fashion brands had to exceed, to meet consumers expectations, in a far more limited time frame.

In this sense Ralph Lauren was a pioneer as the company launched a mobile commerce platform, supported by QR codes, in 2017, although this was initially only available in Europe. If at the beginning luxury fashion brands were engaging with mobile technology in a limited fashion, for example developing apps that worked more as glorified catalogues and allowed only the purchase of selected goods, since then many labels have realised the potential of such strategy and even developed apps to support the consumer experience. In this sense, for example, Chanel offers a Lip Scanner app that allows a user to scan a colour and find a matching shade of lipstick before trying it virtually and then buying it through the app.

An omnichannel strategy involves the integration between the different channels and customer touchpoints to provide a consistent and coherent experience, in opposition to a multichannel strategy where those are not working in synergy but simply alongside each other leading to possible issues in customer experience. Cattapan and Pongsakornrungsilp (2022) observe how, in an onmichannel perspective, the same information and price should feature throughout all channels, and similarly marketing and communication campaigns should feature in a consistent manner throughout all channels. Moreover, the integration of different platforms should allow customers to make seamless transactions throughout and offer information on available stock, whilst also providing integrated logistics and consistent customer services.

This however proved difficult at times for luxury fashion brands to achieve, especially if in different countries certain digital tools were adopted more quickly and a variety of platforms were used. For example, Liu, Perry, and Gadzinski (2019) observed how in China luxury fashion brands had to engage with WeChat, a social media platform that supports miniprograms allowing m-commerce, gaming and also service booking capacity, to meet consumers expectations well before they engaged with similar tools in mature markets. However, issues caused by inconsistent marketing and the lack of desired products availability experienced by Chinese travellers when visiting stores abroad forced labels to widely adopt such platforms to keep up and better cater to this market segment.

In e-commerce and m-commerce platforms, moreover, consumers are more wary of inconsistencies as they fear that this means that products may be fake, affecting trust. In fact, in China authenticity concerns emerged when differences in merchandising selection and presentation in comparison with official brand websites were observed on Tmall, so much so that some brands left the platform and focused on establishing their own e/m-commerce outlets to maintain credibility and trust in the country.

For luxury fashion brands, the omnichannel strategy also involves the need to offer the same quality of customer service online, by making the most of different platforms and touchpoints for relationship-building, which can be problematic as the level of customer service people can experience through physical retail is very high and difficult to convey. This issue is not so relevant for mass-retailers as the level of in-store care doesn't compare with that offered by luxury fashion brands, for the latter to convey the same attentive and personalised service, the same aura of prestige, uniqueness, and excellence is not so straightforward.

Pangarkar, Arora and Shukla (2022) observe how brands such as Burberry aim to add a human touch to their customers' online interactions by offering live chat but also call backs from experienced sales advisors, however significant differences in the standard of online and in-real-life interactions are still present as they are difficult to replicate and convey through different modalities. In order to overcome this obstacle, luxury fashion brands are engaging more and more with digital tools and make the most of their intrinsic potential to convey an experience that is as personalised as possible and that resonates with people's expectations and demands, for example by exploring tools for digital marketing and communication, as examined in Chapter Eight, but also ways to engage consumers through strategies like gaming and dematerialisation, as discussed in Chapter Nine, also blurring the boundaries between retail and entertainment.

5.7 Conclusions

Chapter Five discussed the characterising traits of luxury fashion retail. It examined controlled distribution and issues related to parallel grey markets, and explored the different channels used by luxury fashion brands to distribute their products. Moreover, a case study focusing on Off-White then analysed the rationale and strategies employed when luxury fashion brands collaborate with mass-market retailers. Then the chapter discussed how, when it comes to luxury fashion, customers have high expectations at every stage of their shopping experience, and the pivotal role of flagship stores in this sense was investigated. Furthermore, the chapter addressed the reluctance of luxury fashion brands in joining the e-tail revolution, and explored the strategies they employed when they adopted such method of distribution. In this sense, omnichannel strategies and the evolution of e-commerce and m-commerce were discussed.

5.8 Revision questions

-   What strategies of distribution are adopted by luxury fashion brands?
-   What characterises the luxury fashion consumer experience?
-   What are the challenges faced by luxury fashion brands when selling goods online?

5.9 References

Ahn, S., Kim, H. and Forney, J. A. (2010) 'Fashion collaboration or collision? Examining the match-up effect in co-marketing alliances', *Journal of Fashion Marketing and Management*, 14(1), pp. 6–20.

Arrigo, E. (2015) 'The role of the flagship store location in luxury branding. An international exploratory study', *International Journal of Retail & Distribution Management*, 43(6), pp. 518–37.

Bain & Company (2016) *The millennial state of mind: digital is reshaping how luxury is purchased across generations*. Available at: https://www.bain.com/contentassets/0b0b0e19099a448e83af2fb53a563 0aa/bain20media20pack_the_millennial_state_of_mind.pdf

Boardman, R., Haschka, Y., Chrimes, C. and Alexander, B. (2020) 'Fashion "see-now-buy-now": implications and process adaptations', *Journal of Fashion Marketing and Management*, 24(3), pp. 495–515.

Bonetti, F., Perry, P. and Fernie, J. (2017) 'The evolution of luxury fashion retailing in China', in Choi, T. M. and Shen, B. (eds.) *Luxury fashion retail management*. Springer Series in Fashion Business. Singapore: Springer.

Cattapan, T. and Pongsakornrungsilp, S. (2022) 'Impact of omnichannel integration on Millennials' purchase intention for fashion retailer', *Cogent Business & Management*, 9(1), p. 2087460.

Chadha, R. and Husband, P. (2006) *The cult of the luxury brand: inside Asia's love affair with luxury*. London: Nicholas Brealey.

Chevalier, M., and Mazzalovo, G. (2012) *Luxury brand management: a world of privilege*. Singapore: John Wiley and Sons.

Holmqvist, J., Wirtz, J. and Fritze, M. P. (2021) Digital luxury services: Tradition versus innovation in luxury fashion. *Services marketing: people, technology, strategy*. Singapore: World Scientific, pp. 550–2.

Liu, S., Perry, P. and Gadzinski, G. (2019) 'The implications of digital marketing on WeChat for luxury fashion brands in China', Journal of Brand Management, 26, pp. 395–409.

Luck, E., Muratovski, G. and Hedley, L. (2014) 'Co-branding strategies for luxury fashion brands: Missoni for Target', Global Fashion Brands: Style, Luxury & History, 1(1), pp. 41–56.

Masè, S. and Silchenko, K. (2017) 'The Prada trend: brand building at the intersection of design, art, technology, and retail experience, in Jin, B. and Cedrola, E. (eds.) Fashion branding and communica-tion. Palgrave Studies in Practice: Global Fashion Brand Management. New York: Palgrave Pivot.

Moore, C. M. and Doherty, A. M. (2007) 'The international flagship stores of luxury fashion retailers', in Hines, T. and Bruce, M. (eds.) *Fashion marketing*. Oxford: Elsevier, pp. 277–96.

Moore, C. M., Doherty, A. M. and Doyle, S. A. (2010) 'Flagship stores as a market entry method: the perspective of luxury fashion retailing', European Journal of Marketing, 44(1/2) pp. 139–61.

Nobbs, K., Moore, C. M. and Sheridan, M. (2012) 'The flagship format within the luxury fashion market', *International Journal of Retail & Distribution Management*, 40(12), pp. 920–34.

Okonkwo, U. (2007) *Luxury fashion branding: trends, tactics, techniques*. Basingstoke: Palgrave Macmillan.

Pangarkar, A., Arora, V. and Shukla, Y. (2022) 'Exploring phygital omnichannel luxury retailing for immersive customer experience: the role of rapport and social engagement', Journal of Retailing and Consumer Services, 68, p.103001.

Riewoldt, O. (ed.), (2002) *Brandscaping: worlds of experience in retail design*. Basel: Birkhäuser.

Saviolo, S. and Corbellini, E. (2014) *Managing fashion and luxury companies*. Milan: Rizzoli Etas.

Sresnewsky, K. B. G. B., Yojo, A. S., Veloso, A. R. and Torresi, L. (2020) 'Rapport-building in luxury fashion retail: a collectivist culture case', *Journal of Fashion Marketing and Management*, 24(2), pp.251-76.

Wigley, S. M. and Provelengiou, A.-K. (2011) 'Market-facing strategic alliances in the fashion sector', Journal of Fashion Marketing and Management, 15(2), pp.141-62.

Part III

Luxury Fashion Marketing and Communication

6 Brand Identity for Luxury Fashion Marketing Communications

Case study: Coco Chanel

CHAPTER OBJECTIVES

This chapter:

- discusses sources of brand identity for luxury fashion brands
- explores narratives of country of origin and brand heritage
- examines the myth of the designer

6.1 Chapter summary

Chapter Six focuses on how luxury fashion brands can use different sources of brand identity in their marketing and communication strategies. After discussing different models of brand identity theorised by Kapferer, Floch and Aaker, the chapter examines in detail three pivotal elements that are used by luxury fashion brands to support their prestige and desirability through storytelling. First, the role of country of origin as a source of differentiation and competitive advantage is explored. In this sense, the problematic issues concerning the production practices and business structure of luxury fashion brands are also discussed. Second, the chapter analyses how brand heritage and in particular narratives of history and craftsmanship are mobilised by luxury fashion brands. Finally, the chapter discusses the pivotal role played by the myth of the designer in marketing and communication strategies, issues that are examined in more detail through the case study of Coco Chanel.

6.2 Introduction

Luxury fashion brands invest heavily in promoting and conveying their brand identity through a variety of media. To develop and strengthen their brand positioning through positive and coherent narratives that make them stand out from competitors is a necessity, because at stake is how that brand is perceived by people, as brand image will be affected by incongruences or ineffective communication and branding strategies.

DOI: 10.4324/9781003264811-10

People are influenced by their own personal values and expectations in their interactions with brands, but nonetheless brands should try and work on the elements they can control, and try to manage their brand identity in an effective and strategic way. In order to do so it's important to identify and understand brand identity and convey it in a consistent and coherent manner, which can in itself be challenging as luxury fashion brands can offer a myriad of products and services, communicate through a variety of media and situations, and can involve, through licensing, a number of entities that can contribute to steer the brand in different directions.

There are many different theories that can help identify what a brand stands for, so that the message can then be consistently conveyed through marketing and communication. Here, we examine first the identity prism devised by Kapferer, followed by Aaker's 12 dimensions of brand identity and Floch's semiotic square. Last, we examine Kapferer's theorisation of what constitutes the brand DNA before addressing in more detail the key elements for luxury fashion brands.

Kapferer's brand identity prism

Kapferer (2008) devised a brand identity prism that comprises six elements: physique, personality, culture, relationship, reflection and self-image. Physique consists of a combination of elements which immediately come to mind when people think about the brand. It comprises what the brand looks like, what it does and its prototype, i.e., the flagship product that represents the brand. Brand personality is represented by the kind of person the brand would be, and is something that is gradually created through the brand's communication, so that, for example, for Lacoste that would be sporty and elegant.

Brand culture is represented by the values that inspire the brand and guide its signs, from communication to the products and services it offers, which can be linked to the creator of the brand or its place of origin. For example, in this sense Ralph Lauren embodies WASP. Brand relationship focuses on the transactional side, as brands communicate with people and people communicate through brands.

Brands are also a reflection of their customers, as they represent what people wish to be perceived as when using the brand, whereas self-image represents how consumers see themselves when using the brand. A strong identity prism can help guide brand strategy, especially when decentralised decision making is involved, and is in this sense crucial to support coherent brand communication and marketing strategies.

Aaker's 12 dimensions of brand identity

Aaker (1996) proposes four brand identity perspectives comprising 12 different dimensions. Brands don't have to use all 12, but should at least consider them in order to define what they stand for.

The first perspective is brand-as-product and considers all product-related associations through product scope (in fact if there is a strong link to a product class the brand will then be recalled when the product class is cued), product attributes (that are the functional or emotional benefits of products, which can be enhanced by offering something better than competitors), quality/value (some brands focus on quality as a core identity element), association with use (a strong association with a specific use or occasion can offer competitive advantage), association with users (a strong association with a specific type of user can help position and differentiate brands), and last, country of origin (that can be used to add credibility and allure to brands).

The second perspective is brand-as-organization and focuses on organizational attributes such as innovation, drive for quality, trustworthiness or concerns for the environment. Those attributes are created by the company, its values and staff, and can be used in conjunction with product attributes to create a strong brand. Moreover, by focusing on a local dimension, brands can increase their trustworthiness and credibility.

The third perspective is brand-as-person and focuses on creating a strong brand identity through personality traits, as, for example, brands can be presented as genuine, energetic or rugged. This can help to communicate product attributes but can also be the basis for customer relationships, as it enables people to express their own personality through their association with the brand.

The fourth and last perspective is brand-as-symbol and focuses on improving recollection by offering a cohesive structure through symbols, visual imagery and metaphors that can provide functional or emotional benefits. In this sense, brand heritage can also be used to support strong brand identity.

Aaker also conceptualizes brand identity as including a core and an extended identity. The core identity, which is the central and timeless essence of the brand, is the part that is most likely to be retained as the brand approaches new markets and products, whereas the extended identity includes various brand identity elements that can complete and enrich the brand by adding details.

Floch's semiotic square

Another useful tool to assess and manage brand identity is the semiotic square. Originally devised by Greimas to investigate the production of meaning, the semiotic square was then adapted by Floch (2001) in the field of branding. The square is a versatile and agile tool that enables one to examine in a dynamic way what a brand stands for, what are its core characteristics, how it evolved and how it relates to competitors. The square articulates two categories, existential and utilitarian values, to propose four different types of valorisation: practical, utopian, ludic and critical.

The practical valorisation relies on utilitarian values, that focus on how products are relevant for their practical use, whereas the utopian valorisation involves existential values, where the focus is on the brand universe and the benefits it can propose to consumers, emphasising the dimensions of desire and myth. The utopian valorisation implies that products work as a medium to create identity or achieve status, while on the other hand the ludic valorisation transcends the practical functions of products and focuses on characteristics like beauty or pleasure. Last, the critical valorisation, complementary to the practical one, implies that a product is chosen purely for rational reasons, without taking into account 'unessential' characteristics like beauty, as the main value here is represented by economic convenience in the broader sense.

For example, Chevalier and Mazzalovo (2012: 171) discussed in detail how the semiotic square enables one to map out the evolution of the Ferragamo brand identity as they examine a study by Floch and Schwebel. In the 1990s, the Ferragamo brand was focusing on international expansion and aimed to become a global brand. In this sense, it was decided to move away from the utilitarian dimension and abandon a communication strategy solely based on the founder, Salvatore Ferragamo, as a shoemaker in terms of the comfort and durability of his creations (practical valorisation) and on Salvatore Ferragamo as a quality manufacturer offering a good quality/price ratio (critical valorisation). In fact, the brand worked towards creating a new focus on existential values which saw Salvatore Ferragamo presented as an artist playing with colours and innovative materials (ludic valorisation) and as a 'man of destiny' and shoemaker to the stars who can make those who buy his products feel special and desirable (utopian valorisation).

Kapferer's sources of brand identity

Another useful conceptualisation in this sense is represented by Kapferer's sources of identity. Kapferer (2008) lists seven elements that can create and nourish brand identity: typical products, brand name, brand characters, visual symbols and logotypes, advertising, geographical and historical roots, and the brand's creator.

A brand can in fact be associated with its most symbolic products, for example the trench coat for Burberry. A brand name can also convey meaning, as, for example, Hugo Boss alludes to city life and professional achievement. Brand characters, i.e., the images that are associated with the brand, as, for example, the horse for Hermès, can also be a valuable source of brand identity for luxury fashion brands.

Moreover, visual symbols and logotypes are also pivotal as brands identify with them and often change them when undergoing rebranding or rejuvenation. For example, Burberry in 2018 marked a new direction by abandoning its equestrian knight emblem and signature tartan pattern, opting for a more simple font and a new monogram print featuring interlocking letters (T and B in honour of Thomas Burberry, the brand's founder). Advertising, and any other forms of brand communication, also contributes to brand identity and storytelling.

Last, geographical and historical roots, in addition to the brand's creator, are particularly important elements for luxury labels and will be examined in more detail in the following sections, as country of origin, brand heritage, and the myth of the designer constitute pivotal sources of brand identity that luxury fashion brands can leverage on to create value, reinforce their prestige and status, create emotional attachment and loyalty, and ultimately drive sales.

6.3 Country of origin

Luxury fashion brands often refer to their country of origin, and this is an effective strategy for a number of reasons. Positive associations to a country can help provide differentiation and competitive advantage, but they can also offer a reserve for brands that can support their expansion in different markets or into different product ranges.

In a world that is more and more globalised, the local dimension is not actually cancelled but becoming even more important as people seek differentiation and uniqueness when offerings become more and more homogenised, this is the 'global paradox' theorised by Naisbitt (1994). Being associated with a certain country can offer benefits as it can set a luxury fashion brand apart from its competitors and also offer narratives that can be used for marketing and branding purposes, which are especially useful when brands are circulating in foreign markets.

For example, Italian brand Laura Biagiotti has been consistently using historical landmarks in its communication, and even used ancient Roman columns as inspiration for its Roma fragrances. In this sense, brand names can also offer cues, as, for example, the name Yohji Yamamoto evokes Japan whilst Yves Saint Laurent and Valentino evoke France and Italy, respectively. However, there is not always a congruence between brand names and their country of origin, as, for example, seen in the case of Comme des Garçons, a label with a French name that was founded by Japanese designer Rei Kawakubo.

Moreover, association with country of origin can also offer competitive advantage. This is especially the case for brands linked to specific countries that have acquired a positive reputation in the area where the company operates. For example, France and Italy have a long-standing association with fashion, and their leadership role and prestige in the luxury sector is recognised worldwide, creating a positive image that brands can capitalise on to gain advantage, especially in emerging markets.

In this sense a 'virtuous circle' emerges, one that sees brands taking advantage of positive images and narratives already circulating, which are then in turn strengthened and naturalised in a constant process that sees all parties involved being enhanced and gain traction. For example, as Italy has a long-established association with fashion and luxury, Italian luxury fashion brands can focus on their country of origin to enhance their reputation, but in doing so they also contribute to reinforce the very narratives they relied on, i.e., the prestige of the 'made in Italy' phenomenon.

However, sometimes the traits used to signify country of origin are questionable, as they are meant to be commercially effective but are not necessarily exact nor accurate (Castree 2001), as countries are often romanticised and seen through the lens of an idealised past or through cliché images that already circulate and are recognised by consumers worldwide. For Italian luxury fashion brands, this translates in a focus on art and the cult of aesthetics and quality, on creativity and craftsmanship, and on a slow and romanticised lifestyle rooted in tradition.

Furthermore, traits of national identity can also offer an invaluable reserve that luxury fashion brands can capitalise on when entering new markets, guiding expansion and offering a solid basis for brand coherence that is linked to positive connotations. For example, when Versace entered the hospitality business through Palazzo Versace hotels and restaurants they looked at Italy for inspiration in terms of décor but also for their menus. Similarly, Missoni hotels and restaurants were also rooted in the brand's myth, using signature patterns and brand culture as inspiration, but also used Italy as a reserve to inform service culture and food offerings.

Dallabona (2015) defines this phenomenon as 'cultural opportunism', a strategy that sees luxury fashion brands capitalise on elements linked to their country of origin and employ them to support their marketing, branding, retail and communication strategies, in order to add richness and depth to their brand identity, to support growth in new markets and the development of new products. Elements of national affiliation can provide brands with powerful narratives that can be articulated in their offerings, services and spaces to increase their sensory appeal and to enhance the customer experience by referring to established narratives and myths that involve the socio-cultural dimension.

For example Dolce & Gabbana relies heavily on its country of origin, Italy, with a particular focus on Sicily and the Mediterranean, in a variety of areas. Dolce & Gabbana stores showcase an abundance of marble, and the brand communication has often featured several elements commonly associated with Italy, for example multigenerational families, conviviality, women dressed in black and, more generally, a certain relaxed and fun lifestyle, traits linked to a golden age that does not reflect the pressures of modern-day lives. Dolce & Gabbana features typical Italian patterns such as mosaics and majolica in its products, and has also associated its name to typically Italian food products (such as pasta or panettone) or to iconic Italian brands (such as Martini or Bialetti). Dolce & Gabbana even launched a handbag shaped as a coffee machine. The label emphasised such elements and focused on positive traits of their country of origin even more in response to the controversy that emerged in 2018 with regards to lack of cultural sensibility in China, which is discussed in more detail in the case study of Chapter Nine.

However, sometimes to define the country of origin of luxury fashion brands is not quite so straightforward because even if consumers associate them to a certain country, i.e., the one where they were born, the issues of country of production or brand ownership problematise the notion. Some brands originated in a certain country but are now owned by groups based elsewhere, as, for example, French conglomerate Kering group now owns Italian labels Gucci and Bottega Veneta, in addition to Spanish Balenciaga, whereas Qatari group Mayhoola for Investments LCC owns French Balmain and Italian Valentino.

Moreover, many luxury fashion brands produce their goods abroad, Louis Vuitton makes no secret of producing its shoes in Fiesso D'artico as Italy is associated with excellent craftsmanship in that field, and similarly the fact that Chanel produces its cashmere in Scotland is not associated to negative narratives. However, it is alleged that many luxury fashion brands also produce in countries where labour cost is lower, such as China (Borstrock 2014).

Niu et al. (2020) report that Coach transferred their production from the USA to China in 1996, that British brand Burberry moved production from Wales to China in 2007, and that Prada also uses contract manufactures from the country. However, this is not a complete list, as many more luxury fashion brands are now producing abroad. Despite doing so, luxury fashion brands try to avoid being associated with countries that are not characterised by high prestige in terms of luxury production, and don't usually openly acknowledge that they are manufacturing their products there.

The rationale for this is represented by the fact that consumers generally hold in higher regard goods produced in countries that have a strong association with notions of quality, beauty and prestige, such as Italy or France. Moreover, luxury fashion brands are often criticised for moving production abroad, and want to avoid negative coverage by glossing over the issue.

Sometimes there are exceptions, as, for example, Prada in 2010 launched a limited collection that clearly indicated and drew attention to the fact that their products may not always be made in Italy, launching a series of 'Made in' collections that saw jeans made in Japan, alpaca knitwear from Peru, tartan made in Scotland and Chikan embroidery from India. But again, this strategy was designed to emphasise a valuable dimension of craftsmanship and tradition that was in line with brand identity, which is very different from manufacturing large numbers of cheaper goods in countries where costs are lower.

6.4 Brand heritage

Luxury fashion brands often focus, in their communication and marketing, on their heritage and more specifically on their history and craftsmanship. The rationale for that is represented by the fact that heritage can be leveraged to create and reinforce desirability, distinction but also romance and an idealised aura of timelessness.

Okonkwo (2007) observes that a brand's history offers a background story that people can get attracted to, enhancing the brand's communication power, and similarly Martin and Vacca (2018) also emphasise how heritage storytelling can be a major asset to create engagement. By focusing on heritage, luxury fashion brands create an emotional bond, they make people part of their history, and support connection on a personal level. Moreover, heritage can provide brands with a sense of authenticity, credibility, trust and differentiation.

History is an element that is mobilised and capitalised upon by a number of luxury fashion brands in a variety of ways in their marketing and communication strategies. Many brands have made history a key element of their brand identity, as, for example, Prada features the Savoy coat of arms and knotted rope design as part of its logo (the brand was granted the right to use it in 1919 when Prada became Official Supplier to the Italian Royal Household).

However, it has to be noted that only a few luxury fashion brands trace back to as early as the 19th century (for example Hermès, Luis Vuitton, Burberry and Fendi), as the majority of the brands operating today were founded in the 20th century. For example, Chanel and Balenciaga were established in the 1910s, Valentino and Jil Sander in the 1960s, Moschino and Doce & Gabbana in the 1980s, whereas Stella McCartney was founded in the early 2000s.

The newer the label, the less a luxury fashion brand can leverage on its individual history, but this doesn't mean that narratives of heritage are out of the question. In fact, a number of luxury fashion brands that don't have such a long history capitalise on the history of their country of origin, for example narratives of fashion, beauty and excellent designs are closely associated with Italy and those traits can be mobilised by luxury fashion brands in communication and marketing in a credible way as those narratives are recognised and accepted by consumers.

The history of a brand constitutes a powerful storytelling tool that can provide differentiation, credibility, trust and authenticity, so powerful that it can even grant resurrection, literally, to a label. This was, for example, the case for luxury fashion brand Schiaparelli. The label was founded by Elsa Schiaparelli in 1927 but closed down in 1954, however in 2012 the brand was relaunched. The Schiaparelli rebrand focused heavily on the rich history of the label, its innovativeness and its links to art, through Elsa's long-standing collaboration with iconic artists such as Salvador Dalí, but also on the myth of the designer, that similarly mobilises images of a glorious past that can provide prestige, credibility and distinction.

However, whereas many people in Western countries may have some awareness of the history of luxury fashion brands as those labels were born there and became important cultural references, in new markets where people didn't have a chance to develop the same degree of familiarity because such brands were only recently introduced, more efforts are required to inform new consumers about labels' history and what makes them unique, prestigious, credible and desirable. This can be achieved in a number of ways, through advertising and promotion, by including references in stores and on merchandise, through visual symbols but also through travelling international exhibitions and the launch of brand archives and museums.

Nowadays a number of luxury fashion brands have created spaces that focus on their history. For example, in Spain one can find the Cristóbal Balenciaga Museum, in France the Fondation Pierre Bergé – Yves Saint Laurent, the Musée Christian Dior, and the Pierre Cardin Museum. In Italy one can find the Ferragamo and Gucci museums in Florence, whereas in Milan a permanent exhibition showcasing a selection of Giorgio Armani pieces is presented at the Armani/Silos gallery. Also in Italy, Casa Zegna is a place where the history and craftsmanship of the brand are closely intertwined.

If virtually all luxury fashion brands feature a section, on their websites, where their history, pivotal moments and achievements are listed and disseminated, on the other hand the number of online exhibitions and events launched that focus on such elements is still limited, and in this sense the case of Valentino represents an exception. The Valentino Garavani Museum is fully online and was developed purely as such, featuring a variety of resources, from dresses to sketches, from advertising campaigns to videos of fashion shows to name but a few, that are available to everybody everywhere (Martin and Vacca 2018).

Moreover, Ok (2018) examines how nostalgia is used by luxury fashion brands, for example Louis Vuitton employed vintage inspired looks, old trains and the Louvre Museum as background to convey a sense of timelessness and permanence. A similar strategy has been used for example by Chanel, with a focus on Parisian chic and lifestyle through old buildings to offer a sense of history.

Moreover, luxury fashion brands can focus on craftsmanship in their marketing and communication strategies to achieve distinction, desirability and prestige. Craftsmanship is linked to many traits that characterise luxury, such as ideas of quality in terms of the material used and how a good is made, but also durability and uniqueness.

Some luxury fashion brands originated in a workshop and are associated to a specific know-how, as, for example, Gucci and Prada were born as leather workshops, Fendi as a fur maker, Ferragamo originally only made shoes and Luis Vuitton made luggage and trunks. Craftsmanship is a pivotal element for the very definition of luxury brands but, as we discussed in Chapter One, not every product associated with them is actually handmade. However, as discussed by Chevalier and Mazzalovo (2012), people prefer to believe that they are produced in such a manner.

Okonkwo (2007: 11) observes that it takes almost 20 hours to manufacture a Kelly Bag at Hermès, and that the handmade craftsmanship required by some Gucci products means that some items have to be ordered two years in advance. These narratives of craftsmanship and excellence are reinforced by the brands' communication, as, for example, in France one can visit a Hermès workshop in Bagnolet or a Luis Vuitton workshop in Asnières, where people can see expert craftspeople making goods by hand, but this is only a partial representation of how luxury fashion goods are actually made.

In fact, the majority of products associated with luxury fashion brands, in particular cheaper lines and extensions such as those into cosmetics and eyewear, are mass-manufactured

(Dallabona 2014). Another element that remains hidden under narratives of craftsmanship is also the fact that luxury fashion brands produce their goods abroad, in countries where labour costs are lower.

However, for luxury fashion brands the issue of craftsmanship remains essential for their reputation, prestige and a key element of brand identity. For example, Chanel is particularly active in this sense, as it has acquired a number of its suppliers through their Paraffection subsidiary with the aim to preserve traditional craftsmanship, for example with regards to embroidery, flou and pleating. Some of those suppliers are now housed in Chanel's 19M space and are showcased to the world through the Métiers d'art collection (see also the case study in this chapter).

However, Chanel is not the only label to focus on preserving and promoting craftsmanship, as, for example, LVMH in 2011 launched the Journées Particulières to showcase the group's know-how by opening the doors of artisan workshops in a variety of areas, from jewellery to trunkmaking. The LVMH website also emphasises the links between their brands and history, culture, craft and national identity. Moreover, Gucci has launched a series of initiatives to support the preservation and development of craftsmanship in the areas of leather and foot-wear (through a craftsmanship school and the Gucci École de l'Amour) and in ready-to-wear through a fashion prototyping programme in collaboration with Istituto Secoli.

Issues of history and craftsmanship are an essential part of the heritage of luxury fashion brands, that can capitalise on both elements in their communication and marketing strate-gies. This is, for example, the case of Salvatore Ferragamo. As examined by Ostillio and Ghad-dar (2017), the brand Ferragamo now offers a variety of fashion products but as mentioned before the company originates in the shoemaking business. Salvatore Ferragamo emigrated from Italy to the USA as a teenager to further his shoemaking skills and acquire the most advanced techniques available at the time. There, he discovered, for example, the tanning drum, a tool that allowed production time to be cut from months to days. His craftsmanship was so appreciated that in just a few years Salvatore found himself designing shoes for movie stars both on and off the set.

However, in the USA he didn't have access to the high-quality handmade craftsmanship, like embroidery or lace, that he could find in Italy, so he moved back to his home country and chose Florence in which to settle. There, he bought an historical building, Palazzo Spini Feroni, where the brand's headquarters and museum are still located. The building played an important role in the brand's development, as its image was featured in packaging, advertis-ing and as a pattern on products, emphasising links to the past, capitalising on the reputation of Florence and, more broadly, on Italian history, in order to transfer a sense of timelessness and legitimacy to the label. Moreover, Ferragamo also used heritage as inspiration for new market entry and product development.

In the 1950s, the brand started to move towards large-scale machine-made production but always retained handmade craftsmanship for details and decorations (in addition to a fully artisanal line), and by coupling those two elements Ferragamo was able to increase production and introduce new lines and products whilst retaining the brand's heritage. When Salvatore died, in 1960, his wife Wanda and children developed the business by using the company's archive as a guide for retaining continuity in design, in this sense focusing on the myth of the designer (examined in section 6.5). The narratives in this sense focus on

Salvatore Ferragamo as a great innovator that studied anatomy with the aim to improve the comfort and fit of his shoes, which resulted in almost 400 patents and trademarks.

In 1995, to disseminate and reinforce this legacy, the brand opened the Ferragamo Museum, and launched at the same time a travelling exhibition to further spread the myth of the label and its craftsmanship. History and craftsmanship are also closely intertwined in the case of Burberry. In fact, Burberry often focuses, in its marketing and communication, on its tradition of craft and innovation, emphasising the invention of the weatherproof fabric gabardine in 1879 and its pivotal role in establishing the brand's signature trench coat, which was used by the British military in WWI.

6.5 Myth of the designer

Another element that, like heritage, can offer luxury fashion brands significant advantages in terms of communication and marketing, being mobilised to achieve differentiation, gain media coverage, offer inspiration to products and campaigns, and more generally to support and strengthen brand identity and image, is represented by the myth of the designer.

The myth of the designer appears to be natural and obvious, but it's actually a selective narrative, in this case pursued for financial gain, that hides under an aura of reality (Barthes 1972). This narrative becomes more and more powerful as it is disseminated through all the brands' channels, from websites and online communication to retail spaces, and at times can take on a life of its own, becoming embedded in popular culture and being spread by other players who in turn reinforce such narrative and keep it relevant.

However, to focus on the myth of the designer is not necessarily a strategy that every luxury fashion brand may want to pursue. The industry comprises a variety of enterprises that are at different stages, some of them are still managed by their creators or their heirs, like in the case of Armani and Missoni, whereas some had to face the death of their iconic founders and have seen a number of designers helming the labels. Sometimes the new designers are presented as icons themselves, but this is not always the case. For example, Luis Vuitton opted to support brand equity without creating a myth focusing on the many different designers they have employed.

For brands that are no longer fronted by their founders or their families, the myth of the designer usually involves primarily or solely the former, like in the case of Chanel (see section 6.6 for a more detailed discussion). For many eponymous labels that don't yet have a long history behind them, the myth of the designer-founder can be used productively as a strategy to support differentiation and offer communication and marketing advantages, like, for example, in the case of Stella McCartney.

Sometimes one can observe a complex situation where personal myth and brand myth collide but also remain distinct. This is, for example, the case for Karl Lagerfeld, who became an icon whilst working for three different luxury fashion brands at the same time. Before his death, Lagerfeld had been helming Fendi since 1965, Chanel since 1983 and his own Karl Lagerfeld eponymous brand since 1984. It is interesting to note how the myth of Karl Lagerfeld was created through references to the brands he worked for but also disseminated and commodified through them. In fact, Lagerfeld was known for a specific look, one that was in line Chanel's aesthetics, a severe signature style that involved wearing only black and white, but with personal touches like leather gloves, dark sunglasses and a white ponytail.

A key piece of his iconic look was represented by white shirts with high collars and thick cuffs, so much so that after his death a travelling exhibition and collection of limited-edition white shirts (that would later be sold for charity) was launched, whereas tributes by the general public were shared online through #MyWhiteShirtForKarl, which further confirms how much Lagerfeld's image had become a shared cultural symbol.

During his life, Lagerfeld really pushed the boundaries, becoming an immediately recognisable icon and creating and commodifying his image and myth, especially for Fendi and his own eponymous label. For Fendi, he launched the Karlito bag, which featured a fur version of himself, whilst for his namesake brand he was transformed into a Tokidoki figurine and cartoon-like images of himself were featured on a variety of products. In his last years, his cat Choupette was also added to the myth, and it became an integral part of his image that similarly became iconic and was commodified, further spreading the myth and in turn capitalising on it. However, the myth and cult of a designer can be created and supported through a variety of strategies, as discussed by Dion and Arnould (2011).

Dion and Arnould (2011) observe that to reach the status of myth designers need to acquire legitimacy. This can be achieved in a variety of ways, first by associating with the realm of art, for example either through their own artistic practice, like in the case of Karl Lagerfeld and his work as photographer, or by being an art collector like Miuccia Prada (whose role in this sense was recognised when, in 2010, she presented the Turner Prize for art). Moreover, this can also be achieved by projecting an iconic image or a transgressive one, focused on how the designer breaks and rewrites the aesthetic norms to create something new and unique that itself becomes a work of art.

However, the legitimacy of the designer also depends on the sanction of a series figures. First, by other artists or authoritative figures who are held in high regard and can therefore welcome the designer into their fold and share their aura of legitimacy. Second, by cultural intermediaries in the luxury fashion field, such as journalists, that possess the skills and knowledge, or cultural capital in Bourdieu's (1984) terms, to judge the work of fashion designers and publicly consecrate them. Third, legitimacy can be acquired through opinion leaders such as celebrities, who influence others with their endorsement as people look up to them and trust their judgement. We can see, in this sense, that the myth of the designers is founded on their performance, on their fashion shows and the products they create.

Dion and Arnould (2011) further argue, however, that key clients and the general public also have a role in attributing, or removing, this charismatic authority, as that is the product of a social process of constant reaffirmation. For example, John Galliano had been a successful and critically acclaimed designer for years, projecting an image of eccentricity and innovativeness. He had been working as the artistic director of Dior for over ten years when a scandal erupted and the status he had acquired collapsed. In 2010 Galliano, while at a bar in Paris, made racist and anti-Semitic comments, a behaviour that constitutes a crime in France (a trial ensued and he was ordered to pay a fine). The news spread around the world and LVMH, the group that owned Dior and also the John Galliano label, reacted and quickly and fired the designer from both labels. LVMH had at the time just dealt with a similar scandal concerning racism and anti-Semitism, which involved a descendant of the Guerlain family making offensive comments in an interview which led to demonstrations and calls for a boycott, which explains why the group wanted to immediately distance itself from Galliano to avoid a further public backlash.

To recover from this fall from grace of the iconic designer, LVMH opted to rebrand the Galliano brand and with regards to Dior it focused on emphasising the know-how and craftsmanship of the label but also, interestingly, on the myth of the brand's founder Christian Dior.

In this sense the myth of the designer can be eroded if they fail to retain their legitimacy, but another potentially troublesome situation for brands is constituted by the time a key designer leaves the label, be that because they retire or die. In this sense, luxury fashion brands can retain this charismatic aura through kinship, by passing on key roles to family members. For Versace, the myth of the designer continued after the tragic death of Gianni, murdered in 1997, supported and enhanced after the company's takeover by the designer's siblings.

If passing on the role to a relative is not an option, a brand can continue to focus on the charisma of the former mythical designer by proposing the narrative of the 'spiritual heir', like in the case of Jean Paul Gautier when he joined Saint Laurent. To bring forward designers and their signs and symbols is a powerful tool to strengthen brand identity for luxury fashion brands, as, for example, in the re-launch of the Schiaparelli brand the designer's signature (in the iconic Schiaparelli shocking pink colour) was chosen as the logo.

When adopting a strategy focusing on the myth of the designer, reality and fiction can sometime overlap. For example, in 2016, Burberry, to celebrate its 160th anniversary, released the short movie 'The Tale of Thomas Burberry', a romanticised version of the story of its founder where the focus was Thomas' fictionalised love life.

Other key elements that can feature in the myth of the luxury fashion designer are represented by narratives focusing on the dedication and the sacrifices needed to succeed and on the negative elements often associated with it, especially in terms of mental health, which culminates in images of the tormented genius. The latter aspect is one that is mostly featured in discourses not originating within the luxury fashion brands themselves, as it can offer compelling storylines that can be used for books or movies.

This is, for example, the case for Yves Saint Laurent, as discussed by Moine (2017). Yves Saint Laurent founded the eponymous label in 1962 (with Pierre Bergé) after a few years helming Christian Dior. His brand was a success and he became an icon himself, with his signature look of horn-rimmed glasses. He remained at the forefront of his label, he even posed naked, in 1971, to promote the brand's Pour Homme fragrance. When he retired, in 2002, his myth was sustained through the Fondation Pierre Bergé - Yves Saint Laurent, which aims to conserve and promote the designer's work.

Nowadays, the myth of Yves Saint Laurent is further supported by two museums opened where he lived and worked, one in Paris in rue Marceau and one in Marrakech. However, a series of revelations about his past contributed to a renewed interest and the consolidation of the myth of Yves Saint Laurent.

Yves had battled multiple addictions and suffered from depression, which emerged when he was drafted into military service during the Algerian War. These elements were particularly emphasised by two biopics released in 2014. Their role in spreading the myth of Yves Saint Laurent was recognised by Pierre Bergé, who endorsed one of them, 'Saint Laurent' by Jalil Lespert and even hired the actor playing the late designer, Pierre Niney, to promote the brand's fragrance Nuit de l'Homme. The same strategy, that sees the actor playing the designer in a biopic becoming part of the brand's communication and marketing, was also used in 2009 by Chanel, when Audrey Tautou featured in a Chanel No5 advertising film.

6.6 Case study: Chanel

A brand that has successfully fostered and exploited the myth of the designer to support and nourish the brand is Chanel. This myth was started when Coco was alive, depicting her as fiercely independent, intrinsically chic, and as a successful designer and entrepreneur, but continued after her death, becoming a powerful marketing tool that has been exploited in many ways, from communication to product development, to fashion shows and corporate spaces.

The myth of Coco Chanel is so important for the brand that the company's website features a minisite completely dedicated to its founder, full of images and information aiming to foster a portrait of Coco that resonates with contemporary audiences. The myth of Coco Chanel has become so strong and widespread that it has become part of popular culture, and is reinforced every day through different media, platforms and discourses that don't originate in the brand itself. However, as discussed below, Coco's myth is intrinsically selective, and sees only positive and inspirational elements being featured, leaving out narratives that may prove problematic.

Gabrielle 'Coco' Chanel started her business foray by opening a millinery boutique in 1910 in Paris, in 21 Rue Cambon, before expanding by opening a boutique in Dauville, where her collection of sportswear (with its innovative use of jersey fabrics that up to then were used mostly for men's underwear) was a success. She then founded, in 1913, her first Couture House in Biarritz before moving operations to Paris in 31 Rue Cambon, where the label's boutique, salons and workshops are still located.

Coco recognised the opportunities represented by expanding the brand into fragrances and beauty products and launched her first perfume, the iconic Chanel No5, in 1921 before releasing many more fragrances, and also a makeup collection and a skincare line, within the next ten years. In the 1930s, Chanel designed costumes for Hollywood and launched a high jewellery collection, but during World War II the Couture House was closed down, and only accessories and perfumes where produced and sold. Chanel reopened the Couture House many years later, in 1954, and in the next decade developed many products that became iconic and are now strictly associated with the brand, for example the 2.55 handbag, the trimmed tweed suit and the two-tone pumps.

Gabrielle Chanel died in 1971 and the brand struggled before Karl Lagerfeld became artistic director and started another successful phase for the brand, including a line of watches and more fragrances. Lagerfeld introduced the Métiers d'art collection and supported the acquisition of craft houses, providing another strong element of brand identity (Chanel currently owns over 40 crafts businesses), which complemented the focus on Parisian chic that was reinforced through marketing, communication but also by associating with the iconic Grand Palais (that has hosted the brand's fashion shows for years), whose renovation was sponsored by the brand, and through sponsoring the City of Paris Fashion Museum, Palais Galliera. Nonetheless, Coco Chanel is still the fulcrum of her eponymous brand.

Coco Chanel remained at the centre of the brand even after she sold her shares in the company. She lived next to the boutique and workshop of Rue Cambon, and was used as a public relations tool endorsing a cult based on her past (Riot 2013). After her death her apartment, which has now been designated as a historical monument, has been used as the perfect embodiment of the company's aesthetics, and it continues to inspire brand identity. For example, the Chanel boutique in Hong Kong is inspired by Coco's apartment and reproduces its signature elements. During the reign of Karl Lagerfeld, the fragrances Coco Mademoiselle and Gabrielle were launched as a tribute to the designer, and, moreover, museum exhibitions focusing on her were launched, whilst the brand's communication continuously emphasised her pioneering role and the elements who made her a fashion icon.

Gabrielle Chanel was a successful entrepreneur that made the most of opportunities and managed to create a strong brand centred on her persona, her talent for self-promotion saw her becoming an icon as her designs gathered popularity, and this dimension was greatly emphasised after her death. Coco Chanel's distinctive look consisting of dark hair in a bob coupled with severe black and white garments accessorised with costume jewellery, oversized string of pearls alongside bows, gilded buttons, camellias and quilted bags became legendary. These elements are still used today to signify Chanel, and feature in different levels, from products to advertisements, to fashion shows and store design. For example, they were used as props in the AW2008/9 fashion show, visible symbols of Chanel that worked because they are recognised as such worldwide.

Chanel's communication also emphasises how daring, liberated and ahead of her time Coco was, so much so that she had to create her own clothes to be able to enjoy the active lifestyle she favoured. Her simple and practical style suited the new active role in society played by women after WWII. Coco created a signature style that she successfully commodified, as after the Chanel house reopened the focus was on producing luxury items as cheaply as possible and to dress not just a few hundreds of women anymore but thousands of them (Driscoll 2010).

The brand's minisite presents Coco Chanel as an instinctive and innovative entrepreneur who was the first to pose for company's advertisements and to launch a fragrance. However, actually the first couturier to develop a perfume and cosmetic line was Poiret, but the figure of Coco Chanel resonates more with contemporary values and presented her as the emblem of a new society, a true independent woman that succeeded in business solely thanks to her ability. The creation, in 2011, of the Fondation Chanel, which is aimed at improving the economic and social conditions of women worldwide, is further supporting such narratives.

Coco Chanel came from a poor family, her mother died when she was a child and she was sent to an orphanage with her sisters, there she learned to sew and found employment as a seamstress whilst also singing in cabarets as Coco. She then moved into the chateau of Étienne Balsan, a wealthy heir in the textile business who introduced her to the world of high society and horseraces. It was he who funded Coco's start as milliner while another lover, Arthur Capel, financed her Chanel Mode boutique and, later on, her Couture House (Cattani et al 2022).

However, these elements are not emphasised by the company, as they are not in line with the myth proposed. The Chanel minisite offers some acknowledgement of the situation, but at the same time also minimises the support Coco received, as it mentions only the contribution of Arthur Capel and clarifies that Coco repaid him in full as a question of principle as she wanted to retain complete freedom. The minisite also presents Coco as a patron of the arts, a visionary creative who was fond of signs and symbols, for example naming her No19 perfume as a tribute to her birthday, and featuring the motif of the star and Leo (her star sign) consistently throughout her career.

These narratives about Coco Chanel have been so successful that her myth has developed a life of its own, hiding controversial elements, and becoming disseminated in a variety of media through narratives that transcend the brand, further spreading a positive myth of Coco that the label can capitalise on. For example, three films on Coco's life where released on the occasion of the 100th anniversary of the foundation of Chanel, but none of them mentioned the negative elements like the support she received from her lovers not only in financial terms, but also in terms of suppliers and clientele (Riot 2013) or the fact that she tried to take advantage of Nazi laws to regain ownership of Les Parfums Chanel and that was later suspected of being a Nazi collaborator (Cattani et al.2022).

Questions and activities

- What are the elements that characterise the myth of Coco Chanel?
- How did the brand Chanel spread the myth of Coco Chanel?
- Analyse the strategies adopted with regards to the creation of the myth of the designer by two other luxury fashion brands and compare and contrast the tactics they adopted

6.7 Conclusions

Chapter Six focused on how luxury fashion brands can use different sources of brand identity to create and disseminate narratives about what the brands stand for through their marketing and communication strategies. The chapter discussed how such narratives are intrinsically selective and often present a mix of fact and fiction aimed at supporting the brands' prestige and desirability through storytelling. The chapter examined several sources of identity before addressing in more detail first, the role of country of origin as a source of differentiation and competitive advantage, second, the case of historical roots and heritage of luxury fashion brands and last, the myth of the designer as a powerful communication tool. This was further investigated through a case study focusing on the figure of Coco Chanel in the label's marketing and communication practices.

6.8 Revision questions

- What are the sources of brand identity for luxury fashion brands?
- How do luxury fashion brands use references to their history and country of origin?
- What's the role of the myth of the designer in luxury fashion communication?

6.9 **References**

Aaker, D. A. (1996) *Building strong brands*. New York: Simon and Schuster.

Barthes, R. (1972) *Mythologies*. London: Cape.

Borstrock, S. (2014) 'Do contemporary luxury brands adhere to historical paradigms of luxury?' in Hancock, J., Muratovski, G., Manlow, V. and Pierson-Smith, A. (eds.) *Global fashion brands: style, luxury and history*. Bristol: Intellect, pp. 231–48.

Bourdieu, P. (1984) *Distinction: a social critique of the judgement of taste*. London: Routledge and Keegan Paul.

Castree, N. (2001) 'Commodity fetishism, geographical imaginations and imaginative geographies', *Environment and Planning*, 33(9), pp. 1519–25.

Cattani, G., Colucci, M. and Ferriani, S. (2022) *From the margins to the core of haute couture: the entrepreneurial journey of Coco Chanel, enterprise & society*. Cambridge University Press, pp. 1–43, doi:10.1017/eso.2021.58.

Chevalier, M. and Mazzalovo, G. (2012) *Luxury brand management: a world of privilege*. Singapore: John Wiley and Sons.

Dallabona, A. (2014) 'Narratives of Italian craftsmanship and the luxury fashion industry: representations of Italianicity in discourses of production', in Hancock, J. H., Muratovski, G., Manlow, V. and Pearson-Smith, A. (eds.) *Global fashion brands: style, luxury & history*. Chicago: Intellect.

Dallabona, A. (2015) 'Luxury fashion flagship hotels and cultural opportunism: the cases of Hotel Missoni Edinburgh and Maison Moschino. *Hospitality and Society*, 5(2–3), pp. 117–43 https://doi.org/10.1386/hosp.5.2-3.117_1

Dion, D. and Arnould, E. (2011) 'Retail luxury strategy: assembling charisma through art and magic', *Journal of Retailing*, 87(4), pp. 502–20.

Driscoll, C. (2010) 'Chanel: the order of things', *Fashion Theory*, 14(2), pp. 135–58, doi:10.2752/175174110X12665093381504

Floch, J.-M. (2001) *Semiotics, marketing and communication: beneath the signs, the strategies*. Basingstoke: Palgrave.

Kapferer, J. N. (2008) *The new strategic brand management: creating and sustaining brand equity long term*. London: Kogan Page.

Martin, M. and Vacca, F. (2018) 'Heritage narratives in the digital era: how digital technologies have improved approaches and tools for fashion know-how, traditions, and memories', *Research Journal of Textile and Apparel*, 22(4), pp. 335–51. https://doi.org/10.1108/RJTA-02-2018-0015

Moine, R. (2017) Saint Laurent on screen: fashion icon, doomed artist, or celebrity?, *Fashion Theory*, 21(6), pp. 733–48, doi:10.1080/1362704X.2017.1357369

Naisbitt, J. (1994) *Global paradox*. New York: Avon Books.

Niu, B., Chen, L. and Xie, F. (2020) 'Production outsourcing for limited-edition luxury goods with consideration of consumers' origin preferences', *Transportation Research Part E: Logistics and Transportation Review*, 140, p. 101975.

Ok, P. (2018) 'European luxury fashion brand advertising and marketing relating to nostalgia', *Studies in Communication Sciences*, 18(2), 307–24. https://doi.org/10.24434/j.scoms.2018.02.007

Okonkwo, U. (2007) *Luxury fashion branding: trends, tactics, techniques*. Basingstoke: Palgrave Macmillan.

Ostillio, M. C., Ghaddar, S. (2017). 'Salvatore Ferragamo: brand heritage as main vector of brand extension and internationalization', in Jin, B. and Cedrola, E. (eds) *Fashion branding and communication*. Palgrave Studies in Practice: Global Fashion Brand Management. New York: Palgrave, https://doi.org/10.1057/978-1-137-52343-3_3

Riot, E. (2013) 'Woman in love, artist or entrepreneur? The edifying, mystifying life of Coco Chanel', *Society and Business Review*, 8(3), pp. 281–313. https://doi.org/10.1108/SBR-12-2012-0054

7 Luxury Fashion Promotion and Advertising
Case study: Fear of God

CHAPTER OBJECTIVES

This chapter:

- discusses the methods luxury fashion brands employ in terms of promotion and advertising
- explores the role of fashion shows, advertising campaigns and celebrity endorsement
- examines the pivotal role of PR

7.1 Chapter summary

Chapter Seven discusses issues related to promotion and advertising within the luxury fashion industry. The chapter analyses in particular the pivotal role of fashion shows, that nowadays are a spectacle for the wider public but that were originally meant for fashion insiders only. Moreover, the chapter addresses how advertising is employed by luxury fashion brands, also considering the differences arising from the variety of products associated with labels. Furthermore, the role of celebrity endorsement within the marketing strategies of luxury fashion brands is also discussed, and illustrated through the case study of Fear of God. Finally, the chapter focuses on PR, discussing the different activities and opportunities for luxury fashion brands, but also its role in terms of crisis management through a number of examples.

7.2 Introduction

To promote and advertise their products and brands is essential for luxury fashion labels, and they put significant efforts into informing consumers of new collections or products, into spreading brand awareness, disseminating their brand values and reinforcing brand identity whilst enhancing their aura of prestige and exclusivity. The most established tools

DOI: 10.4324/9781003264811-11

used in this sense are fashion shows, advertising, celebrity endorsement and public relations, which are the focus of this chapter (most recent strategies concerning digital marketing and social media are examined in Chapter Eight). In the following pages it will be discussed how these elements have evolved following a series of changes affecting the socio-economical dimension.

Luxury fashion brands showcase new designs through lavish and extravagant fashion shows, create narratives and employ storytelling also through association with celebrities and influential figures, and employ a variety of tools and strategies to engage with different stakeholders, gain media coverage, nourish their brand and drive financial profitability. For luxury fashion brands it is essential to communicate with their clients, potential customers and the wider public in order to boost sales, retain high brand awareness, and capture people's attention and imagination, supporting their desirability and aspirational nature. Before the Internet and social media, brand communication was a one-way process, whereas now technology has created a new situation that sees people becoming more engaged and an important part of the narrative surrounding the brand, sometimes co-creating discourses and spreading positive images and values but also, on the other hand, sometimes working against the brand to disseminate criticism.

Luxury fashion brands spend considerable amounts on advertising, it's not unusual for brands operating in fragrance and beauty to spend as much as 50% of revenues following the launch of a new product. Chadha and Husband (2006), report that LVHM spends approximately 11% of sales on advertising, whereas Gucci is thought to invest about 12%. However, the details concerning practices of luxury fashion brands are not generally made public (Chevalier and Mazzalovo 2012).

Luxury fashion brands have to make sure to create appropriate content that can reach relevant target markets, which has become a much more complex exercise now that labels operate globally and aim to entice both the higher market segment and less affluent consumers. Moreover, the situation has been made more problematic by the fact that the strategies employed by luxury fashion brands to promote and market their labels have somehow lost some lustre as mass retailers and prestige brands have been adopting many of them. In this sense, for example, elements such as fashion shows, extravagant product launches and celebrity campaigns have become more commonplace and have lost the ability to unequivocally convey notions of prestige, status and exclusivity, and forcing luxury labels to push the boundaries and explore new strategies to differentiate themselves and capture people's attention in a competitive and saturated mediascape.

The next section explores issues concerning the evolution and role of fashion shows in creating and supporting the aura of luxury fashion brands, whereas section 7.4 examines advertising and celebrity endorsement (also through the case study of brand Fear of God), and last, section 7.6 discusses in detail the multifaceted role of PR.

7.3 Fashion shows

Fashion shows are considered essential to promote luxury fashion brands. The most important luxury fashion brands present mainly at the four main fashion weeks taking place in Paris, Milan, London and New York, although other locations are commonly used for resort collections shows. Fashion shows today are a media spectacle aimed at the general public, and not anymore simply a way to propose new designs to customers and to address fashion insiders such as journalists and buyers. Nowadays fashion shows are streamed live on a variety of platforms, receive significant coverage, and content is quickly disseminated by users through social media. In this sense fashion shows have evolved greatly.

Pinchera and Rinallo (2021) observe that in the second half of the 19th century clothes started to be presented on living people, following years of using wax or wooden dummies to show off designs to potential customers. Lucile, founded by Lady Duff Gordon, is believed to have been the first luxury fashion brand, in 1901, to adopt a theatrical parade of models (who were instructed not to talk or smile, and to strike dramatic poses) and to use music and lighting to stage a distinctive experience. However, these elements were quickly adopted by other fashion houses and became the norm. Fashion shows were initially aimed at buyers and the press, but concerns about design piracy and counterfeiting meant that luxury fashion brands were very selective in allowing access to their fashion shows, and also enforced a series of restrictions, for example forbidding sketching or taking photos and by dictating when reports could be made public.

It was only in the 1970s that fashion shows started to become the media spectacle they are today, with designers creating striking displays and exaggerated looks to capture attention and encourage the media to record and share images with the public. In the 1980s fashion shows became extremely popular with the general public, fashion houses started to pursue the presence of celebrities and to employ supermodels like Naomi Campbell, Linda Evangelista and Cindy Crawford, a phenomenon that was driven by Gianni Versace. It was in the 1980s that fashion shows started to be primarily considered as promotional events aimed at generating media coverage.

Since then, the biggest revolution has been represented by the Internet and social media, which consolidated fashion shows as events targeting the general public even more. In this respect, New York fashion week was the first to allow taking and sharing digital images and to offer infrastructure to support social media coverage. Social media is now ubiquitous at fashion shows, and it's not unusual for luxury fashion brands to select some models also because of their social media visibility, in order to gather media interest and increase circulation and awareness online.

However, the recent focus on social media has also created some issues and generated a power struggle between bloggers/influencers/content creators and figures that are more established and authoritative, at least within fashion circles, such as fashion editors and buyers for example. This struggle is epitomised in the politics of seating at fashion shows, as front-row places are more desirable and given to those who are seen as the most important guests, which are now represented by those linked with celebrity culture and social media, whilst fashion journalists and buyers are sometimes relegated to less desirable seating. In order to avoid this impasse some luxury fashion brands have experimented with novel catwalk designs, for example creating really long runaways so that everyone is offered a front-row seat, or through technological means, for example by adopting virtual fashion shows.

Luxury fashion brands have often experimented with technological tools to offer novel experiences and gain media exposure, as, for example, in 2006 Alexander McQueen presented a hologram of model Kate Moss on the catwalk, whilst in 2018 Dolce & Gabbana had drones flying handbags on the runaway. However, fashion houses started to engage more and more with the digital dimension of fashion shows in the aftermath of the COVID-19 pandemic, as travel restrictions and social distancing made it problematic to host fashion shows with a live international public in an indoor setting. Fashion weeks held over the summer of 2020 took place completely digitally due to the restrictions, but luxury fashion brands had already engaged with different forms of fashion shows in the past, although they did not become commonly used until the pandemic

As discussed by Linfante and Pompa (2021), the idea of having a film instead of a live fashion show was first explored by Paul Poiret in 1911, when the parade of designs shown at his 'The thousand and second night' was projected to foreign buyers months later. In the 1990s many luxury fashion brands like Helmut Lang presented their designs through CDs or Internet broadcasts, and this practice became more and more popular in the 2000s as cheaper and faster connectivity was available, further fuelled by the development of mobile technology. However, those practices only become consolidated during the pandemic, before losing their primacy once again when restrictions were gradually eased.

At first luxury fashion brands were able to show in person again, but either in open spaces (as, for example, Balmain presented its FW2021 fashion shows along the river Seine in Paris whereas Chloé used the deserted streets of Saint-Germain-des-Prés) or through hybrid formats where some guests were in attendance while screens were used in place of digital guests (for SS2021 Balmain featured rows of monitors whilst Vuitton featured columns holding smartphones). Some brands were more imaginative, as, for example, Moschino created a puppet-show with both models and guests, like renowned fashion journalists Anna Wintour and Anna Dello Russo, for its SS2021 collections.

Fashion shows are nowadays very expensive spectacles, as high costs are associated with the use of exclusive locations, extravagant productions, sought-after models and celebrities but also PR activities. Fashion shows have become more and more flamboyant as their aim evolved from being an opportunity to show designs to buyers to a media spectacle focused on increasing brand awareness and support notions of prestige and desirability.

In this sense, the quest for more memorable and striking locations has led luxury fashion brands like Dolce & Gabbana to host fashion shows in the Valley of Temples in Sicily, whereas, in Paris, Yves Saint Laurent showcased their collections at the Tour Eiffel and Louis Vuitton at the Louvre Museum, whilst, for example, Gucci held shows at Westminster Abbey in London. However, also in this respect Pierre Cardin was a trailblazer, as he was the first Western luxury fashion designer to host fashion shows in China. He also celebrated the brand's first 40 years in the country with a lavish show on the Great Wall, a location that was also used by Fendi in 2007 and Bottega Veneta in 2022.

At times luxury fashion brands opt to hold their fashion shows in a place they are supporting in terms of restoration, as, for example, Fendi hosted several events at the Trevi Fountain in Rome. This practice of associating a brand name to the preservation of a specific historical site, and to heritage and country of origin (as examined in Chapter Six), can have a positive impact on the reputation and prestige of brands, provide authority and a sense of timelessness and also support valuable narratives that can contribute to brand identity and enhance brand equity. Unusual locations such as subway or railway stations have also been used by luxury fashion brands to host fashion shows, and Maison Martin Margiela is renowned for this.

To gain media coverage, luxury fashion brands have to offer extravagant and innovative fashion shows, a strategy that, for example, has been actively pursued by Chanel. In fact, Chanel is renowned for its imaginative fashion shows, as, for example, it has recreated a life-size beach, a spacecraft, an airport, a supermarket, a giant PC, and a carousel featuring Chanel symbols. The brand even recreated a protest for women's rights in a Parisian street in 2014, and replicated the Eiffel Tower. Similarly, in 2019 Louis Vuitton recreated the Pompidou Centre inside the Louvre Museum in Paris.

However, sometimes the takeover of public spaces by luxury fashion brands can be met by criticism, as people are not always very forgiving of the closures and restrictions caused by holding fashion shows there. However, it's not only the general public that may disapprove, as, for example, in 2022 Dior asked Valentino for 100,000 Euros compensation arguing that the fashion show held by Valentino in Piazza di Spagna in Rome caused limited access to its store and damaged the brand. However, as reported by Mendes (2021), other forms of takeover can also be controversial as, for example, in 2013 Louis Vuitton faced criticism when the giant trunk they built in Moscow's Red Square partially obscured St. Basil's cathedral, leading to the trunk's removal.

7.4 Advertising and celebrity endorsement

Advertising and celebrity endorsement are a strategic communication tool used by luxury fashion brands to manifest the brands' values, stand out from competitors and fascinate consumers. There are significant differences in the way the assorted products associated with luxury fashion brands are advertised, as, for example, TV ads for fragrances or beauty products are not rare but clothing lines are not usually promoted this way, as such goods are not aimed at the broader mass-market, unlike the former. Fashion houses are primarily associated with campaigns in specialised fashion magazines such as *Vogue* or *Elle*, but also in-flight and hotel publications, alongside luxury lifestyle magazines, as they offer a more targeted approach to the relevant audience.

Window display is also considered a strategic tool to advertise and promote a brand, leading many brands to create striking and imaginative displays in their shops, sometimes even collaborating with renowned artists like in the case of Louis Vuitton. Similarly, street advertising can offer the opportunity to target relevant cities or specific areas, usually those where luxury fashion brands operate. This can range from posters to scaffolding or media screens, but we are also seeing brands employing more creative and striking strategies, as, for example, in 2022 Valentino took over the coastal town of Qinhuangdao in China, generating significant media attention. Moreover, Bottega Veneta has increasingly been adopting an experimental approach, as, for example, it launched a series of big and unusual adverts on roofs near the airport in Los Angeles so that people could see them while flying.

When it comes to goods produced under a license agreement, which are very common especially in areas where particular expertise is required such as fragrances, beauty products or eyewear, usually advertising is funded by the licensor, which generally is left with some contractual freedom to decide how and where to advertise, although in some cases contracts can have tighter requirements. For goods that are not associated with licensing, it is the luxury fashion brand that has sole responsibility for advertising and promotion.

Advertising for luxury fashion goods usually involves high costs and notions of excellence and prestige, which are conveyed through a variety of strategies. For example, campaigns are shot in exclusive locations with famous models and by renowned photographers or directors as the rationale is represented by supporting narratives of distinction and status. Moreover, they feature in prestigious magazines and in prominent positions. Magazines command higher prices if they have higher circulation (this now also includes their online circulation and social media engagement) and, for their print editions, cost can vary according to the position of the ad, as, for example, the back cover, the first part of the magazine and right-hand pages are characterised by higher prices (Lea-Greenwood 2013: 45).

Luxury fashion adverts often refer to an idealised past or to specific locations that are closely intertwined with brand identity. That is, for example, the case for Chanel, that has often used and been inspired by Paris and café culture, or for Dolce & Gabbana and Sicily, although the brand also refers more generally to Mediterraneanness through references to elements such as traditional lifestyles and close-knit multigenerational families. Luxury fashion brands can also convey a coherent brand image by focusing consistently on specific themes for their advertisements as, for example, Louis Vuitton has centred their communication on the theme of travelling.

Luxury fashion adverts often feature recurrent themes to capture people's attention. Kim, Lloyd and Cervellon (2016) identify seven themes: exclusivity and uniqueness, romance and seduction, involvement in a fantasy world, the comparison with others in terms of self-definition, power and success, sensory appeal and heritage, and ownership and consumption. Moreover, luxury fashion brands are characterised by specific modalities of communications in advertising.

Gurzki, Schlatter and Woisetschläger (2019) observe how luxury fashion brands tend to use storytelling, symbolism and rhetoric, distancing techniques and more abstract messages that could lead to multiple interpretations. The authors examine how Hermès features a complex set of visual symbols in their ads to supplement and enrich the brand's narratives, as, for example, alongside the use of the label's iconic orange, adverts present references to ephemerality and the transformative nature of butterflies and the companionship and loyalty of horses. Metaphors are also commonly used by luxury fashion brands.

Moreover, Gurzki, Schlatter and Woisetschläger also argue that luxury fashion brands tend to adopt more complex templates, as they feature more elements as meaning carriers, use backdrops and settings to provide additional context, and adopt a variety of distancing strategies to anchor themselves to a dimension outside of the ordinary. This can occur in temporal terms, as adverts are often set in a highly stylised past rooted in heritage, in spatial terms as campaigns are often set in remote and aspirational locations (and moreover products and models are often presented in the context of abstract artworks and architecture), but also in social terms as models can strike arrogant looks, showcase status symbol elements or other features to signify exclusion, and, last, in hypothetical terms as adverts can depict situations that are unrealistic or surreal.

In this sense, it has to be observed that luxury fashion advertising can also be reshaped all of a sudden by external forces, like economic crises for example. In fact, as discussed by Ahn and Mundel (2018), the economic crash in Argentina saw some luxury fashion brands leave the country altogether whilst those that remained adopted an advertising style that was much more factual and realistic, and much less decorative and emotional to fit in better with contemporary sensibilities.

Luxury fashion brands are also increasingly focusing on notions of prestige and authority through the use of celebrities and renowned directors to create artistic films, a practice that has increased greatly in the last few years. For example, David Lynch directed 'Lady Blue Shanghai' for Dior in 2010 starring Marion Cotillard (who also starred in other advertising campaigns for the brand), whereas in 2012 Roman Polanski created 'A Therapy' for Prada featuring Ben Kingsley and Helena Bonham Carter. Luis Vuitton has explored 'the spirit of travel' that characterises the brand in 2016 through a video ad campaign featuring movie stars Alicia Vikander and Michelle Williams. Moreover, in 2009 Jean-Pierre Jeunet directed the commercial film 'Train de nuit' for Chanel, starring Audrey Tatou, who also played the role of the brand's founder in a movie.

Lea-Greenwood (2013) defines celebrity endorsement as the use of someone who is well-known in the public domain to represent a brand in a variety of ways, from traditional advertising campaigns to covert endorsement, which happens when PR secures the collaboration of celebrities to use the brand in a way that is seen as spontaneous by the public because it is not presented as an official partnership.

Celebrities can also be used to create or front special collections, as, for example, seen in 2023 when Kim Kardashian curated a collection for Dolce & Gabbana consisting of updated selected vintage pieces. Another effective partnership between celebrities and luxury fashion brands can be seen when charity is involved, as, for example, significant media coverage was achieved when Louis Vuitton stated that the personalities featured in a 2007 campaign (politician Mikhail Gorbachev, actress Catherine Deneuve, and tennis legends Andre Agassi and Steffi Graf) had donated their fees to environmental causes. Celebrities are also used by luxury fashion brands to attend events and achieve media attention; this is often the case for fashion shows as renowned stars are seated in the front row to generate press coverage.

Another powerful strategic tool consists in supplying clothes and accessories to celebrities for events, as the media attention can generate significant publicity and drive sales. For example, *The Business of Fashion* reported that, during the Cannes Festival in 2022, Bollywood star Deepika Padukone, the first Indian Louis Vuitton brand ambassador, generated alone more than a quarter of the earned media value (EMV) during the event, and topped the brand's social media posts. Moreover, luxury fashion brands are also known to capitalise on celebrity associations by naming products after celebrities, for example the Jackie bag by Gucci is a tribute to Jackie Kennedy, whereas the Kelly and Birkin bags by Hermès are named after Grace Kelly and Jane Birkin, respectively. More recently, Marc Jacobs named a bag BB, after fashion blogger Bryaboy, whilst Louis Vuitton named the SC bag after film director Sofia Coppola.

Through celebrity endorsement luxury fashion brands can achieve a series of benefits. In fact, as discussed by Okonkwo (2007), the purpose of celebrity endorsement is to make the brand's message stand out, to support the credibility of a brand's offerings, to create brand awareness, to position and re-position brands, to sustain a brand's aura, to revive and revitalize brands, to generate extensive PR leverage and to offer opportunities for brands to reach a global market. Moreover, as observed by Carrillat, O'Rourke and Plourde (2019), advertisements featuring celebrities are better recalled, brand names are better recognised and more generally the association has a positive effect on consumer attitudes and the brand's value.

The allure of celebrities and the hold they have in terms of fascinating and influencing audiences has been long recognised by luxury fashion brands, as, for example, Charles Worth was one of the first, in the 19th century, to engage with this dimension very actively, as he pursued the most influential figures of his time, i.e., royals and aristocrats such as Empress Eugenie and Princess Mitternich. Nowadays luxury fashion brands are focusing their attention more on figures working in the entertainment industry and, in particular, leading figures in sports, movie and music, although they still pursue the visibility associated with endorsements by socialites and aristocrats. Movie stars like Jennifer Lopez, Halle Berry, Scarlett Johansson and Zendaya have featured in campaigns and promoted brands such as Vuitton, Versace and Valentino. Music artists like Rihanna and Harry Styles have been the face of Gucci, Lady Gaga posed for Versace and Lily Allen for Chanel, whereas sportsmen David Beckham and Victor Cruz were chosen, respectively, to front campaigns for Armani and Givenchy.

Interestingly, in an era where digital technology offers worlds of opportunities, luxury fashion brands can even 'resurrect' deceased celebrities as Dior did for their J'Adore fragrance, as the ads featured Charlize Theron alongside Marilyn Monroe, Marlene Dietrich and Grace Kelly. Fashion bloggers and influencers are also employed by luxury fashion brands, as those figures tend to be perceived by the general public as more authentic and effective in terms of building trust.

Usually luxury fashion brands seek highly recognisable celebrities, but they might do the opposite, as, for example, Celine did when they hired American writer Joan Didion to front a campaign in 2015. Although Didion may be recognisable in the USA in intellectual circles due to her work and signature look she is not a household name worldwide. However, Celine chose Didion precisely because it aimed to reinforce its reputation as an intellectual brand by choosing a celebrity that would be recognised as such only by the target audience (Jerslev 2018), playing on an exclusion-inclusion dimension based on cultural capital, to use Bourdieu's terminology.

Luxury fashion brands have to select a suitable celebrity, one that can add allure and credibility to the fashion house due to the nature of their notoriety, as, for example, usually only high calibre VIPs are chosen to front campaigns or become brand ambassadors. Moreover, as luxury fashion brands have gone global, it's more and more important to choose a celebrity that has international appeal and whose characteristics can resonate with a wider audience.

This means that there is a real competition between labels to secure a collaboration with the most sought-after celebrities, which is inflating costs, and, moreover, it can be difficult at times to secure exclusive contracts. This can lead to unfortunate associations, as, for example, Madonna has been the face of Versace for several campaigns, but on one occasion, in 2016, the artist was simultaneously also advertising her own partnership with mass retailer H&M, which created confusion and diluted the Versace message.

Moreover, celebrity endorsement can also hurt the brand if the partnership is perceived to be inauthentic or, to a greater extent, if celebrities are embroiled in scandals or controversies. However, sometimes luxury fashion brands may strategically use controversial celebrities. This was, for example, the case for Kate Moss, who was dropped by Chanel and Burberry when she was involved in a drug scandal, but was hired by Longchamp with the aim to modernise its image. The strategy worked, as it did for Calvin Klein when the brand hired Justin Bieber in the midst of driving under the influence and assault charges.

It might appear counter-intuitive to hire a controversial celebrity, but provocation and controversy have historically been used by fashion brands, and in particular in the luxury industry, to achieve differentiation and acquire an exciting and uncommon personality, an effect that is further boosted if the celebrity in question is inherently controversial (Carrillat, O'Rourke and Plourde 2019). However, it seems that the nature of the controversy has to be taken into consideration, as, for example, in Western countries drug scandals in the entertainment industry are common and nowadays generally considered as less serious than those involving racism or domestic violence.

7.5 Case study: Fear of God

As discussed in section 7.4, celebrity endorsement can offer great advantages to brands in terms of gaining media attention, retaining or attracting customers, providing an appealing and memorable communication strategy and raising awareness about the brand and its values. This of course comes at a cost, as prices are driven up by competition to entice the most sought-after celebrities and the fact that more and more celebrities are exploiting the opportunities offered by their personal brands to launch product lines such as clothing, accessories, fragrances and cosmetics. This is, for example, the case for Hollywood superstar Jennifer Lopez, who recently fronted campaigns for Versace and Dolce & Gabbana, but also created a variety of products under her own name.

Celebrity endorsement these days rarely comes for free, as more and more celebrities capitalise on their celebrity status in a variety of ways and are deeply aware of the value of being seen wearing a certain brand or product. However, in this sense the case of the Fear of God brand is unusual, as not only many celebrities endorsed the brand willingly and without having a financial agreement in place, but because the brand itself actually became known for its strong celebrity following in the first place.

Fear of God is an independent luxury streetwear brand founded in Los Angeles in 2013 by Jerry Lorenzo. Initially offering only unisex pieces under the main Fear of God line, the brand has since expanded into several lines for children, men and women with its Essential second line (initially called F.O.G.), and Athletics line launched in 2023 in partnership with sportswear giant Adidas. Not trained in fashion design, Lorenzo actually developed his brand because he could see a gap in the market for comfortable yet stylish clothes during the years he spent organising very successful parties attended by celebrities.

His work as a party promoter gave him the connections that proved so fundamental in putting his brand on the world map. Soon Fear of God was worn by sports, film and music stars like Colin Kaepernick, David Beckham, Micheal B. Jordan, Beyoncé, Gigi Hadid and Queen Latifah to name but a few, and images of celebrities wearing the brand were picked up by the media, providing invaluable exposure for the label which quickly translated into sales. Moreover, it was reported that so strong was the brand's cult following in the fashion world that Alessandro Michele, the artistic director of Gucci, allowed Jared Leto, who was at the time a spokesperson for the company, to appear in the sixth collection for Fear of God.

An early fan of Fear of God was also the late Virgil Abloh (artistic director of menswear for Louis Vuitton and founder of luxury brand Off-White), who is said to have introduced Lorenzo to music artist Kanye West, who hand-picked him to work initially on his A.P.C. collaborations, then for his Yeezus tour and the early collections of Yeezy, the luxury fashion brand he created. The name of Fear of God and Jerry Lorenzo further gained attention for its cult following as he worked on creating garments and merchandise for music stars Kendrick Lamar and Justin Bieber. The latter collaboration was so successful that it was even distributed outside of the tour, through pop-up stores and also in upmarket department store Barneys alongside the main Fear of God collection.

Fear of God, that does not show its collection at fashion week, is a small independent company that supports its development through its very commercially successful second lines, that appeal to a wider clientele due to the lower entry price. The label has a strong digital presence and doesn't directly operate any retail stores, preferring to sell on-line through their official website and through selected stockists only.

Fear of God has launched a series of collaborations, for example several collections for Nike, Vans, Converse and, in 2020, with luxury fashion brand Ermenegildo Zegna for a capsule collection that was launched with a number of worldwide events and which saw, unsurprisingly, the presence of many celebrities. Through those collaborations Fear of God is capitalising on the status, prestige and awareness that associations with celebrities have granted the brand, which is the primary reason that the label became an instant success and was able to retain its independence. In fact, to launch and promote a luxury fashion brand is extremely expensive, and in this sense it's difficult to compete with the resources of luxury groups and conglomerates.

Questions and activities

- What's the origin of the brand Fear of God?
- How did Fear of God use celebrity endorsement?
- Select a luxury fashion brand that has used celebrity endorsement and compare and contrast the strategies it has adopted in this sense

7.6 Public Relations

PR aims at managing relations between luxury fashion brands, the media and the wider public. With regards to the latter, Lea-Greenwood (2013) observes, PR is used, for example, to remind consumers of the brand, to make people recall previous advertising from the brand, to promote the recognition of the brand's image and to reinforce the fashion credentials of the brand.

PR often involves creating a story to make a lasting impression of a brand, circulate its messages and entice consumers through other means than paid advertisement, which can be perceived by the public as more credible and gain more attention than paid partnerships. Often luxury fashion brands employ external PR agencies alongside their own PR operations, mostly due to their global presence and the complex and competitive current mediascape.

PR involves many activities:

- cultivating relationships with the media, celebrities and other relevant stakeholders
- sending out press releases and other content to support circulation
- supporting events, store openings and fashion shows
- organising sponsorship and charity events
- supporting exhibitions, publishing opportunities and product placement
- mitigating the effects of any scandals and controversies the brand might be involved in.

Cultivating relationships with the media, celebrities and other relevant stakeholders is an essential part of PR. In today's mediascape, it's becoming more and more important for luxury brands to be associated with celebrities that can support their aura of prestige and desirability, be that through official endorsement agreements or through extensive gifting and loaning (which is the norm for outfits worn by VIPs at events) that is overseen by PR departments. Some fortunate pairings have created immense publicity for all parties involved, as British actress Elizabeth Hurley suddenly became known worldwide thanks to a Versace safety-pin dress worn on the red carpet in the 1990s, whereas in 2000 Jennifer Lopez wore a green Jungle dress by Versace that gained so much coverage that it is said to have inspired the creation of Google images.

To cultivate media relationships is also essential for luxury fashion brands, as positive and extensive coverage can offer invaluable free publicity. In this sense PR works less overtly than advertising, but is still closely related to it as brands that advertise in a magazine, or other media, usually also receive some PR coverage. Featuring in editorials or being mentioned by renowned figures through features that don't look like they've been paid for by the brands can make the endorsements appear more credible. However, media relationships have to be nurtured, as the case of Yves Saint Laurent demonstrates.

In 2012, Yves Saint Laurent underwent significant changes in order to revitalise the brand and a dispute emerged in the media. The brand name was changed and a significant online backlash ensued, as the logic behind the change (a case of retro-branding that took inspiration from the font and name of Yves Saint Laurent's ready-to-wear collection of 1966, called 'Saint Laurent Rive Gauche') had not been communicated effectively to stakeholders. When *The Business of Fashion* (2012) wrote about the re-brand they were asked to remove the article by the company's PR team, which clarified that the label should be correctly referred to as 'Yves Saint Laurent' but that the ready-to-wear collection by Hedi Slimane was to be referred as 'Saint Laurent', whereas 'Saint Laurent Paris' should be used in the logo but not when spoken/written about the collection, and, last, that collection credits should be presented as 'Saint Laurent by Hedi Slimane'.

The publication wrote about this communication and highlighted the many confusing names associated with the brand, which wasn't appreciated by Yves Saint Laurent's PR team. An unpleasant series of exchanges ensued, culminating in the threat of not collaborating any more with the publication and the revocation of the invitation to the label's fashion show for Imran Amed, founder and editor of *The Business of Fashion*. Amed, in turn, published a very critical piece about the PR team of the label, that he accused of considering the media as their mouthpiece as they aimed to dictate, and not nurture, the conversation about the brand.

To send out content and support its circulation is another key aspect of PR. In the past, the most common types of content produced by PR were constituted by press releases, images and sketches to support the new collections. However, as the advertising and media landscape changed, nowadays more varied content needs to be constantly produced to capture the attention of both the press and consumers alike. For example, now PR teams routinely work on delivering content showing what happens behind the scenes at luxury fashion brands, for instance the craftsmanship involved in creating haute couture pieces or the backstage of fashion shows to name but a few elements, but also proposing interviews with designers, brand ambassadors and brand muses and more generally creating and supporting opportunities to reinforce and disseminate the brand's message.

Moreover, PR involves organising a variety of events, from product launches to store openings and fashion shows. PR also curates a relationship with buyers, and in this sense also organises events to present new collections, promote new retail venues, with the aim to create a buzz and support engagement with relevant stakeholders.

Furthermore, PR also involves organising sponsorship and charity events. By sponsoring elite events, luxury fashion brands can enhance their prestige whilst also gaining media coverage and access to wealthy individuals who can afford their most exclusive services. For example, Louis Vuitton has sponsored for over 20 years an American regatta competition that was renamed the Louis Vuitton Cup, whereas French label Hermès has been sponsoring the horse race Prix de Diane Hermès and the jumping competition Saut Hermès, both events that fit in perfectly with the brand's identity and core values of exclusivity and tradition.

By associating with charitable causes, luxury fashion brands can gain media attention and position themselves in a positive light in the consumer's mind, whereas charities gain vital funds to support their work. Breast Cancer Awareness is one of the most active charities in this sense, partnering with a number of brands such as Burberry, Ralph Lauren, Tommy Hilfiger and Prada. However, virtually all luxury fashion brands now engage with charity, sometimes through special events, as, for example, Jimmy Choo auctioned photos of celebrities wearing nothing but their shoes to raise fund for the Elton John AIDS foundation, or by creating their own charitable foundations to permanently anchor themselves to positive narratives.

More recently, luxury fashion brands have been actively disseminating information about their own charitable effort during the COVID-19 pandemic, as, for example, Armani donated three million Euros to help hospitals and the Italian Government's Civil Protection Department, converted production to make single-use hospital gowns to donate to medical facilities and also donated a portion of profits from 2020 sales to 52 different non-profits working in different cities. Similarly, Chanel produced and donated hospital gowns and face masks, and collaborated with over 80 nonprofit partners worldwide through their Fondation Chanel, whilst also creating the Chanel Emergency Response Fund. Burberry funded research by the University of Oxford to develop a vaccine for COVID-19, and also contributed to the UNICEF appeal to support equal access to vaccines. The LVMH group on the other hand converted production to manufacture hand sanitiser gel, associating its name with a narrative of compassion, empathy and goodwill.

PR also involves supporting exhibitions, publishing opportunities and product placement in a variety of settings. Exhibitions are often organised by luxury fashion brands in collaboration with museums or other cultural institutions as a means to raise media interest and brand awareness, whilst increasing their art and prestige credentials. Ferragamo has been particularly active in this field but there are countless examples of this strategy as permanent and travelling exhibitions have mushroomed in recent years. Sometimes books are launched as tie-ins, as, for example, in 2008 Ferragamo published a book to celebrate its 80th anniversary linked to the exhibition held at the Triennale museum in Milan.

Product placement can also offer luxury fashion brands a valuable platform to reach wider audiences and foster their aspirational values. This is, for example, the case for the movie *American Gigolo*, that in the 1980s contributed to making Giorgio Armani a household name worldwide or, more recently, for the *Sex & The City* series, that introduced some brands like Manolo Blahnik to the wider public whilst also reinforcing the prestige of labels such as Chanel or Prada. Similarly, *The Devil Wears Prada* movie featured a variety of references to luxury fashion brands. Moreover, movies that focus on specific luxury fashion brands can also offer valuable opportunities, as, for example, in the case of the 2021 movie House of Gucci by Ridley Scott. The film was supported by the fashion brand and allowed access to its spaces, and in turn gained extensive media coverage and significant social media engagement.

To create costumes for Hollywood films can also offer great visibility to luxury fashion brands, as was the case for Prada and *The Great Gatsby* movie released in 2013. However, to mitigate the effects of any scandals and controversies the brand may be involved in is perhaps the most common aspect associated with PR.

In this sense PR often leverages on positive elements, like craftsmanship or heritage for example, that can offer beneficial narratives to counterbalance negative associations. As discussed in the case study of Chapter Ten, Dolce & Gabbana employed such tactics to try to mitigate the effects of its scandal in China. However, the label also used that strategy previously, in 2015, when it was caught in a controversy as its founders appeared to express a negative view concerning gay people having children. This resulted in a highly publicised call for a boycott led by celebrities such as Elton John, that the brand attempted to overcome by launching a series of campaigns focusing on family in the broadest sense, as, for example, the #DGfamily project encouraged people to upload photos of their own family, resulting in a more inclusive and diverse display.

Controversies surrounding luxury brands are actually not that uncommon, as demonstrated by the cases of Louis Vuitton, Balenciaga, Comme des Garçons and Tommy Hilfiger examined below, and in this sense is something that all luxury fashion brands should prepare for by having procedures in place that can be mobilised quickly should the necessity arise.

In 2019, Louis Vuitton faced controversy as a few days after its menswear collection featured references to Micheal Jackson, the documentary *Leaving Neverland* debuted, focusing on accusations of sexual abuse by the singer on minors. PR efforts focused on distancing the collection from the scandal, emphasising that it was not a licensing agreement with Jackson's estate nor an official partnership whilst the designer, Virgil Abloh, declared that he was not aware of the documentary when working on the collection. Also, the pieces referring to the singer were withdrawn from the market.

Another big scandal emerged in 2022 when Balenciaga launched an advertising campaign featuring young children holding teddy bears dressed up in bondage-style garments. As soon as the campaign was released accusations of inappropriateness and child pornography emerged, and quickly spread through social media and the press. At first the brand didn't take action, and further backlash ensued as it emerged that a previous Balenciaga campaign featured documents related to court rulings on child pornography. In the following days there were rumours that Balenciaga was launching legal actions against the photographer who took the teddy-bear campaign photos, who ultimately spoke to the press to distance himself from the shoot and to clarify that he did not have a say on the products advertised nor the models or set.

Boycott campaigns were launched by the public, and celebrities were urged to re-evaluate their relationship with Balenciaga. Then, a few days later, the brand finally released a statement admitting to failures in their assessing and content validation procedures and declared that from then on a new image board and an external agency were being tasked with evaluating in detail any content to be released. Balenciaga also declared that it was committed to learning how to better protect children, in this sense pursuing training on responsible communication and by giving money to organisations working on child protection.

However, the effects of this kind of scandal can be difficult to contain these days, even if action is taken swiftly by luxury fashion labels, as all digital traces are hard to erase and controversies can resurface at a later time and negatively affect brands. In the past the situation was different, as, prior to the Internet, scandals didn't go viral and didn't spread so quickly and widely, and in this sense mitigating procedures were more effective, as shown by the Comme des Garçons scandal in the mid-1990s.

In 1995, Comme des Garçons became embroiled in a scandal when the label was accused of referencing the Holocaust in its collection, as discussed by Zborowska (2014). The scandal was caused by the unfortunate date of the show (the day of the liberation of the concentration camp at Auschwitz) and the juxtaposition of images of the Holocaust to some pieces from the collection, such as a striped pyjama and jackets featuring numbers. This commentary took hold in the media, despite the fact that the numbers did not appear on the striped pyjamas and that the collection comprised over 80 designs that didn't raise any concerns.

The brand claimed that the scandal was the product of a coincidence and not an intended reference, but public opinion disagreed and in the end Comme des Garçons destroyed the collection, whilst considerable efforts were also made to make sure to obliterate all traces, including photographs and mentions to the event. This example highlights the importance of decisive and swift action by luxury fashion brands when a scandal emerges, but unfortunately this was not the case for Tommy Hilfiger.

In the mid-1990s, rumours started to circulate over emails that designer Tommy Hilfiger made racist, anti-Semitic and homophobic comments while appearing on a popular US talk show, *The Oprah Winfrey Show* (Anti-Defamation League 2013). He was alleged to have stated that his clothes were intended for upper-class white people and that had he known that minorities were going to wear them then he wouldn't have made them so nice, which allegedly led Oprah to throw out the designer and call for the boycott of his brand.

There was no truth in those rumours. At the time Tommy Hilfiger was a firm favourite for rappers and hip-hop artists, something that was encouraged by the brand and supported by extensive gifting. The brand issued a series of denials and released multiple statements, and even Oprah stated that Hilfiger had never even appeared on her show. However, the rumours continued to circulate and damaged the brand, and experts have voiced criticism of the PR strategy adopted, as Tommy Hilfiger only featured as a guest on *The Oprah Winfrey Show* to quash the rumours in 2007, many years after the scandal emerged (Sherman and Pearlman 2010: 4)

7.7 Conclusions

Chapter Seven examined the different tools used by luxury fashion brands to promote and advertise their products. First, it focused on fashion shows and mapped its evolution from an event aimed at fashion insiders to spectacle for the wider public, and the consequences arising from the latter. Moreover, the multifaceted issue of advertising in luxury fashion was investigated. Furthermore, the role of celebrity endorsement within the marketing strategies of luxury fashion brands was discussed, and the concepts outlined were illustrated through the case study of Fear of God. Last, the key role of public relations in managing communication between luxury fashion brands, the media, and the wider public was explored. In particular, the chapter examined the pivotal role of PR in terms of crisis management, addressing a number of recent controversies.

7.8 Revision questions

- What are the methods used by luxury fashion brands to promote themselves?
- How do luxury fashion brands use fashion shows, celebrity endorsement and advertising?
- What is the role of PR within the luxury fashion industry?

7.9 References

Ahn, H. and Mundel, J. (2018) 'Luxury brand advertising in Argentina: changes following import restrictions', *Journal of Marketing Communications*, 24(3), 291-303, doi:10.1080/13527266.2015.1079548
Anti-Defamation League. (2013) Rumor: Tommy Hilfiger fashion not intended for minorities. Available at: https://www.adl.org/resources/news/rumor-tommy-hilfiger-fashion-not-intended-minorities
Business of Fashion. (2012) 'A wake-up call for YSL's PR team'. Available at: http://www.businessoffashion.com/articles/opinion/a-wake-up- call-for-ysls-pr-team
Carrillat, F. A., O'Rourke, A. and Plourde, C. (2019) 'Celebrity endorsement in the world of luxury fashion – when controversy can be beneficial', *Journal of Marketing Management*, 35(13-14), 1193-1213, doi:10.1080/0267257X.2019.1634632

Chadha, R. and Husband, P. (2006) *The cult of the luxury brand: inside Asia's love affair with luxury.* London; Boston: Nicholas Brealey International.

Chevalier, M. and Mazzalovo, G. (2012) *Luxury brand management: a world of privilege.* Singapore: John Wiley and Sons.

Gurzki, H., Schlatter, N. and Woisetschläger, D. M. (2019) 'Crafting extraordinary stories: decoding luxury brand communications', *Journal of Advertising*, 48(4), pp. 401–14.

Jerslev, A. (2018) 'The elderly female face in beauty and fashion ads: Joan Didion for Céline', *European Journal of Cultural Studies*, 21(3), pp. 349–62.

Kim, J. E., Lloyd, S. and Cervellon, M. C. (2016) 'Narrative-transportation storylines in luxury brand advertising: motivating consumer engagement', *Journal of Business Research*, 69(1), pp. 304–13.

Lea-Greenwood, G. (2013) *Fashion marketing communications.* Chichester: John Wiley & Sons.

Linfante, V. and Pompa, C. (2021) 'Space, time and catwalks: fashion shows as a multilayered communication channel', *ZoneModa Journal*, 11(1), p. 1542. doi:10.6092/issn.2611-0563/13100.

Mendes, S. (2021) 'The instagrammability of the runway: architecture, scenography, and the spatial turn in fashion communications', *Fashion Theory*, 25(3), 311–38, doi:10.1080/1362704X.2019.1629758

Okonkwo, U. (2007) *Luxury fashion branding: trends, tactics, techniques.* Basingstoke: Palgrave Macmillan.

Pinchera, V. and Rinallo, D. (2021) 'Marketplace icon: the fashion show', *Consumption Markets & Culture*, 24(5), 479–91, doi:10.1080/10253866.2019.1703699

Sherman, G. J. and Perlman, S. S. (2010) *Fashion public relations.* New York: Fairchild.

Zborowska, A. (2014) 'Uses and abuses of history: a case of a Comme des Garçons fashion show', *Critical Studies in Fashion & Beauty*, 5(2), pp. 233–52. doi:https://doi.org/10.1386/csfb.5.2.233_1

8 Digital and Social Media Marketing for Luxury Fashion

Case study: Cyber Valentine's Day (520 festival)

CHAPTER OBJECTIVES

This chapter:

- outlines the different tools for digital marketing within the luxury fashion industry
- explains what strategies are used by luxury fashion brands
- explore how luxury fashion brands can extract value through data analytics

---

8.1 Chapter summary

Chapter Eight discusses recent changes in the media landscape affecting marketing and communication practices of luxury fashion brands. Initially luxury fashion brands were reluctant to embrace the digital revolution, but they are now engaging with digital and social media in a variety of ways. First, the chapter addresses the issue of digital marketing, discussing a number of tools and techniques, before focusing on social media marketing. In this sense, the chapter discusses the different strategies adopted by luxury fashion brands and examines the challenges and opportunities involved. This is further investigated through a case study focusing on Cyber Valentine's Day (also known as 520 festival), a digitally native celebration of love that luxury fashion brands are using to connect with Chinese consumers. Finally, the chapter examines how digital and social media do not only offer luxury fashion brands platforms to reach the wider public, but also to gather valuable data that can inform and drive marketing and communication alongside branding and management strategies.

8.2 Introduction

Luxury fashion brands have been notoriously reluctant to embrace the digital revolution, opting finally to engage with the opportunities of online retail much later than mass-market companies, and they have similarly been cautious about engaging with the seismic changes

DOI: 10.4324/9781003264811-12

concerning the media landscape that are affecting marketing and communication practices. New technologies have changed the way companies relate to and communicate with people. The Internet allows information to be available at all times everywhere, and offers an insight into products and practices of luxury fashion brands that was previously unattainable for the general public.

Companies are engaging more and more with digital tools and tactics for a variety of reasons. First, due to mounting evidence about the effectiveness of online word-of-mouth as a powerful driver of both desirability and consumption, and second because digital tools offer opportunities for mobilisation of online communities that can be exploited by companies, which also seek to foster and capitalise on the emotional relationship forged through the digital world. Brands are focusing more and more on creating meaningful relationships that can support trust, loyalty and brand growth, be that by fostering a relationship with the brand, its products or between consumers. Through digital means, brands can stay relevant and support their communicative efforts, address a wider audience and reach potential customers, and even support the co-creation of products and services by analysing consumers data.

With the advent of user-generated content, first through blogs and communities and then through social media and virtual worlds, there's been a change of perspective as users are no longer simply the recipients but also the creators of digital content that contribute to the reputation and success of companies. Brands have gone from a situation where they controlled the communication flow, for example through advertising campaigns, to new forms of co-creation of meaning, as now people can share information and create new content about luxury fashion brands, which can affect brand image and reshape what the brands stand for. In this sense it is important for brands to adopt an integrated approach that uses digital means in a coherent manner to support brand identity and create value.

8.3 Digital marketing for luxury fashion

Digital media offer brands an opportunity to communicate with their audience and interacting in real time in a relatively low-cost manner through different media and platforms. In this section, we propose a classification of digital elements that can be leveraged by luxury fashion brands that is based on Heine and Berghaus (2014), who discuss digital marketing through eight digital luxury brand touchpoints spanning from owned channels, that are characterised by maximum control, to consumer-driven platforms like social media and third-party channels.

Here the model has been updated and adapted to changes in the mediascape. In this sense some elements have also be renamed, what Heine and Berghaus define as 'phone and tablet apps' we have renamed here as 'apps and digital products', as the original label no longer represented the variety of digital elements created by brands. For the same reason we have also renamed the sixth type of consumer touchpoint from 'social campaigns' to 'social media'. In this respect, this section examines eight elements: luxury brand website, search engine optimisation (SEO), direct mailing, online advertising, brand communities, social media, apps and digital products, and e-commerce.

Luxury brand websites

The official website of luxury fashion brands is now seen as the most important digital asset for labels, as it constitutes a brand-building tool that should reflect the brand philosophy and offer as much information as possible about the brand, its products, campaigns and vision (Heine and Berghaus 2014). However, this strategic role was not immediately recognised by many luxury fashion brands, as initially their websites were rather simple, offering limited information and customer services.

For example, Okonkwo (2007) recalls how initially Prada's website consisted of a single-page and featured no information apart from the occasional message about news and events, and how websites were closed during redesign, which resulted in Versace's website being unavailable during the launch of its global campaign starring Madonna.

Okonkwo (2007) also discusses that initially Chanel's website consisted of three different main sections that featured a puzzling incoherence of styles and layouts, whilst also showing extremely low-quality images in their fragrances and beauty section, and that Hermès did not include a section outlining its core values. In this sense, for example, Gucci really stood out when it introduced an in-store inventory search on its website and offered a version tailored for smartphones and tablets. This strategy saw Gucci increase its online traffic significantly, although this did not immediately translate into more sales (Bug and Haussmann 2017).

Websites can offer a space for luxury fashion brands to reinforce their identity, and virtually all luxury fashion brands now include information on their heritage, history and vision. Burberry was one of the first labels to fully engage with this dimension during its rebranding in the 2000s to showcase the brand in all of its facets, linking it to its social media and other digital touchpoints. As discussed in the case study of Chapter Six, Chanel dedicates a whole mini site to the label's legendary founder. Nowadays, virtually all the websites of luxury fashion brands also feature information on issues such as sustainability, inclusivity and the charitable causes supported by labels, as those elements now resonate with consumers, especially in more mature markets.

Search engine optimisation (SEO)

Another digital tool for luxury fashion brands is represented by search engine optimisation (SEO), that concerns efforts to increase website traffic by making it more visible on search engines like Google. Although it may seem obvious that labels would want to engage with this dimension, this was not always the case, leading to disastrous consequence. For example, Heine and Berghaus (2014) observe that when luxury fashion brands started to launch their websites, they neglected SEO in new and profitable markets such as China, resulting in an oddity of not appearing first when people searched for the brand name.

Direct mailing

Moreover, a useful digital touchpoint for luxury fashion brands is represented by direct mailing. This method is one of the most established digital marketing tools, and one of the first to be adopted by luxury brands. For example, in the mid-2010s, the Armani brand was known to discretely use emails to interact with people (Grilec, Vukusic and Dujic 2020). However, direct mailing still constitutes an opportunity to efficiently convey information and foster customer relationship.

The fact that people choose to join newsletters, coupled with the fact that often they can also select the particular product categories they are interested in, increases the likelihood of proposing relevant information and reach the right market segments (Heine and Berghaus 2014). Direct mailing nowadays is also a tool that is intertwined and can support other digital touchpoints, as, for example, emails usually feature links to product pages on official websites but also to other digital means, such as apps and social media.

Online advertising

Luxury fashion brands also adopt online advertising, which is seen as a powerful customer acquisition tool. Sometimes online advertising is represented by the simple transposition of marketing communication created for traditional media, such as magazine advertising campaigns. However, this strategy is more effective when brands make the most of the opportunities offered by the digital media chosen to create engaging, memorable and creative content that encourages people to share with others (Heine and Berghaus 2014).

Brand communities

Brand communities are platforms where people share their admiration for luxury brands and develop a sense of belonging that transcends physical distance. They can either involve third-party platforms, such as blogs and social media networks, or be implemented through proprietary-media (Heine and Berghaus 2014), this was the case for Burberry and their 'Art of the Trench' platform, which offers people a place to upload their photos wearing the iconic garment, becoming part of the Burberry story, and engage with a network of people sharing the same interests.

Social media

One of the most interesting opportunities of the digital revolution is represented by social media, which is the focus of section 8.4. Social media transformed word-of-mouth and made people willingly share and champion brands by supporting and disseminating their content through different platforms, for example by sharing video campaigns.

This method is considered to be most effective when digital channels are considered when creating content, in view of supporting engagement and virality but also customer loyalty, as seen in the case of Chanel and its 'Little Black Jacket' exhibition in 2012. The exhibition travelled in fashion capitals around the world and offered a constant stream of content for all the label's digital touchpoints but especially social media, whilst at the same time providing an opportunity for the brand to engage in real life with their most affluent and important customers through exclusive events (Heine and Berghaus 2014).

Nowadays, luxury fashion brands feature many different types of content on social media, from product or campaign showcases to filters and fashion shows, from behind-the-scenes videos to sophisticated short movies shot by leading directors to name but a few. The first luxury brand to engage with social media in a significant manner was Burberry, which streamed its fashion show live on Snapchat in 2010, and was also the first to use the 'buy now' function on Twitter (Roberts and Armitage 2017).

At the moment, social media offer brands the opportunity to pursue consumer-generated content and have people contribute to narratives about the labels. Bug and Haussmann (2017) for example discuss the case of #GucciGram, a contest created by Gucci in 2015 that encouraged artists to submit, through social media, their work inspired by Gucci. Selected entries featured on Gucci's social media and website and the initiative was so successful that it dominated the top ten on Instagram.

Social media can also act as an entry point for other digital touchpoints, such as brand websites, apps and direct mailing, a role that became even more important recently. In fact, social media became particularly prominent during the COVID-19 pandemic, as luxury fashion brands used them to communicate their humanitarian efforts (such as donating equipment or money to worthy causes) but also to interact with consumers and promote their labels.

Grilec, Vukusic and Dujic (2020) discuss how during the pandemic, for example, Burberry joined Tmall's luxury live stream promotions for the first time, whereas Louis Vuitton started to use live streaming more extensively in a variety of social media platforms and also launched a playlist and a cine club. The brand also created a new Instagram filter to mark the reopening of its boutiques. Chanel on the other hand used social media to disseminate the playlist it created and to feature concerts to entertain people during lockdowns.

Apps and digital products

Moreover, as mobile technology offered new opportunities, luxury brands started to launch new apps. At first many apps were primarily acting simply as a digital showcase of brands' collections, and often offered no additional benefit to consumers apart from their format, whilst they were also plagued by technical issues.

However, the app 'Silk Knot' by Hermès, launched in 2013, was an exception in this sense, because it offered consumers a real benefit as it aimed to teach how to tie scarves and ties in a creative manner, representing a perfect fit with the brand identity and providing a credible service for users. Similarly, the Louis Vuitton City Guide Apps offer people content and relevant shopping information in line with the established associations of the brand with travelling.

Most luxury fashion brands are now offering a variety of apps beyond shopping, as, for example, Louis Vuitton has launched its Louis Vuitton Pass application (relaunched in 2023) to offer people enriched and exclusive content when they scan any of the brand's campaigns. However, there are a variety of other digital products and services launched by luxury fashion brands to promote themselves. For example, in 2008 Louis Vuitton created Soundwalk, an MP3 journey were the sounds of three Chinese cities, coupled with the narration by three Chinese actresses, evoked the spirit of travel. Moreover, Hermès developed its 'Contre-Temps' digital assistant, based on OLED technology, which was the perfect size to fit into one of the label's iconic bags, unlike laptops (Okonkwo 2010). Augmented reality, virtual reality and gaming are also adopted by luxury fashion brands more and more, as examined in more details in Chapter Nine.

E-commerce

Last, e-commerce can also be a tool for luxury fashion brands to promote their brands, communicate with their customers and more generally support engagement and loyalty. In fact, despite the initial reluctance of luxury fashion brands in adopting this method of distribution, now virtually all of them engage with such dimension (although as discussed in Chapter Five in many cases only limited products are available for purchase online) in terms of marketing and promotion.

8.4 Social media marketing

Social media has changed marketing, created novel tools to negotiate meaning for people and brands but also changed the time frame for communications, as consumers now seek new content constantly and brands have to keep up. Moreover, as information can spread very fast on social media, luxury fashion brands have to act more quickly in a variety of areas, for example when a crisis arises, to fight negative associations and try to contain worldwide backlash. The sense of immediacy and proximity conveyed by social media also has to be negotiated through strategic focus as the notion of prestige, status and exclusivity associated with luxury fashion brands needs to be preserved.

Social media has created new figures in the mediascape, first introducing the figure of the fashion blogger in the fashion industry. They paved the way for other contemporary figures such as influencers and content creators, and disrupted established hierarchies within the luxury fashion industry. In fact, before the mid-2000s information and authority on luxury fashion was mostly associated with gatekeeper figures such as fashion journalists, industry insiders or celebrities, and primarily conveyed through traditional media such as fashion magazines.

Dolce & Gabbana was the first label to put bloggers in the first row at fashion shows, causing a furore, and also offered media stations they could use to blog from the shows to further support this new marketing tool. Fashion bloggers became a way for luxury fashion brands to reach younger audiences and gain publicity and media attention. At times luxury fashion brands even exploited media traction associated with this phenomenon by using fashion bloggers as inspiration for products, as, for example, Marc Jacobs named a bag after Filipino-born blogger Bryanboy (real name Bryan Grey Yambao).

Literature suggests that bloggers, influencers, content creators and other leading figures in social media constitute trustworthy sources for users, that see them as more approachable and similar to them, meaning that their endorsement can be more effective than traditional adverts. This was especially true at the beginning of social media, when lack of legislation meant that partnerships and gifting were not publicly declared, contributing to the idea that influencers were genuinely endorsing products and brands for no financial gain. However new regulations are bringing more transparency in this sense, challenging established associations and the way brands promote themselves in this area.

The popularity of this strategy was also driven by low costs in comparison with advertising through leading publications, as sometimes brands only need to provide free products to influencers. However, nowadays fees can be significant for the most popular figures that have a solid fan base, this was, for example, the case for Senegal-born Khaby Lame, international Internet sensation who in 2022 became the global brand ambassador for Hugo Boss, later also launching his own capsule collection for the brand, and who was instrumental in the label's rebrand to showcase a clear change of direction.

Moreover, technological innovations are also allowing social media to become embedded into other parts of the luxury fashion brands, such as physical retail. In this sense Burberry has, for example, launched a social retail store in Shenzhen (China), where customers are given an animal avatar that evolves as they explore different rooms to unlock exclusive content and rewards.

There are several advantages associated with social media marketing. Social media allow brands to strengthen their relationship with current customers and to reach out to potential ones, to increase their visibility and boost sales, to nourish a positive brand image and to support brand loyalty, but also trust and commitment. Social media enable brands to create engaging messages using multiple modalities, from photos to videos, to capture people's attention. Moreover, social media allow people to share their thoughts and emotions towards the brand in a similarly rich and nuanced way.

Fetais et al. (2022) argue that luxury fashion brands use social media to provide entertainment, offering an enjoyable and fun experience focused on escapism and relaxation, which can positively affect brand awareness and purchase intention. Moreover, social media offer the opportunity to customise messages and support a dialogue with consumers, whilst interaction facilitates information sharing and the ability to disseminate new trends.

On the other hand, electronic word-of-mouth (eWOM) from other people offers users credible sources of information. The popularity of this approach is driven in particular by younger consumers such as millennials (see case study in Chapter Four). The main advantages of using social media are represented by the low costs associated with such strategy and the fact that it allows brands to reach a wider audience, in this sense supporting brand awareness. But luxury fashion brands can also use social media to target top consumers, for example by creating events or other opportunities to showcase their appreciation and support loyalty and advocacy.

However, the use of social media for marketing and promotion is also associated to problematic issues. Social media is an umbrella term that comprises different platforms, from social networking sites (such as Facebook), to those focusing on a particular medium (such as videos for YouTube) to professional networking platforms (such as LinkedIn) that have revolutionised marketing as they allow people and companies to connect on a vast scale. Social media allow two-way communication and offer users the opportunity to engage with brands in a way that was previously impossible, but this strategy also has a significant disadvantage, as brands have lost the level of control they previously held over the way they are portrayed.

Social media allow users to share their dissatisfaction and discontent concerning luxury fashion brands, sometimes even fuelling calls for boycotts. However, luxury fashion brands can also exploit online criticism and turn the tables, as, for example, in 2020 the #GucciModelChallenge went viral on social media. The challenge consisted in encouraging people to pile up mismatching clothes and mimic the looks presented by Gucci at their latest show, but the brand saw the funny side and hijacked the viral trend, sharing some of the outfits created by users on their social media profiles and even launching its own challenge (that asked people to live a Gucci life for a day).

Initially luxury fashion brands were also cautious in entering the world of social media due to concerns that they could affect negatively their exclusivity and prestige. Burberry is perhaps the luxury fashion label best known for having embraced social media marketing and using such strategy effectively to rejuvenate the brand. Other early adopters are represented by Gucci and Louis Vuitton.

However, it has to be noted that luxury fashion brands in this sense have been careful to adopt strategies to support their aura and status, for example by emphasising through their social media activities their heritage and history but also by not adopting some social media functions. For example, luxury fashion brands do not usually engage in one-to-one conversations with individuals (Louis Vuitton was the first to offer a dedicated social media account, on Twitter, to deal with queries) or use some social media functions, such as real-time streaming, only in limited circumstances (Athwal, Istanbulluoglu and McCormack 2018).

Lee, Hur and Watkins (2018) discuss how a highly curated visual feed can support notions of luxury and exclusivity by eliciting perceptions of scarcity through images showcasing low visual complexity and fewer objects, which is in line with the way luxury stores focus on simple and uncluttered presentation. Park, Im and Kim (2020) suggest that, in order not to be perceived as too accessible, luxury fashion brands should only follow and engage on social media with selected and high-profile individuals such as celebrities. However, it has been observed that concerns over the negative impact, for luxury fashion brands, of being seen as more accessible are less relevant in collectivist cultures, which led luxury labels to adopt social media marketing earlier and more consistently in the valuable Chinese market.

Ng (2017) discusses how in China consumers, and especially younger ones, value information from social media and e-commerce platforms before and after purchase. This is the rationale that saw many luxury fashion brands focus on their online presence on different social media, hoping to capture people's attention and new clients in a country where people spend more time on those platforms than elsewhere in the world. However, the more consistent and extensive engagement with social media in China was also influenced by some specific technological developments. In fact, social media in China were far more advanced, offering functions that were not yet widely employed in other markets, as in the case of WeChat.

WeChat, is a Chinese developed social media platform that early on offered many functions such as an integrated payment and booking systems, as discussed by Liu, Perry and Gadzinski (2019). WeChat also allows the creation of third-party sub-apps, also called miniprograms, that companies can use to independently create and manage different functionalities. Luxury fashion brands have used WeChat to develop their own e-shops, to run their loyalty programmes and marketing initiatives and to effectively integrate all of their services, for example supporting customer-related management through the ability to book appointments and engage with customers in a more personalised manner than seen in other markets. Ng (2017) argues that by adopting a very active social media strategy luxury fashion brands did not damage their prestige and exclusivity in China, but that, nonetheless, problematic issues still emerged.

In fact, luxury fashion brands initially faced some problems because the decentralised approach negatively affected consumer experience. As sales assistants in other countries were not aware of the content shared in China, they were unable to quickly respond to the specific expectations and needs of Chinese customers travelling worldwide. Chinese tourists are a very important and lucrative market segment for labels, so much so that specific training and roles were introduced abroad to better cater to those customers.

Liu, Perry and Gadzinski (2019) also highlight that the global presence of luxury fashion brands implies that their social media presence should not only be creative and engaging, and seamlessly blend in an omnichannel strategy perspective, but also be adapted to specific cultures, which involves not only celebrating local festivities but also collaborating with local teams and opinion leaders. At the same time, all localised strategies should also fit with the brands' identity and showcase coherence in order not to negatively affect the brand.

Social media should be employed by luxury fashion brands carefully, because if a more active social media strategy could work in some circumstances, on the other hand by sharing the same content on different platforms could lower engagement. In fact, consumers can experience fatigue and get tired of seeing the same things all the time, which means that new content needs to be constantly produced to retain people's attention.

Moreover, another challenge is constituted by the fact that it is increasingly difficult to stand out in a very competitive environment where similar communication strategies are employed by many companies. Sometimes, in this sense, one strategy to create difference is to abandon social media altogether, as, for example, in 2021 Bottega Veneta closed all its social media accounts, and launched instead an online quarterly magazine to disseminate information and spread the brand's message.

Through social media marketing, luxury fashion brands aim to promote and create positive brand outcomes through fostering engagement behaviours, which can vary greatly.

In this sense Pentina, Guilloux and Micu (2018) have identified 11 types of social media engagements, characterised by different levels of active interactions. The behaviour characterised by the least effort is represented by liking or following a brand on social media, which can be motivated by informational needs as people like to be the first to know about new products or offers, or occur because people feel attachment to the brand or rate their aesthetics, or due to social motivations such as sharing their interest with people whilst adding to their virtual identities, as following and likes are visible to others.

Second, commenting on brands' posts and advertisements constitutes a more active form of engagement, although users are aware that in the luxury sectors brands are not likely to show reciprocity and reply. Pentina, Guilloux and Micu (2018) observe that liking, tagging and sharing brands' posts on social media is the most commonly seen behaviour, and that this is valuable for brands because it can increase their reach whilst also being easily measurable. Mentioning friends in comments is similar to commenting on brands posts, but is more socially motivated and contributes to eWOM by sustaining a dialogue about the brand.

Tagging brand names and using fashion-related hashtags in posted photo combines social and self-presentation needs through increasing their posts' visibility and showcasing a relationship with brands. Publishing photos of brands' products, or publishing photos of oneself with brands, can be motivated by the need for approval, to offer advice, or to signify and elevating one's social standing. On the other hand, initiating and maintaining brand related conversations in personal social networks refer to users' need for self-validation, social approval and belongingness, but this practice can impact brand perceptions as it creates links between people's personality and brand image.

Pentina, Guilloux and Micu (2018) also argue that publishing multimedia shopping stories showcases more engagement and creativity, and is based on social, self-presentation and emotional needs that make people want to share the way they consume the brand. An even higher form of engagement is represented by modifying branded products or suggesting new interpretations, and consists in a focused use of creativity directed primarily to those in the know about the brand to validate one's taste and skills.

Interactions that are directed primarily to the brand, such as likes and comments, cause less impact on brand meaning as they don't involve feedback and have lower dissemination potential, whereas on the contrary engagement behaviours that involve people's personal social accounts or other users cause a bigger impact by spreading the message and creating new associations with the brand. However, because of this, brands should monitor more carefully high-effort engagement behaviours and try to avoid negative or trivial associations by creating content that focuses on uniqueness, heritage and other elements that can support brand exclusivity and desirability.

In this sense, luxury fashion brands can support engagement behaviours on social media by providing quality content in terms aesthetic value or by interacting with celebrities, by fostering an emotional response in users through what their messages evoke and, in online communities, by supporting socio-psychological motives such as self-presentation and status, which differ but are equally important in collectivist and individualistic cultures. Furthermore, luxury fashion brands can support brand image and sustain its aesthetic appeal, whilst using platforms that are easy to use and support engagement behaviours (Bazi, Filieri and Gorton 2020).

8.5 Case study: Cyber Valentine's Day (520 festival)

The 520 Festival, also called Cyber Valentine's Day, is a digitally native celebration of love that originates in the assonance between the sentence 'I love you' and the number 520 in Chinese. Over the Internet suggestions were then made to use this similarity as the basis to create a new festival on the 20th of May (5/20), an idea that got traction and resulted in the creation of Cyber Valentine's Day.

However, this festival is not the only celebration of this kind, as China also celebrates Western Valentine's Day on the 14th of February and the Qixi Festival, occasions that have been seized upon by luxury fashion brands to promote their products, labels and drive sales. In particular, Cyber Valentine's Day and Qixi Festival are used by luxury fashion brands as a means to show commitment and foster engagement in China through the celebration of local culture.

To show appreciation of Chinese cultural elements is something that luxury fashion brands are exploring more and more, as they try to gain favour and increase market share in such an important market. In this sense a variety of strategies have been employed, from engaging with local traditions in marketing to using them as inspiration for products, as, for example, in 2013 Loewe launched a monochrome bag collection inspired by traditional Chinese ceramics craftsmanship, and even sponsored the creation of a new monochrome ceramics educational programme to preserve this cultural heritage.

Many luxury fashion brands engaged with the 520 Festival already in the late 2010s, mostly using digital means and social media to promote the special collections created for this digitally native event. However, the COVID-19 pandemic caused a shift, as more and more brands invested heavily launching campaigns and limited-edition capsule collection available for purchase through physical retail and online platforms such as WeChat and Tmall Luxury Pavilion. Early examples of engagement with the 520 Festival are represented by Cartier, that created a 1980s-style video game that on completion gave users the opportunity to buy the pieces presented as a prizes in the game, whereas Coach and Michael Kors encouraged people to send a message to their loved ones through their platforms (Jing Daily 2017).

In 2020, Prada launched the successful 'Mathematics of Love' campaign, where singer/songwriter Cai Xukun, also known as KUN, professed his love through a series of numbers adding up to 520, i.e. 'I love you'. The campaign comprised a series of posters, filters, and videos that were released on different social media and that promoted the capsule collection designed specifically for Cyber Valentine's Day. In the same year Louis Vuitton launched its 'Treasure Hunt' through a collaboration with actress Song Jia and popular live-streamer Austin Li, capitalising on the traction of this communication method at the time.

Also in 2020, Gucci teamed up with eight celebrities, including singer/songwriter Chris Lee and actress Ni Ni, for a campaign that involved all major Chinese social media platforms. However, in order to keep the message fresh and avoid alienating consumers through the repetition of similar content through different platforms, Gucci employed a strategy which saw different elements emphasised through each channel.

For example, on WeChat the focus was on the idea of love, whereas on Weibo the focus was on a radio-style format where celebrities discussed how they fell in love with the brand. In particular, the latter element was considered to be particularly effective in order to differentiate the Gucci campaign from those of its competitors, as they focused on romantic love, which is more traditionally associated with 520.

Vogue in 2021 observed that during the pandemic luxury fashion brands were communicating about and engaging with the 520 Festival more than they had ever done for any other festival of love (be that Western Valentine's Day or Qixi Festival), and that their campaigns generated significant social media buzz, boosting views and sales for the likes of Gucci, Valentino and Balmain. WWD (2021) argued that the 520 Festival offered a 'perfect commercial moment' as due to national lockdowns both Chinese New Year and Valentine's Day celebrations were halted, which led to the digitally native festival to become top priority in terms of liquidating inventories linked to the cancelled events.

This may explain why, despite the fact that some claim that the popularity of the 520 Festival is declining in certain market segments due to consumer fatigue as a result of the variety of events held in China that are linked to love and romance, the luxury sector was still investing heavily in it. For example, Dior launched a capsule collection through a massive campaign of celebrity endorsement, whilst Gucci heavily promoted their limited collection on social media. Prada and its sister label Miu Miu, but also Celine launched products, as did Valentino.

Questions and activities

- What is Cyber Valentine's Day?
- What strategies have luxury fashion brands used to celebrate it?
- Identify other digital events and compare and contrast the strategies adopted by luxury fashion brands in this sense

8.6 Marketing analytics

Advancements in technology are enabling more and more data to be captured at different points of the consumers journey, both online and offline. This involves a variety of information gathered through different channels, for example tracking what people see on social media and how they respond to it, recording point-of-sale (POS) transactions, capturing personal data such as colour preferences and sizing information, and more generally acquiring data through omnichannel touchpoints.

As the amount of data captured grows, brands face significant costs to store and make sense of the dense information they have acquired and to exploit the potential it holds to drive sales and support brand equity. In fact, more and more companies, including in the luxury fashion industry, are creating specific roles and recruiting figures that can help them unlock the potential hidden in the data they hold.

Customer data can provide luxury fashion brands significant insight into how effective their communication strategies are, which in turn can be used to support brand awareness, enhance brand identity and boost sales by offering more relevant and personalised marketing campaigns to the right market segment. Data analytics can also be used to gain a better insight into people's lifestyle, to suggest other goods that are likely to be in line with customers' needs and taste, and to entice them through personalised communication and offers.

Analysing data from social media can offer brands a way to understand and manage more effectively the way they are seen by people. Data analytics can trace geographical differences and local trends by mining information on social media, and the resulting insight can be used to inform the strategies of luxury fashion brands and guide product development.

Co-creation with consumers in the luxury fashion industry is commonly associated with customers employing personalisation tools (such as Gucci Garage, which allows users to create their own sneaker shoes) or made-to-measure services, but through data analytics more discrete forms of co-creation can be brought forward to create products that are more likely to be accepted and desired by current and potential consumers. In fact, by gathering and examining data, be that from owned or non-proprietary platforms, brands can better understand and more appropriately target people that are not yet clients but who in the future could purchase their products, and devise strategies to entice and retain them in the long-term.

McKinsey & Company (2021) published a report that focuses more specifically on the opportunities available to those fashion and luxury companies that integrate data analytics throughout their business. They claim that a 10% increase in sales was observed when decisions on stock and store optimisation were driven by data, for example through optimising store-network for omnichannel, real-time sales and stock visibility. McKinsey & Company estimate that fashion brands could see a 30–50% online sales growth if they use data to personalise the e-commerce journey of customers. This also involves reducing return rates by using more effective fit predictions.

In fact, currently a large number of customers order garments in many different sizes to try on at home as inconsistencies in garment measures among different products and brands make finding the right fit not very straightforward. This leads to high return rates, which is undesirable because it entails significant extra costs for brands and the environment. Moreover, McKinsey & Company claim that data-driven decisions could also increase margins by supporting full-price sell-through and develop a more efficient range when applied to merchandising and go-to-market.

In terms of logistics and supply chain, more efficient stock positioning, a streamlined inventory management, more accurate return forecasting and transport optimisation could result in a 10–15% reduction in inventory costs. With regards to sustainability, data analytics can drive a more effective tracking and management of sustainability impact, avoid overproduction, support the selection of appropriate suppliers and the traceability of both virgin and recycled materials.

This complex scenario involves significant costs as new infrastructure, digital tools and skilled staff are needed to make the most of big data. Moreover, McKinsey & Company observe that challenges in making the most of the data companies already possess also revolve around the non-standard formats of data, as, for example, stock keeping unit (SKU) information provided by suppliers can differ greatly. Furthermore, the richness of information that big data contains is complicated to analyse, and also involves challenges as personal and sensitive information such as payment details are recorded.

The Business of Fashion (2023) observes how privacy implications have changed the digital marketing scenario in a variety of ways, and that the cost of acquiring new customers has trebled in the last ten year. If at the dawn of the Internet era luxury brands enabled cookies without informing users and used the data collected primarily for their own benefit (Okonkwo 2007: 170), nowadays we see people becoming more wary of giving companies access to their data.

A technical shift concerning online privacy security risks, coupled with landmark legislations in the EU and USA (respectively, the General Data Protection Regulation of 2016 and the California Consumer Privacy Act of 2020) meant that digital strategies such as third-party ads targeting or social media hacking were no longer as effective. As more and more users decide to not allow cookies, and as a number of operating systems like Apple's iOS give the opportunity to opt out of tracking, it's becoming more difficult and costly for brands to reach their target audiences. However, there are strategies that can still allow brands to obtain data, as it's been argued that people are more willing to share information if they are given something is return. Moreover, brands are investing more heavily and prioritising new proprietary channels in their quest to obtain valuable first-party data.

There are many challenges involved in the analysis and integration of big data in business strategies, from the costs involved in storing the data, to the choice of appropriate tools and software among the myriad on offer, to the hiring or training of staff in this area whilst also ensuring that information is shared and made available by the relevant departments, which impacts the traditional compartmental structure of many companies. Moreover, it has to be observed that if some metrics can be used in a rather straightforward manner, for example to quantify the number of likes and shares on social media, the reality is that the different types of data that can be gathered from all the sources available to luxury fashion labels make the task of analysing it much more complex

Furthermore, as discussed by Liu, Shin and Burns (2021), there are other challenges concerning big data as there are intrinsic limitations concerning what information can be extracted from it. In fact, first, it's hard to obtain data on certain behaviours that are difficult to observe, like consumer's motivations or attitudes, and second it's complicated to untangle and make sense of huge sets of data and the richness of information they may contain. Even when it comes to social media (that are generally regarded as being the most commonly used type of big data examined by brands) the majority of relevant information lays in unstructured data that requires several steps, tactics and tools to be analysed.

For example, Liu, Shin and Burns (2021) discuss the difficulty in analysing unstructured behavioural data because, unlike structured numerical data such as number of likes or comments (which are easy to store and process with traditional marketing softwares), they involve complex data that is created through different formats and that need to be unpacked accordingly. In fact, social media posts feature information both in textual form, for example in posts or replies, but also in non-textual formats, such as emojis, images and videos.

Liu, Shin and Burns explain that when they needed to examine a dataset of over 3.5 million tweets concerning luxury brands, the process involved first pre-processing data through natural language processing (NLP) techniques for semantic categorisation, before coding a large quantity of textual elements. They emphasise that different processes such as tokenisation (which involves splitting a sentence into words and punctuation) and tagging (involving finding the part of speech for a word) as part of NLP are essential to guarantee analytical accuracy and the usefulness of the unstructured data studied.

However, despite the difficulties and challenges involved, companies still engage with big data because of the significant benefits that it entails. For example, Forbes (2022) discusses how big data can give companies the opportunity to create customer intimacy whilst increasing engagement and customer retention. They examined the case of Bucherer, a leading luxury watches' distributor that invested heavily in data analytics capabilities to benefit all consumer touchpoints, leading to the development of an app that uses machine learning to offer personalised recommendations. Forbes also discusses the case of luxury furniture brand Poltrona Fau, that similarly uses AI to drive more accurate demand and support supply change predictions.

8.7 Conclusions

Chapter Eight addressed the challenges and opportunities for luxury fashion brands arising from recent changes in the media landscape affecting marketing and communication practices. It discussed how luxury fashion brands were initially reluctant to be online, and examined the different tools and strategies adopted when engaging with digital marketing and social media. In this sense, the opportunities but also the challenges involved in balancing exclusivity with reaching a wider audience were explored. A case study focusing on Cyber Valentine's Day (also known as 520 festival) in China offered a detailed discussion on how social media can create a connection with consumers.

Last, the chapter examined how digital means and social media can also offer luxury fashion brands the opportunity to gather valuable data that can be productively used to support strategic development in a variety of areas, from marketing and communication to branding and management.

8.8 Revision questions

-   What are the digital marketing tools used by luxury fashion brands?
-   How do luxury fashion brands engage with social media?
-   How can luxury fashion brands extract value through data analytics?

8.9 References

Athwal, N. K., Istanbulluoglu, D. and McCormack, S. (2018) 'The allure of luxury brands' social media activities: a uses and gratifications perspective', *Information Technology & People*. ISSN 0959-3845

Bazi, S., Filieri, R. and Gorton, M. (2020) 'Customers' motivation to engage with luxury brands on social media', *Journal of Business Research*, 112, pp. 223-35.

Bug, P. and Haussmann, N. (2017) 'Using social media for luxury fashion management', in Choi, T. M. and Shen, B. (eds.) *Luxury fashion retail management*. Springer Series in Fashion Business. Singapore: Springer. https://doi.org/10.1007/978-981-10-2976-9_8

Business of Fashion. (2023) The year ahead: digital marketing in the age of privacy. Available at: https://www.businessoffashion.com/articles/marketing-pr/the-state-of-fashion-2023-report-digital-marketing-privacy-customer-acquisition-retention/

Fetais, A. H., Algharabat, R. S., Aljafari, A. and Rana, N. P. (2022) 'Do social media marketing activities improve brand loyalty? An empirical study on luxury fashion brands', *Information Systems Frontiers*, 25(2), pp. 795-817.

Forbes. (2022) How luxury brands keep up with fast technological change. 14 December 2022. Available at: https://www.forbes.com/sites/stephanegirod/2022/12/14/how-luxury-brands-keeps-up-with-fast-technological-change/

Grilec, A., Vukusic, D. and Dujic, D. (2020) 'Communication strategies of luxury brands during COVID-19 crisis', *Economic and social development: book of proceedings*, pp. 281-90.

Heine, K. and Berghaus, B. (2014) 'Luxury goes digital: how to tackle the digital luxury brand consumer touchpoints', *Journal of Global Fashion Marketing*, 5(3), pp. 223-34.

Jing Daily. (2017) China's '520 Day' puts luxury brands in the mood for love, 20 May. Available at: https://jingdaily.com/china-520-day-love-wechat/

Lee, J. E., Hur, S. and Watkins, B. (2018) 'Visual communication of luxury fashion brands on social media: effects of visual complexity and brand familiarity', *Journal of Brand Management*, 25, pp. 449-62.

Liu, S., Perry, P. and Gadzinski, G. (2019) 'The implications of digital marketing on WeChat for luxury fashion brands in China', *Journal of Brand Management*, 26, pp. 395-409.

Liu, X., Shin, H. and Burns, A. C. (2021) 'Examining the impact of luxury brand's social media marketing on customer engagement: using big data analytics and natural language processing', *Journal of Business Research*, 125, pp. 815-26.

Ng, M. (2017) 'Luxury brands and social media in China: new trends and development', in Choi, T. M. and Shen, B. (eds.) *Luxury fashion retail management*. Springer Series in Fashion Business. Singapore: Springer. https://doi.org/10.1007/978-981-10-2976-9_10

Okonkwo, U. (2007) *Luxury fashion branding: trends, tactics, techniques*. Basingstoke: Palgrave Macmillan.

Okonkwo, U. (2010) *Luxury online: styles, systems, strategies*. Basingstoke: Palgrave Macmillan.

McKinsey & Company. (2021) Jumpstarting value creation with data and analytics in fashion and luxury. Available at: https://www.mckinsey.com/industries/retail/our-insights/jumpstarting-value-creation-with-data-and-analytics-in-fashion-and-luxury

Park, M., Im, H. and Kim, H. Y. (2020) '"You are too friendly!" The negative effects of social media marketing on value perceptions of luxury fashion brands', *Journal of Business Research*, 117, pp. 529–42.

Pentina, I., Guilloux, V. and Micu, A. C. (2018) 'Exploring social media engagement behaviors in the context of luxury brands', *Journal of Advertising*, 47(1), pp. 55–69.

Roberts, J. and Armitage, J. (2017) 'Luxury fashion and creativity: change or continuity?', in Tsan-Ming, C. and Bin, S. (eds.) *Luxury fashion retail management*. Singapore: Springer doi:10.1007/978-981-10-2976-9

WWD. (2021) China's 520 Valentine's Day pivots to kickstart 618, 17 May. Available at: https://wwd.com/feature/china-520-valentines-day-618-shopping-festival-1234816922/

Part IV

The Future of Luxury Fashion Branding and Marketing

9 Luxury Fashion Marketing and Emerging Technologies
Case Study: Gaming and Luxury Fashion Brands

CHAPTER OBJECTIVES

This chapter:

- outlines the ways luxury fashion brands use technology to support consumer engagement
- examines the different tools and tactics used with regards to dematerialisation
- considers how technology can support the fight against fakes

---

9.1 Chapter summary

Chapter Nine first examines the use of technology to support consumer engagement by luxury fashion brands. In this sense the chapter considers radio frequency identification (RFID) and QR codes but also augmented reality (AR), virtual reality (VR), artificial intelligence and chatbots through a series of examples. Moreover, the chapter addresses the issue of dematerialisation in luxury fashion, which sees brands associating their names to virtual products of varying prices, and the different strategies and tools, such as non-fungible tokens (NFTs), used in this sense. A case study focusing on the relationship between luxury fashion brands and gaming is also provided. Finally, the chapter examines the role of AI and blockchain technology in supporting luxury fashion brands in their constant fight against fakes. Counterfeits are a major and ever-present issue for luxury fashion brands, and one that has become even more prominent since the advent of social media and e-commerce.

9.2 Introduction

In 2022, McKinsey reported that fashion brands were increasing spending on technology in a variety of areas, as technology offers opportunities to streamline manufacturing, increase personalisation and traceability, and support community creation and consumer experience.

DOI: 10.4324/9781003264811-14

Technology can offer luxury fashion brands opportunities for PR and marketing communication to create hype to promote their label, products or services. Luxury fashion brands invest in technology to create engagement because people are spending more and more time online not only to shop and to socialise but also for entertainment. This is a particularly relevant trait of millennials and Gen Z consumers, which is a market segment of growing importance for luxury fashion brands.

Other drivers is this sense are represented by pursuing a trailblazing reputation, the need to respond to demands for innovation by consumers and the fact that in the luxury fashion industry brands tend to adopt new tactics if they have been trialled successfully by other labels. Moreover, brands also engage with technology because it could lead to revenue streams in the future.

9.3 Consumer engagement through technology

For a number of years luxury fashion brands have employed their platforms and social media to forge connections with consumers, foster brand awareness and loyalty and drive sales, creating engaging content to capture people's attention and create lasting impressions. They have used technology in their flagship stores, sometimes driven more by notions of novelty or by the opportunities in terms of media coverage and PR than by the will to improve the customer experience.

However, nowadays luxury fashion brands are also using technology to support engagement and create communities in a variety of ways. For example, in 2002 the 'Adidas for Prada re-source' project saw the launch of an interactive platform that enabled the community to create a large-scale artwork, and benefit from the sale of the resulting NFTs. Luxury fashion brands have also entered the wearable technology market, for example creating smartwatches like the Louis Vuitton Tambor Horizon watch or the Apple Watch Hermès collection. Pioneer in this sense was Ralph Lauren, which in 2015 launched a Polo shirt that could track vitals such as heart rates and breathing, which were then picked up by an app that devised personalised workout plans.

However, the available technology doesn't currently offer cheap and easy-to-use solutions to convey haptic qualities, and in this sense luxury fashion brands are still unable to convey the sensory characteristics of their products, or to offer a definitive solution to issues of fit. Those issues represent the main reasons people return items, increasing costs and the environmental footprint for labels, but such concerns are less relevant in virtual worlds, encouraging brands to engage more with dematerialised products, as also discussed in section 9.4.

Especially during the COVID-19 pandemic, a number of luxury fashion brands have experimented with different technological tools to launch a variety of services to entertain and engage consumers, boosting emotional connection and loyalty. During the pandemic online fashion shows, which had been used before but that had rarely been designed specifically for streaming, became the norm and allowed for more imaginative displays, like seen, for example, in Moschino's puppet show for SS2021. Moreover, online fashion shows also offered opportunities beyond the main lines and fashion weeks, as, for example, Dolce & Gabbana launched its DG Digital Show in November 2021 to mark the release of a collection that would be immediately available to purchase, and that was meant to be more wearable and accessible than the main collection. During the pandemic new initiatives where devised or reinforced, from movie clubs like the Louis Vuitton LV Cine Club to designers interacting on social media with users. For example, Miuccia Prada and Raf Simons in 2021 launched 'Possible Conversation', an online dialogue with selected students from around the world.

In terms of achieving consumer engagement through technology, some luxury fashion brands have emerged as trailblazing. This is the case for Burberry, that, for example, created, within the brand's first social retail store in China, a living sculpture that responded to body movement of customers. The brand had previously also adopted RFID (radio frequency identification) and then QR codes to offer a more personalised service. Gucci has been another pioneer label in this sense, as, for example, users can access a virtual tour of the Gucci Garden Boutique in Florence.

Gucci also implemented AR functionality allowing users to try on a number of goods, from make-up to accessories, and even to position the home collection in their own house. Moreover, Gucci partnered with Zepeto to personalise worlds and avatars and even recreated its physical sustainable fashion line, Gucci Off The Grid, for videogame *The Sims 4*. Furthermore, in 2023 Gucci launched the Gucci Cosmos exhibition, a physical exhibition where technology allowed people to explore nine immersive 3D installations focusing on the history of the brand. For those who couldn't attend the physical exhibition, Gucci made it also available online through The Sandbox.

However, many other brands have experimented with technology to create engagement, for example through exhibitions. This was the case for Chanel that, following its 'Little Black Jacket' exhibition in 2012, launched a virtual museum on its website that mimicked the real experience by including the sound of other people walking around. In 2022, on the other hand, for the Le Grand Numero de Chanel exhibition, the label used virtual reality to provide visitors an immersive experience which saw them embody the company's perfumer, Ernest Beaux, and participate in the creation of iconic fragrance Chanel No. 5.

In terms of the specific technology used by luxury fashion brands, RFID and QR codes were among the first tools to be used to create engagement. In particular, RFID was used primarily to convey more information on products but adoption was limited by the fact that specific devices are needed to release information, whereas QR codes are more flexible as they can simply be read through an app. This factor has enabled QR codes to be featured on a number of elements, and in particular in advertising, to provide additional information and content. Other tools employed by luxury fashion brands are augmented reality (AR), virtual reality (VR), and artificial intelligence (AI).

Augmented reality has been used by luxury fashion brands to create filters and allow users to try on products. This was, for example, the case for Dior, that in 2019 launched a Snapchat filter that allowed users to try on new looks, or for Off-White that in 2021 used AR to superimpose its face masks on selfies. It has to be noted that AR has been initially used by luxury fashion brands as a tool to enable users to try on limited categories of goods, such as on sunglasses or shoes, but now it has wider applications.

For example, Louis Vuitton uses AR to allow people to visualise designer objects and furniture of its Objects Nomades collection in their own homes. Moreover, AR has been used by Gucci in 2019 to create an immersive experience at Art Basel Miami, whereas Off-White has been experimenting with it in different window displays around the world. Furthermore,

Burberry used AR in 2017 to promote the brand and create hype by teaming up with Apple, allowing users to digitally alter their surroundings with Burberry-inspired drawings by artist Danny Sangra.

Luxury fashion brands have also used virtual reality to create engagement. Harba (2019) observes that Dior was the first label to launch its own VR headset (Dior Eyes) in 2015, although it was not for sale but only available in selected stores. However, at the time Yves Saint Laurent had already used VR technology to offer make-up tutorials and Ralph Lauren had featured headsets in some stores to allow customers to watch a fashion show in 3D. In 2017, Givenchy announced the launch of its own headset, that would combine VR and AR, but nowadays luxury fashion brands don't seem to focus anymore on creating their own VR devices but on providing experiences instead.

For example, in 2020 Balenciaga staged a VR fashion show presented through Oculus glasses sent to selected guests worldwide. On the other hand, Prada has used VR to release a number of experiences, from visits to key spaces like the Epicenters in Tokyo, New York and Los Angeles or the Fondazione Prada in Milan and Venice, and to offer behind-the-scenes accounts of how a number of handmade goods are made in the company's workshops. Moreover, in 2016 to launch two new fragrances Prada created an app that became fully immersive through the use of VR headsets.

Another tool that has been adopted by luxury fashion brands to support engagement is artificial intelligence (AI), but this technology has a number of applications in a variety of areas. In fact, in the fashion industry, AI is also used behind the scenes, to assist in design and production, for example to minimise environmental impact through more efficient practices, to monitor social media, to predict trends and to offer more customisation of products and personalisation of experiences.

For example, in 2018 Tommy Hilfiger collaborated with IBM and The Fashion Institute of Technology (FIT) to introduce students to the potential of AI for a project that saw thousands of images from the brand and other sources analysed to create a series of patterns, silhouettes and prints that could be used to inform future design. In 2020, Acne Studios used AI to create its FW collection, but Xu and Mehta (2022) observe that this strategy can be off-putting in luxury fashion, as dream value and emotional value are impacted as people feel brands are losing their essence by delegating creativity to a machine.

AI can also offer new ways to promote luxury fashion brands and create engaging content. In 2018, Balmain used AI to create three CGI models, whilst virtual influencers Lil Miquela (also known as Miquela Sousa) has featured in a number of luxury campaigns. Moreover, Bulgari in 2021 launched Serpenti Metamorphosis, a project led by Turkish artist Refik Anadol that saw AI creating an ever-changing display based on millions of images from nature that would later launch as a NFT. However, the most common application of AI in the luxury fashion business is represented by chatbots.

As discussed by Chung et al. (2020), chatbots, also known as virtual assistants, allow brands the opportunity to offer 24/7 assistance to their customers, providing a solution to the fact that the internationalisation of luxury fashion labels has created a consumer base that lives in different time zones. In this sense, brands hope to emulate the attentive touch of their in-store staff to boost satisfaction, loyalty and sales, but current technological barriers such as the limited ability to deal with communication subtleties mean that chatbots are not yet able to convey the same levels of competence, credibility and trust of human agents. Ralph Lauren was a pioneer in this sense, introducing a chatbot on Facebook Messenger dedicated to the TommyXGigi Hadid collection in 2016.

Zeng et al. (2023) observe that many luxury brands nowadays offer chatbots on their websites and social media platforms, mostly to offer product information and sale services, but those are still primarily text-based. Chatbots can only deal with limited queries, and human agents are still required for more complex issues. Most luxury fashion brands use a professional tone and aim to convey authority and prestige through chatbots, and therefore, so far, references to playfulness and irony are limited. However, this is the case for Gucci, that through chatbots provides a more fun and engaging experience for consumers by featuring games and quizzes.

If other technologies are used in conjunction with chatbots they usually have limited scope, as, for example, the authors observe that Dior offers VR try-on functionality through chatbots, but only for limited products. There is great disparity in the way luxury brands use chatbots, with some only using them for some categories of goods such as cosmetics as in the case of Chanel and YSL, whereas other labels adopted such tools widely at first and then abandoned them, like in the case of Burberry, at least in some countries. Zeng et al. (2023) also highlight the issue of information security and privacy for chatbots, as the lack of explicit authorisation and knowledge of how data is going to be used can provide a barrier for adoption.

This is an important issue, because if consumers are reluctant to engage with chatbots as they are wary of giving away information then they are depriving brands of an invaluable insight that would allow them to better understand people's motivations, concerns and interests. It has to be noted that AI can also be used to increase accessibility, as, for example, Gucci uses alt text to assist people with visual impairments through screenreaders on social media and in stores (this service was launched in the US and is currently available in limited locations).

Last, another technological development that is increasing in popularity in the luxury fashion industry is represented by non-fungible tokens (NFTs), which are examined in the following sections from a variety of perspectives. Moreover, luxury fashion brands have also experimented with gaming to support consumer engagement, as examined in the case study of this chapter.

9.4 Dematerialisation of luxury fashion

This section examines the issue of dematerialisation in luxury fashion, which sees brands associating their names to virtual products. In this sense, luxury fashion brands are launching different products and adopting different strategies. Dematerialisation broadly refers to moving away from physical products towards digital ones. This is a growing market because people live more and more of their lives online, leading to new needs and aspirations as people pursue identity-making and uniqueness.

Dematerialisation has also been associated with sustainability as it can reduce the impact on the environment by limiting the need for physical objects. For the fashion industry, that has a very high environmental impact, to minimise the number of goods produced in real life and increase production of digital goods instead seems to offer a potential solution. However, digital products are not necessarily as sustainable as one might think, as, for example, to mint NFTs involves significant energy consumption, as examined in more detail below.

NFTs are digital goods that are authenticated through blockchain, they are timeless, don't decay and can offer luxury fashion brands a series of benefits. As discussed by Alexander and Bellandi (2022) NFTs are seen as valuable assets by collectors and investors as they are scarce and unique, unlike other digital goods created by luxury fashion brands. NFTs can provide traceable proprietary information that can support authenticity (as discussed in more detail in section 9.5) and can be used for more than digital products, as they can act as a 'digital twin' of real-life goods. Moreover, NFTs can be used by labels to provide access to exclusive experiences.

However, NFTs are also characterised by a number of downsides. First, the minting process of NTFs requires a lot of energy, leading to a big environmental footprint that goes against the calls to make the industry more sustainable. Moreover, NFTs have so far generated a lot of hype but are not yet linked to a stable revenue stream for brands. Furthermore, they are perhaps not as safe as people may think, as Alexander and Bellandi (2022) observe that NFTs can be vulnerable to cyber-attacks and may possess questionable legal status as the copyright of NFTs is currently separate from assets, and in this sense copyright still belongs to the creator.

Moreover, barriers to NFTs adoption are also represented by cryptocurrency volatility and its low use among target market segments for luxury fashion brands, which labels are trying to overcome by pursuing the use of more commonly used forms of payment. Last, another limiting aspect is represented by fragmentation and the inability to use digital assets on various platforms, in fact the NFTs created by luxury fashion brands, even if sold at exorbitant prices, cannot currently be used on all the virtual platforms and social media profiles of their owners.

However, this aspect is mitigated when technology conglomerates are involved, as, for example, Meta featured virtual clothing stores where users can buy luxury fashion items by the likes of Prada and Balenciaga, and use them in all the group's social media platforms. Meta's commitment to luxury fashion was further manifested by the launch, in 2022, of the first Metaverse Fashion Week, which saw luxury brands like Etro and Alexander McQueen participating.

Despite the limits and challenges, luxury fashion brands are engaging more and more with dematerialisation. For example, Kering declared in 2022 that they had created a group-wide team dedicated to the metaverse and Web 3.0, and that further teams for each of the brands owned by the group, like Gucci and Balenciaga, had also been established.

Initially, the digital products created by luxury fashion brands were not NFTs, but this area has expanded greatly in the last few years. Sometimes both approaches are used by luxury fashion brands as, for example, Prada has launched several limited edition NFTs since 2019, mostly as digital twins of its 'Timecapsule' drops (sometimes also associated with the chance of winning access to exclusive events). Originally the Prada 'Timecapsule' collection consisted of monthly drops of products not always associated with NFTs, but the brand aims to close the gap, as it announced in 2023 that it was working on gifting a NFTs digital twin to all those who bought the collection in the past.

Another divide in the luxury fashion industry is represented by the fact that some brands focus on cheaper products that are accessible to many whereas others pursue elevation strategies that focus on limited edition goods that are sold at high prices. The first strategy sees luxury fashion brands launching cheaper products and is, in this respect, similar to the one employed in real life through brand extension in the lower market segment. They in fact share the same risks, those of affecting brand equity and diluting the brand through negative association caused by over diffusion.

However, by launching low-price digital goods labels can create hype, increase brand awareness and pave the way for future sales. An example of such strategy is represented by Gucci Garage, that sells virtual sneakers costing less than £20 and that can be worn through AR. This strategy is not associated with real scarcity, as products are not usually NFTs, but nonetheless some form of exclusivity can be maintained, for example by limiting sales to specific platforms or making goods available for a limited time only.

The second strategy in approaching dematerialisation within the luxury fashion industry is represented, on the contrary, by focusing on producing digital goods that are expensive and elevate the brand. Those type of goods are characterised by real scarcity, as they are produced in a limited number or as one-offs, and minted as NFTs, and represent the digital equivalent of the most exclusive pieces associated with luxury fashion brands. This is, for example, the strategy pursued by luxury conglomerate LVHM, as chairman Bernard Arnault has declared that the group doesn't intend to follow a cheapening downscale vertical brand extension logic like its competitors, but on the contrary to differentiate themselves by adopting dematerialisation tactics that can sustain the aura of status, prestige and exclusivity of the brand. This is also the rationale behind the recent digital collection launched by Dolce & Gabbana.

In 2021, Dolce & Gabbana launched Collezione Genesi, comprising nine pieces ranging from womenswear, menswear and jewellery minted as NFTs. Items were sold at auction, totalling almost $6 million. For some items, physical goods were also released, as in the case of the Glass Suit, a silk men's suit embellished with Murano glass beads and Swarowski crystals, and of two women's dresses and crowns that were also offered physically with a digital twin. However, three men's jackets were offered in digital format only, as their design would not be possible to achieve through current methods, and similarly one of the three jewellery pieces created, 'The Impossible Tiara', was presented as being made of gems that cannot be found on earth. What made those items extra special was also the fact that each item was to be exhibited at the brand's flagship in Milan and in another store selected by the buyers, that the NFTs also included the original sketches of the items, and that it guaranteed access to exclusive Dolce & Gabbana couture shows and events, plus a private tour of the brand's atelier in Milan.

However, a number of brands are employing both strategies, to maximise benefits and minimise risks. This is, for example, the case for Gucci, that sells cheap digital goods that are accessible to many, as, in addition to the virtual sneakers mentioned above, the brand has also released a number of goods on gaming platform Roblox, but also some more exclusive goods characterised by intricate methods of acquisition to support exclusivity (McDowell 2022).

In 2022, in fact Gucci launched Gucci Grail, a project that saw the brand create New Tokyo, a floating city, and offered NFTs, but released a long list of requirements to gain access. First, people had to in fact register in order to qualify for one of the 5,000 passes available. Special access was reserved for those who had shown significant engagement, for example within the Gucci Discord community, or had purchased previous Gucci NFTs, but there were also other requirements, all in order to create buzz and reward brand loyalty and engagement. In 2021, Gucci also sold 'Aria', a NFTs video inspired by its collection, at action in Christie's, in line with elevation strategies.

Moreover, dematerialisation in luxury fashion is also closely intertwined with gaming, as explored in the case study.

9.5 Case Study: gaming and luxury fashion brands

In the last few years gaming has emerged as a very important tool for consumer engagement in the luxury fashion industry. Pioneer in this sense was the brand Armani, that in 2007 recreated its Milan Flagship in Second Life, an iconic 3D virtual world. Other early adopters were, for example, Moschino, that partnered with 'The Sims' to develop a series of collections, and Louis Vuitton, that in 2012 launched a partnership with the developers of the game 'Final Fantasy', whose character Lightning then featured in the brand's SS2016 campaign (Rathore 2017).

Luxury fashion brands have engaged with this dimension more and more to cater to the needs of younger consumers worldwide, that, as discussed in the case study of Chapter Four, are becoming a pivotal market segment for the industry. In this sense, luxury fashion brands aim to provide entertainment whilst increasing brand awareness, support brand loyalty and also boost sales, both in real life and online. In fact, many luxury fashion brands are not only using gaming as a way to generate hype and promote their brands, but also as platforms to distribute dematerialised products.

Luxury fashion labels have employed a series of different strategies for their foray into gaming. First, luxury fashion brands have associated their names with established gaming platforms to release digital collections (sometimes also using co-branding with mass-market brands) and NFTs, or used them as inspiration for physical collections. Moreover, luxury fashion brands have collaborated with established gaming platforms to launch promotional campaigns. Furthermore, luxury fashion brands have released their own branded game consoles and games. In this respect games can either be launched in collaboration with established platforms, or using owned-media. Most recent developments have also seen luxury fashion bands partnering with developers to revolutionise their digital offerings.

Many luxury fashion brands have associated their names with established gaming platforms to release digital collections. For example, *Animal Crossing* has featured special collections from labels such as Valentino, Gucci and Marc Jacobs, the platform also launched a social media account chronicling its high fashion collaborations. Moreover, many luxury fashion brands have also launched virtual stores on Roblox, as, for example, in 2022 Ralph Lauren released there a gender-neutral limited edition that allowed users to enjoy winter activities adorned in the brand's products.

In this sense, some brands have also employed co-branding strategies, as, for example, in 2021 Gucci dressed Pokémon GO avatars in garments created in collaboration with North Face, and created a sense of exclusivity and scarcity by making the collection available at selected PokéStops around the world. This tactic is in line with those adopted by luxury fashion brands when collaborating with mass-market brands in order to protect their status and prestige. If many luxury fashion brands are using gaming platforms to release dematerialised products, some brands are now also expanding through NFTs, as, for example, Burberry has so far collaborated twice (in 2021 and 2023) with Mythical Game to launch limited-edition NFT items such as skins and accessories in Blankos Block Party.

In some cases, luxury fashion brands used gaming as inspiration for their physical collections. For example, in 2019 Louis Vuitton partnered with League of Legends to develop skins for the game but also a physical capsule collection (the brand even crafted the Summoner's Cup's trophy trunk), whereas the FW2021 collection of Balenciaga took inspiration from the PlayStation game console.

Moreover, some labels have also used gaming to create advertising campaigns, as, for example, Balenciaga in 2021 not only dressed *Fortnite* characters in a capsule collection that was offered in a physical version too, but the game's developer Epic also created 3D billboards to be shown in key cities worldwide to promote the collaboration. In this sense it is not unusual to adopt different strategies at the same time, as also demonstrated by Gucci. In fact, in 2020 Gucci partnered with e-sports organisation Fnatic to launch a limited edition of Gucci Dive watches inspired by *League of Legends*, a collaboration that was promoted through a series of videos starring real game players and also celebrated through the launch of a new game on Gucci Arcade.

Another area that luxury fashion brands have explored with regards to gaming is represented by the release of their own branded game consoles, as, for example, in 2021 Gucci launched its Xbox Series X. Only 100 units of this special edition console were available, comprising two controllers and a hard case engraved with the words 'GOOD GAME', in this sense fostering the brand's association to gaming through the happy coincidence that in gaming vocabulary the initials GG, that are one of Gucci's symbols, are the abbreviation of the iconic sentence used at the end of a match.

Moreover, many luxury fashion brands have released their own games, either in collaboration with established platforms or developing their own. One example of such partnership is represented by Gucci, that in 2023 collaborated with mass-market brand Vans to create a treasure hunt on *Roblox*, which led to special items to wear on the platform. After many collaborations with the platform, Gucci has now launched a permanent Gucci Town on *Roblox* where people can shop and personalise avatars, socialise, and take part in challenges, games and competitions, earning GG Gems. However, Gucci has also created games on an owned-platform, as it launched a 'Gucci Arcade' section on its app, where users can engage in a variety of games with retro 1970s and 1980s aesthetics.

However, many other luxury fashion brands have launched their own games independently by established platforms. For example, Hermès in 2018 released a game to promote and celebrate its jumping competition in Paris, whereas in 2019 Burberry launched the *B Bounce* game. The game saw a deer-shaped character wearing a monogram puffer jacket bouncing to the moon, with winners awarded custom made GIFs and virtual Burberry puffer jackets edited onto a digital picture of their choice, whereas in some countries users also had a chance to win a real Burberry jacket. The game was made available to play on the huge screen inside Burberry's flagship in London. Then, in 2020, Burberry launched a second game, *Ratberry*, to celebrate the Year of the Rat for its New Year campaign, associated with stickers on WeChat.

Moreover, in 2020 Balenciaga launched the game 'Afterworld: The Age of Tomorrow' on its website to support its AW2021 collection. Furthermore, in 2021 Louis Vuitton launched 'Louis the Game' to celebrate the late founder's 200th birthday. In the game users, through a customizable character, had to explore 200 virtual worlds to find 200 birthday candles, upon completing the mission they could then search for 30 hidden collectible NFTs. Through the game, users learnt about the brand, and this allowed Louis Vuitton to reach younger potential customers and increase brand awareness and emotional connection.

Gaming has also been used by luxury fashion brands in terms of localised practices, to better engage and entice consumers in specific areas. For example, Louis Vuitton in 2022 created the game 'Mah Jump' to further reinforce its commitment to Chengdu when launching its first restaurant in China, next to its flagship in the city. Chengdu was added to the brand's City Guides before the launch, and the game celebrated its culture, for example mahjong and tea traditions.

Moreover, a number of luxury fashion brands, like Dior, Valentino and Gucci, have also released mini-games on popular Chinese social media WeChat but also through Taobao Life (linked to retailer Tmall), fostering engagement, brand awareness and loyalty through those popular Chinese-developed platforms that allow brands to create their own content through mini-programs.

However, another facet of the relationship between luxury fashion brands and gaming is represented by the foray into this area by luxury retailers. For example, Luisa Via Roma, an established luxury retailer with physical stores in Italy but that operates online worldwide, created *MOD4*, a free mobile game that allows users to buy, collect and use digital pieces from leading luxury fashion brands. Products can be collected by participating in challenges and missions, and users can create special looks and moodboards that can be then featured in the Magazine feed for everyone to see.

Socialising is supported through the introduction of chat functions, and encouraged as commenting and liking the Magazine feed, but also supporting players' challenges, is necessary for users to gain items and game currency. Items can be only used for a certain number of times, after which they need to be regenerated, but they can also be resold on the platform, that retains a commission on the sales (currently 30%). This platform offers Luisa Via Roma a way to engage and increase customer loyalty, offer an opportunity to diversify income streams, but also benefit luxury brands more broadly as it supports engagement and brand awareness in a key target market.

Most recent developments have also seen luxury fashion bands partnering with developers to revolutionise their digital offerings. This is, for example, the case for LVMH, that in June 2023 announced a partnership with Epic Games (creators of the iconic game *Fortnite*) to support the group's new online strategy in virtual worlds and though immersive experiences. The first projects announced involved virtual fitting rooms, 360 product carousels and augmented reality. In this sense, LVHM announced it would also continue to implement the use of 3D creation tool Unreal Engine (developed by Epic Games), technology that the conglomerate used in 2022 to create a Virtual Ancient Rome for Bulgari and to launch Livi, their first virtual ambassador.

Questions and activities

- How have luxury fashion brands engaged with gaming?
- What are the strategies adopted in this sense?
- Identify the latest examples of the relationship between luxury fashion brands and gaming, comparing and contrasting the strategies adopted in this sense.

9.6 The fight against fakes, from AI to blockchain

In this section we examine how luxury fashion brands are using technology in their constant fight against fakes and counterfeits, an issue that plagues the industry and that has become even more prominent since the advent of social media and e-commerce has challenged established models of controlled distribution.

We have examined in Chapter Five how luxury fashion brands have traditionally used controlled distribution as a way to fight against fakes, using monobrand stores and choosing the retailers that are allowed to sell their products. However, it is difficult to eradicate fakes altogether, as parallel grey markets, where merchandise is sold by retailers that are not authorised do so, can offer opportunities for counterfeits to flourish.

Now that counterfeits have moved online, the battle against fakes is even more costly and complex. In this sense, luxury fashion brands are trying to implement online the same strategies of controlled distribution they use in physical retail. Moreover, some luxury fashion brands have also collaborated with pre-loved and second-hand platforms to offer safe alternatives to buy authentic used goods in the re-sale market. However, even in this case it's difficult to eradicate fakes, as seen, for example, in the legal battle between Chanel and reseller platforms TheRealReal and What Goes Around Comes Around, that were accused of selling counterfeit handbags.

Fakes and counterfeits represent a major issue in the luxury fashion industry, and can hurt brands in a variety of ways. Near perfect fakes can hurt the brand in terms of loss of sales, and moreover if they are presented as the genuine article and are similar, but not an exact match in terms of quality or performance, then they may also create negative associations in those that are not familiar with the originals. To spot that an item is fake can be difficult, as it has been reported that near perfect fakes are getting more and more similar to the originals as they are being produced by former suppliers, licensees or partners in Asian countries where luxury fashion brands delocalised their production, creating the know-how that is now used against them (Chada and Husband 2006). In this sense, luxury fashion brands that employ third parties to design or produce their goods are particularly vulnerable, and this vulnerability is one of the contributing factors that are leading many labels to regain control of their supply chain and productive capabilities.

Literature observes that in the past the majority of fakes were bought by people that were aware they were not originals, with cues being differences in design, lower prices, lower quality and unofficial retail channels. However, with the advent of social media and e-commerce things have become more complex as a flourishing second-hand market, fuelled by controlled distribution and scarcity of certain iconic products, like the Birkin bag by Hermès for example, led to the fact that the boundaries between genuine articles and fakes are becoming more blurry, as more people can be misled into thinking that they are buying authentic goods when it's not the case. These fakes can make luxury fashion goods become more overexposed, making them commonplace and leading key target segments to abandon them in favour of less heavily seen items. Disappointment concerning the quality of goods received can also negatively influence brand image, impact future sales of genuine articles and hurt brand equity.

Fighting against fakes is costly for luxury fashion brands, Okonkwo (2007) reports that Louis Vuitton spends €10–15 million each year to fight fakes in different ways. Using lobbyists, the brand aims to achieve more effective legislation against counterfeits, as, for example, in France it supported the creation of a law that made illegal not only selling but also buying fake goods. Agents for Louis Vuitton travel the world to identify factories making counterfeits, and the brand also assists local authorities in seizing and destroying merchandise.

For example, in 2004 Louis Vuitton led over 6,000 raids and filed over 8,000 copyright complaints. Moreover, the company is also targeting those turning a blind eye to illegal activities, as, for example, it filed complaints against the landlords of a notorious counterfeit location in New York City. So far, the damages awarded to luxury fashion brands in those litigations are small in comparison with the damage done, and in many cases they are unlikely to ever be collected, because the international nature of the counterfeit business and the different jurisdictions involved add another layer of complexity in this sense.

A recent case concerning Burberry showcases those difficulties (ManagingIP 2007). Burberry had been monitoring eBay since the early 2000s looking for counterfeits when they discovered that a factory in Thailand had been supplying vendors in the UK and Germany, but it took years to see anyone convicted and the fines are probably never going to be recovered. However, Burberry is not the only brand searching the Internet for counterfeits, as nowadays luxury fashion brands routinely employ specialised teams in this sense.

Zargani (2020) discusses how Valentino sued, jointly with Amazon, a US company selling counterfeits of the brand's iconic Rockstud shoes, whilst also seizing thousands of other products and listings from websites, online marketplaces and social media. Zargani also details how Ferragamo succeeded in 2018, when a US court awarded to the brand damages and the transfer of over 150 domain names that infringed its copyright. In fact, fakes are sold online through a variety of platforms, from social media to own websites and through retail giants like Amazon and eBay for example, and so far despite the efforts to eradicate this phenomenon listings for fakes keep re-emerging. Chaudhry (2022) examines how dupe influencers also fuel consumer demand for counterfeits, facilitating knowledge transfer and the purchase of fakes through a model dubbed 'order this, get this', where consumers are directed to a non-infringing listing with the knowledge that in reality a counterfeit good will be delivered.

Recently, to monitor the Internet more effectively and accurately in search of counterfeits, luxury fashion brands have turned to AI. In this sense AI can facilitate the task by allowing more data to be carefully analysed, for example to identify design similarities, looking for copyright or intellectual property infringement.

However, issues of copyright can be problematic, and technology can provide new challenges in this sense. This is, for example, the case for the lawsuit brought forward by Hermès, that sued a digital artist for releasing a MetaBirkin NFT, a fuzzy digital version of the brand's iconic handbag. The MetaBirkin actually costs more than the original Hermès counterpart, and its creator stated that it was an artistic reinterpretation of the iconic bag that didn't mean to mislead the public. However, Hermès argued that at the heart of the issue was the fact that although the label's current trademarks cover only leather and fashion, the brand wanted to avoid confusion, preserve brand equity and protect its right to offer digital version of Hermès goods in the future. Hermès ultimately won the lawsuit and also a permanent injunction, but the creator of the MetaBirkin stated that an appeal would be pursued.

However, luxury fashion brands are also engaging with technology to explore ways to guarantee authenticity for their goods, therefore making it easier to spot fakes. In this sense some brands have adopted RFID and near field communication (NCF) whereby chips can communicate with devices and confirm their authenticity. However, luxury fashion brands nowadays are increasingly using blockchain, a decentralised network created in 2008 whereby information and transactions are sealed and cannot be changed unilaterally, to make it easier to check if goods are authentic.

Currently, in fact, authentication through official channels such as flagship stores or auction houses, and also through the authentication services offered by pre-loved platforms such as Vestiaire Collective, are not easily accessible to all. Moreover, people may not want to use them in countries where even the possession of fakes is a criminal offence if they are not completely sure of the goods' origin. Blockchain allows keeping a record when genuine products are sold, offering people the traceability and confidence that is especially needed in the second-hand market. In this sense luxury fashion brands aim to extend to physical goods the same level of authenticity guaranteed to NFTs through blockchain technology.

Blockchain is especially useful as it can be used to authenticate both real-life products and digital ones, supporting the expansion of luxury fashion brands into gaming and dematerialisation. For this reason, in 2021, luxury fashion conglomerates LVHM, Richemont, the Prada Group and the OTB Group, alongside Cartier and Mercedes-Benz, created the Aura Blockchain Consortium. Loro Piana joined in 2023 and more brands are expected to do so as the non-profit association of luxury brands aims to promote the adoption of blockchain solutions worldwide for the luxury industry, offering enhanced transparency and traceability, to improve consumers experience through supporting selling, reselling and recycling luxury goods.

However, blockchain can also be used by luxury fashion brands beyond the fight against fakes, for example to offer sustainability information or for storytelling purposes. This is the case for the archive of the late Karl Lagerfeld, that is being digitalised and authenticated through blockchain to provide a rich experience where photos are linked to exclusive information, behind the scenes anecdotes and extra content.

9.7 Conclusions

Chapter Nine addressed the issue of how to support and increase consumer engagement through digital means. In this sense elements considered were radio frequency identification (RFID), QR codes, augmented reality (AR), virtual reality (VR) and also artificial intelligence and chatbots. A series of examples regarding both older and more recently established luxury fashion brands, such as Gucci and Off-White, were provided. Moreover, the chapter examined the issue of dematerialisation in luxury fashion and presented a case study focusing on luxury fashion brands and gaming. Last, the chapter discussed the role technology can play with regards to the fight against fakes and counterfeits, a major issue for luxury fashion brands that has become even more complex to tackle since the advent of social media and e-commerce.

9.8 Revision questions

- How do luxury fashion brands use technology to support consumer engagement?
- What are the different tools and tactics used with regards to dematerialisation?
- How can technology support luxury fashion brands in their fight against fakes?

9.9 References

Alexander, B. and Bellandi, N. (2022) 'Limited or limitless? Exploring the potential of NFTs on value creation in luxury fashion', *Fashion Practice*, 14(3), pp. 376–400.

Chadha, R. and Husband, P. (2006) *The cult of the luxury brand: inside Asia's love affair with luxury*. London: Nicholas Brealey.

Chaudhry, P. E. (2022) 'Dupe influencers exploiting social media to peddle luxury fakes', *Business Horizons*, 65(6), pp. 719–27.

Chung, M., Ko, E., Joung, H. and Kim, S. J. (2020) 'Chatbot e-service and customer satisfaction regarding luxury brands', *Journal of Business Research*, 117, pp. 587–95.

Harba, J. N. (2019) 'New approaches to customer experience: where disruptive technological innovation meets luxury fashion', in *Proceedings of the International Conference on Business Excellence*, 13(1), pp. 740–58.

ManagingIP (2007) Check mate for Burberry. Available at: https://www.managingip.com/article/2a5cnh8udkg66wspcvv9c/check-mate-for-burberry

McDowell, M. (2022) 'Gucci goes deeper into the metaverse for next NFT project'. Available at: https://www.voguebusiness.com/technology/gucci-goes-deeper-into-the-metaverse-for-next-nft-project

McKinsey. (2022) State of Fashion Technology Report. Available at: https://www.mckinsey.com/industries/retail/our-insights/state-of-fashion-technology-report-2022

Okonkwo, U. (2007) *Luxury fashion branding: trends, tactics, techniques*. Basingstoke: Palgrave Macmillan.

Rathore, B. (2017) 'Exploring the intersection of fashion marketing in the metaverse: leveraging artificial intelligence for consumer engagement and brand innovation', *International Journal of New Media Studies: International Peer Reviewed Scholarly Indexed Journal*, 4(2), pp. 51–60.

Xu, L. and Mehta, R. (2022) 'Technology devalues luxury? Exploring consumer responses to AI-designed luxury products', *Journal of the Academy of Marketing Science*, 50(6), pp. 1135–52.

Zargani, L. (2020) 'Valentino, Amazon file suit against N.Y.-based counterfeiter', *WWD*, p. 3.

Zeng, N., Jiang, L., Vignali, G. and Ryding, D. (2023) 'Customer interactive experience in luxury retailing: the application of AI-enabled chatbots in the interactive marketing', in *The Palgrave handbook of interactive marketing*. Cham: Springer International Publishing, pp. 785–805.

10 Diversity, Inclusivity and Cultural Sensitivity
Case study: Dolce & Gabbana

CHAPTER OBJECTIVES

This chapter:

- explores how narratives of diversity are employed by luxury fashion brands
- considers issues of inclusivity within the industry
- defines cultural appropriation and discusses other forms of cultural references by luxury fashion brands

---

10.1 Chapter summary

Chapter Ten focuses on issues that have become more and more topical in the last few years as a function of changes in societal values, and that are shaping the way luxury fashion operates in a variety of areas, from marketing to staff management. First, the chapter explores notions of diversity and investigates how luxury fashion brands are engaging with this dimension through a variety of strategies both in front of the camera and behind the scenes, addressing the issue of tokenism. The latter is also considered when it comes to inclusivity, which is another element that luxury fashion brands are increasingly engaging with. Finally, the chapter examines the issue of cultural sensitivity, exploring how international expansion and the advent of the Internet and social media have made labels vulnerable to criticism when local cultures and values are not respected or when issues of cultural appropriation are at play. In this sense, the case study of the Dolce & Gabbana Love China scandal is explored.

10.2 Introduction

Over the last few years a major shift has occurred in luxury fashion, as practices in a variety of areas have come under scrutiny by the media and the general public. In this chapter we examine those related to diversity, inclusivity and cultural sensitivity, whereas issues related

DOI: 10.4324/9781003264811-15

to environmental sustainability, animal welfare and social responsibility are addressed in the following chapter.

Nowadays, people are becoming more aware of discriminatory practices and also more vocal in stating their dissent, primarily through social media. Recently, many brands have faced scandals and have, more broadly, been criticised for not doing enough for minorities and disadvantaged groups. This effect is more notable in Western countries, but discourses concerning equality, diversity and inclusion are becoming more commonplace in a number of countries. In this sense, to fight or prevent accusations, but also to project a positive brand image and attract a market that is increasingly value-driven, many luxury fashion brands have engaged more and more with those issues, launching initiatives, promoting causes and changing their communication and marketing practices.

Diversity concerns issues of representation, and examines whether a group is an homogenous entity or not. Diversity can involve observable characteristics such as age, ethnicity, gender or disability, but also less evident ones like cultural background or cognitive patterns. In many countries, to discriminate people on the basis of such characteristics is illegal, and more protection has been gradually offered to more and more categories, for example in terms of transgender rights. However, even when legislation offers some degree of protection, minorities are often still stigmatised, isolated, mistreated and face discrimination in a variety of ways.

Discourses of diversity in the luxury fashion industry refer primarily to representation in public-facing practices, such as marketing, communication and promotion. In fact, it's the image projected by luxury fashion brands that is especially scrutinised in this sense, with a particular focus on the people that are in front of the camera, such as models. The issue of diversity with regards to the actual workforce of companies has been featuring more in public debate, but also in this sense the emphasis is often placed on the most evident symbols of labels. For example, in the luxury fashion industry the focus seems to be more on the characterising traits of designers and managers than those of other company employees, which, however, represent the majority of the workforce.

If discourses of diversity focus on legal compliance, fair treatment and notions of equal opportunities and representation, inclusion on the other hand involves developing practices that nurture people's talent regardless of their characteristics and background, with the aim to promote participation, to support people's involvement in decision making and to foster a sense of belonging. The concept of inclusivity focuses on how diversity is mobilised.

Inclusivity goes deeper than diversity in this sense, as it considers not only whether a company has a diverse workforce, but how that diversity is implemented in practice. For example, a company could have 80% of staff belonging to minorities or under-represented groups and receiving praise in this sense, but the situation would be interpreted differently if it was to be revealed that this 80% of staff members belonging to minorities or under-represented groups were all in low-pay and low-responsibility roles, whereas management was solely represented by people coming from the most traditionally represented segments in a country.

It is important to observe that issues of diversity and inclusivity refer to elements that are culture specific, as, for example, one of the most relevant dualities in the USA in this sense is represented by a Black/White opposition, as examined in the next sections. With regards to fashion, issues of inclusivity primarily revolve around notions of inclusive design, consumer experience and workforce practices, as examined in section 10.4. However, there are other cultural elements that luxury fashion brands need to consider in their quest to appeal to societal values, for example with regards to cultural appropriation and cultural sensibilities. As discussed in section 10.5, luxury fashion brands have struggled with those issues at times, and one of the reasons scandals and controversies have emerged has been attributed to the fact that labels are not diverse nor inclusive enough, as they seem to focus on the issues more at surface-level, without implementing practices to valorise difference.

10.3 Diversity

The fashion industry has often been criticised for its lack of diversity, initially the controversies involved the models used in shows and marketing campaigns, and only recently the attention has shifted to what happens behind the scenes and to brands' management.

Cavusoglu and Atik (2023), in particular, observe how current narratives within the industry revolve primarily around the dichotomies Black/White and skinny/plus size, leaving out other skin tones and different body types. However, when it comes to diversity, more elements could and should be considered, such as social class, age, sexual orientation, gender identity, having disabilities or living with health conditions. The latter is, in particular, an area where luxury fashion brands could do more, as, for example, models with albinism such as Stephen Tompson, who modelled for Givenchy in 2011, are still under-represented. Similarly models with vitiligo, a skin condition that causes loss of pigmentation, were rarely seen before Winnie Harlow became the first model to walk the catwalk for a luxury fashion brand.

As luxury fashion brands are more and more under scrutiny for their practices, they focus their efforts on trying to convey a more diverse image in order to achieve reputational benefits, create buzz and deflect criticism, especially in their most visible public-facing practices such as fashion shows and advertising campaigns. In particular, the ethnicity of models chosen by luxury fashion brands has been scrutinised, with many reports criticising the limited number of non-White models used. Werner (2020) observed how, particularly in the USA, despite some pivotal moments, the industry remained primarily White. In fact, defining moments like the first Black model (Donyale Luna) to feature on the cover of a major magazine in 1965, the ethnic diversity featured in the 'Battle of Versailles' in 1973, and the first Black model (Beverly Johnson) to appear on the cover of Vogue USA in 1974, remained isolated occurrences. So much so that still in 1988 supermodel Naomi Campbell featured on the cover of French *Vogue* only after Yves Saint Laurent threatened to stop advertising in the magazine.

In this sense, fashion magazines have long been criticised for their role in spreading a certain aesthetics, and criticism of tokenism are rife, but signs of a shift in terms of more racial diversity can be seen, for example, in the July 2008 issue of *Vogue* Italy, that only featured Black models, and in the appointment of Edward Enninful to British *Vogue* in 2017.

Many luxury fashion brands have demonstrated very little engagement with diversity, as, for example, when in 2013 Prada featured a Black model in its campaigns this happened after a 19 year gap where no such models were employed. Moreover, Phoebe Philo was criticised for not having any Black models in any Celine fashion shows between 2009 and 2014.

On the other hand, luxury fashion brands that have been commended for their diversity are Gucci, that, for its 2017 pre-fall campaign, recreated a 'soul scene' reminiscent of the

1970s, and Balmain, that, in its 2016 show, saw each model being from a different heritage and ethnicity. In fact, if the debate is currently primarily focused on the Black/White dichotomy, representation of Asian, Hispanic, Middle Eastern and other ethnicities is also on the rise, as the debate is slowly broadening to include a more varied definition of diversity in fashion.

Representation in the luxury fashion industry matters and can help change established beauty standards with regards to a variety of elements. For example, many Asian countries have adopted Western beauty ideals and a focus on fair skin, which many luxury brands including Chanel have capitalised on through the introduction of Whitening beauty products. However, the influence of the luxury fashion industry in this sense can work both ways, as reports have observed that, for example, the use of Black models in China, that had been traditionally low, has been increasing in recent years as local brands mirror the practices of Western luxury labels in this respect.

But it's also the modalities whereby representations of diversity occur that are pivotal in this sense. In fact, studies have highlighted that beauty standards of different ethnicities still tend to be rejected and undervalued in fashion discourse, but also exoticised and often presented in a stereotypical manner. For example, Cavusoglu and Atik (2023) observed that Latinas and Black models on fashion magazine covers were found to be more over-sexualised, whereas Asian models featured in more passive poses, whilst both Black and Asian models also often wore ethnic clothes. Furthermore, a number of reports have highlighted discrimination based on skin darkness, as lighter tones are more represented within the fashion industry. Also, many models have criticised the widespread tokenism attitude of the industry, as many claims have emerged of models not getting jobs because a brand already employed 'one like them'.

Behind the scenes, the luxury fashion industry has been criticised for a general lack of diversity and the debate has been focusing, especially in the USA, on the small number of Black designers. This has been attributed to the low number of students in major American fashion schools, but representation in this sense is rising, the 2015 New York fashion week only featured four Afro-American designers but the number had risen to nearly 30 in 2023. In this sense the appointment of Virgil Abloh as creative director of Louis Vuitton in 2018 became a watershed moment for more representation.

After that, more Black designers have been appointed creative directors of luxury fashion brands, for example in 2022 Maximilian Davis, of British-Caribbean heritage, became creative director at Ferragamo, Ib Kamara, from Sierra Leone, was hired to replace Virgil Abloh after his death, whereas American artist Pharrel Williams succeeded him at the helm of Louis Vuitton's menswear line. Similarly, when LVMH revealed they were partnering with global superstar Rihanna to launch the Fenty luxury fashion house the news created buzz worldwide and the group was praised for creating the first luxury fashion brand led by a Black woman. The Fenty brand was also commended for its approach to diversity, that translated into a very diverse range of models for the label's debut show in 2019. The brand was, however, discontinued two years later, with claims that the pandemic and also the lack of a strong customer appeal, unlike the one seen for the very successful mass-market lines launched by Rihanna, were to blame.

In this sense, the initiatives launched by US brands Ralph Lauren, Michael Kors and Tommy Hilfiger to increase Black representation in the fashion industry have been praised. Such initiatives included, for example, the launch of scholarships, providing funding to organisations and launching schemes to support internal career progression and boost inclusion. Ralph Lauren in 2022 also launched a collaboration with two historic Black colleges, releasing a film and ad campaign that featured real students, staff and alumni, led by a Black production team. The importance of racial inclusion within the US market is particularly evident in the fact that Gucci only releases data regarding race and ethnicity for their US workforce, as, for example, the majority of the workforce as of 2021 was Hispanic or Latino, followed by White, Black or African American and Asian, whilst at management levels White represented almost 40% followed by Hispanic or Latino, Asian and Black or African American.

However, other mature markets are quickly catching up as the issue gains more attention. For example, in 2019 in Italy (a country that so far isn't as multi-ethnic as others like the USA) a number of protests led to the country's fashion association, the Camera della Moda, to launch a series of initiatives to support Black Italian designers and also support diversity in fashion shows. This involves not only offering professional hairstylists and make-up artists that specialise in textured hair during fashion week, but also offering training to others in this respect. Many models, like Naomi Campbell, have been vocal about this facet of racial discrimination behind the scenes, as darker models often have to carry their own make-up to shoots, and at times they even have to apply it themselves, whilst hair care is also an issue.

However, luxury fashion brands are realising more and more the potential that lies within a diverse clientele and are devising strategies to reach that target market. For example, Dolce & Gabbana was among the first luxury fashion labels to enter the modest market with a range of hijabs and abayas, but since then many luxury fashion brands have produced goods that can cater to that lucrative market segment. Representation in this sense is also making its way into other market-facing initiatives, as, for example, models such as Rawdah Mohamed have worn a veil on the catwalks of a number of luxury fashion brands such as MaxMara, which has been hailed as one of the most inclusive brands in this sense.

Another area of diversity that luxury fashion brands are engaging more with is represented by notions of beauty. The fashion industry has often been accused of promoting unattainable standards of beauty focusing on Whiteness, and a number of traits such as big eyes and lips, thin nose, long straight hair and high cheekbones. In particular, the luxury fashion industry has been criticised for its use of extremely thin models (more so than their mass-market counterparts) as literature has observed that the gap between the idealised fashion model body type and the average person has been increasing. Despite many Western nations launching enquiries and introducing legislation aimed at monitoring models' BMI (for example banning models below a certain BMI threshold or asking for certificates of health), those have so far proved ineffective in changing strongly-rooted practices that see larger bodies being under-represented or used as tokens.

Model sizes had decreased in particular between 1980 and 2000, and despite the occasional use of models like Sophie Dahl or Ashley Graham it seems that any progress so far has been at surface-level as often only one model with a diverse body type is featured in a campaign or fashion show. Even if luxury fashion brands have occasionally showcased more diversity in respect to some traits, their practices are still focusing on a certain body ideal that is characterised by thinness and youth. For example, the Kering group still uses underage models (they only banned the use of models under 16 years of age) and even though the group similarly made a stand by banning models below a size 34 for females and a size 36 for males those ranges still reflect a very slim body type. Moreover, a number of designers such as Karl Lagerfeld have praised extreme thinness and shared unkind views about other sizes and body types.

Some countries, like France, are also forcing brands to state in a clearly visible manner when they use photo editing to alter images, as they try to fight the widespread practice, within the fashion industry, of making thin models look even thinner. In terms of products, the luxury fashion industry has been criticised for the limited sizing offered. Notable exceptions in this sense are Marina Rinaldi, a dedicated plus-size luxury brand, and Dolce & Gabbana, that go up to a XXXL international size (or a 54). With regards to that, the mission of extending sizing by retailer 11Honoré has been pivotal in supporting labels such as Diane Von Furstenberg to become more inclusive and expand their size range.

The fashion industry has similarly been accused of presenting models of masculinity that are difficult to attain. The mass market has been progressively adopting a more muscular silhouette since the 1980s, whereas luxury brands have been adopting a more slender body type since Hedi Slimane reintroduced the silhouette whist at Dior. Barry (2014) observes that the Rootstein male mannequin, the industry standard, has decreased significantly from the 1960s, and that model sample size has currently gone down from an Italian 50 in the 1990s to a size 46. What the muscular and slender type have in common is the narrow range of age and ethnic characteristics featured and a lack of representation, for example, when it comes to different heights, receding hairlines or disabilities.

Sometimes the luxury fashion industry has been praised for promoting alternative ideals of beauty, even though elements are often used for shock value, to provoke and to gain media coverage, and do not represent a true change of direction. For example, Mugler featured Rick Genest, aka Zombie Boy, an artist with a skeleton tattoo covering all of his body, in their AW2011 campaign. Gucci's 2019 make-up campaign also received significant attention for featuring models whose teeth were not completely straight and not unnaturally white. Dolce & Gabbana has also been praised for sometimes not using professional models in its fashion shows, opting for celebrities but also common people, resulting in a more diverse range of body shapes, heights and ages. Moreover, Valentino over the last few years has been praised for its diversity drive, that saw models of different ages, body types and ethnicities grace the catwalks.

In terms of age, it has been reported that in 2019 the four major fashion weeks featured only 3% of models over 45, but they have since become more common in advertising campaigns, as brands aim to capitalise on the ageing population in Western markets. However, in many cases the bodies associated with luxury fashion brands seem to differ from established ideals of beauty only with regards to one element. In fact, for example, in 2012 Lanvin featured an 82-year-old model in its advertising campaign, but she was still thin, and so is Joan Didion, a renowned US writer that starred in a Celine campaign in 2015. In many cases older individuals are actually celebrities, therefore aligning more with celebrity endorsement strategies. For example, in 2012 Prada had actors Willem Dafoe and Gary Oldman walking the runaway, followed by Jeff Goldblum and Kyle MacLachlan in 2022.

The number of transgender and non-binary models in the luxury fashion industry is currently very low, even though 'feminine' male models have often graced the catwalk, the most notable case being Andreja Pejic, who modelled both womenswear and menswear before transitioning to female. Since the 2000s, luxury fashion brands have engaged more and more with the LGBTQIA+ communities, for example supporting causes and organisation, especially for Pride Month, often through special collections that donate a portion of profits. Most recently, Balenciaga, Ralph Lauren, BOSS and Versace have done so, but some brands have been criticised for engaging at a superficial level by only releasing rainbow-themed items. In this sense, Acne Studio showcased more commitment, as its Fall 2017 campaign featured Black LGBT Kordale Lewis and Kaleb Anthony and their family, in an industry first. More broadly, the fashion industry still features limited commitment in this sense, as the number of transgender individuals that have appeared on *Vogue* covers is still limited (for example Valentina Sampaio and Laverne Cox), and similarly non-binary people are also currently under-represented.

Moreover, luxury fashion brands have featured narratives of disability only sporadically, and are seen more as tokenism than a real commitment to more representation. For example, in 1999 athlete Aimee Mullins walked the runaway for Alexander McQueen with intricately carved prosthetic legs, whereas Gucci featured Ellie Goldstein, a model with Down Syndrome, in its Unconventional Beauty 2020 campaign. However, not many labels have followed in those footsteps, although more representation is slowly being introduced.

In this sense the work of Edward Enninful, the editor-in-chief of *Vogue* UK, who himself has a hidden disability as he is partially blind and with a hearing impairment, is notable, as in 2023 the magazine featured a number of disabled people on its cover and in its pages, in line with the diversity drive he introduced.

10.4 Inclusivity

In the discourses of luxury fashion brands, issues of inclusivity primarily revolve around issues of inclusive design, creating a more inclusive consumer experience, and develop workplace practices that valorise diversity. However, it's the latter that seems to be more prominent.

When it comes to inclusive design, the fashion industry is yet to fully engage. Only a limited number of companies, like Nike and Target, have developed adaptive design ranges, and these are often limited in scope. In the luxury fashion industry, a pioneer in this sense is Tommy Hilfiger, that in 2016 launched an adaptive collection for children called Tommy Adapted. Several collections have since been released, and the range has been expanded to include adults too. Tommy Adapted offers practical and stylish solutions to everyday issues, for example in terms of fastening by adopting velcro fasteners and magnetic buttons instead of traditional ones.

Tommy Adapted has also featured disabled models and people living with health conditions consistently in its marketing and communication, which is an exception in the luxury fashion industry, where tokenism is rife as labels only sporadically engage with difference in this sense, and seem to use it to create buzz and project a positive, caring image whilst in reality keeping the focus still firmly on able bodies. In this sense the fashion industry is seeing this market as a niche, and brands are primarily focusing on the benefits that adaptive design could offer to people living with disabilities or medical conditions, but it is believed that in the future, especially in mature markets where the population is getting older and the stigma associated with such conditions is easing, more consumers would appreciate and adopt garments that focus on comfort and function.

Another area of inclusivity where the fashion industry can do so much more is represented by consumer experience. In fact, companies are often putting little or no effort in making shopping, both physical and online, more accessible to those with disabilities, and similarly initiatives to make communication and marketing practices more inclusive are few and far between. In this sense the initiatives recently launched by Gucci are pioneering.

Gucci entered a partnership with a visual interpreting service to improve access to visual information for the blind and sight impaired in their stores (initially only in the USA) and also used AI to improve consumer experience by featuring alt text in social media posts, so that images can be described for those using screenreaders. Gucci was also voted best place to work by the Disability Equality Index in 2023 due to a series of initiatives such as mandatory accessibility training for staff and Guccibility disability resource groups. The brand also stated its commitment to create more opportunities in the workplace for people with disabilities. Prada also launched schemes to increase inclusivity in this sense, and in 2021 was the first luxury fashion group to join The Valuable 500, an organisation aiming to end disability exclusion, with a first commitment to hire individuals affected by Down Syndrome in their Italian retail network.

Usually, when it comes to inclusion and diversity, luxury fashion brands tend to establish a number of initiatives to support claims of authenticity and convey an image of real engagement and to deflect accusations of tokenism, as consumers are wary that many of those schemes may be limited in scope and motivated more by reputational needs than by a real commitment to improve lives. In fact, if in their public-facing activities many luxury fashion brands are projecting images of diversity, and initiatives have been launched to increase inclusivity behind the scenes, key roles remain primarily linked to certain characteristics.

In addition to race and ethnicity, as seen in the previous section, issues of education and social class have also been claimed to be barriers towards reaching relevant positions, limiting inclusion. For example, nowadays luxury fashion designers are often educated in the most exclusive fashion schools, where fees are high, and despite the fact that a number of institutions and brands support scholarships or training programmes, lack of diversity is still seen at the top of the hierarchy, leading to questions of how inclusive the industry really is.

Prada created a scholarship programme to support students in the USA and Africa. Prada also offers aspiring fashion industry professionals paid internships within the group, and supports internal development through training programmes ranging from technical know-how on leather work and footwear to sustainability. Similarly, Gucci offers scholarships and exchange programmes with fashion schools around the world. Moreover, luxury fashion brands like Hermès and See by Chloé have been supporting the Casa 93 project, a fashion training programme aimed at underprivileged students in partnership with the Institut Français de la Mode.

Moreover, many luxury fashion brands have also created committees dedicated to diversity and inclusion in the aftermath of scandals and controversies, with the aim to restore their reputation and clean up their image. This was, for example, the case for Gucci, that after being accused of racism in 2019 promptly announced that a Global Equity Board was going to be established and a series of initiatives would be launched to increase diversity and inclusion in-house. In the same year Prada introduced its Advisory Council on the subject.

In the late 2010s, as debate over inclusion and new sensibilities became more prominent, also in reaction to a number of scandals within the industry, many luxury fashion brands established committees and launched initiatives in this sense, and many have followed since. Nowadays, virtually all luxury fashion brands have created initiatives to support inclusion and diversity, because, as in other areas, trailblazing initiatives are quickly emulated by other luxury fashion brands as they don't want to fall behind.

In response to consumer's scepticism about the real impact of their initiatives with regards to issues of inclusivity and diversity, a number of brands have sought certifications to attest to their commitment (often employing a third-party to assess their practices to further showcase the rigorousness of their approach) or joined forces with leading organisations to convey an image of credibility and authority to their practices. For example, Gucci has collaborated with UN Women and UNHRC (the UN refugee agency) to convey trust with regards to the brand's commitment to worker's rights and equal opportunities.

In this sense, an area that more and more luxury fashion brands are associating themselves with is women's rights and gender equality. For example, Gucci in 2013 launched its Chime for Change campaign, becoming the first Italian luxury fashion brand to obtain a Certification of Gender Parity. Gucci also partnered with an Italian bank to offer its suppliers funding if they supported women's career and gender equality within their companies.

In its communication Gucci also highlights how the brand supports female leadership in the workforce, stating that as of 2023 the company featured 57% female members in management roles (they make up 63% of total staff) and that they are aiming to close the gender pay gap for equivalent positions within the organisation by 2025. Similarly, Prada highlights that, as of 2022, 63% of their workforce was female and that 59% of managerial positions were occupied by women (although nearly 70% of the workforce came from Italy, Europe and America).

For the luxury fashion industry, more inclusivity at managerial level is associated with a series of benefits. As Quarato et al. (2017) discuss, in fact female directors are found to improve operating profitability, whereas multicultural teams are associated with more efficient problem solving, increased innovation and more diverse perspectives. Benefits are also associated with the co-existence of different generations, whereas professional and educational background diversity was also found to improve the ability to assess opportunities and make strategic decisions.

Inclusive and diverse teams can also provide increased innovation and commercial advantage through being more in tune with the target market. On the contrary, the lack of inclusion of different voices has been linked to a number of scandals dealing with issues of cultural appropriation and cultural sensitivity, as explored in the following section.

10.5 Cultural sensitivity

Luxury fashion brands have recently been embroiled in a number of scandals concerning lack of cultural sensitivity. This is the result of changed sensitivities within society, meaning, for example, that nowadays the homeless-inspired collections launched in the early 2000s by the likes of Vivienne Westwood and John Galliano would be met with much more criticism.

The whole industry has faced widespread claims of lack of due diligence and nonchalant attitudes towards other people's values and cultures, and this situation has often been linked to a lack of diversity in decision-making positions and a lack of inclusion in the workplace. This means, for example, that dissenting voices are not listened to when concerns are raised, that people with detailed knowledge of issues or coming from the cultures referred to are not involved nor asked for approval, and that the industry lacks comprehensive final checks over product development and marketing communications.

This situation has led to many scandals in the last few years. For example, in 2018 Prada was accused of Blackface for its Pradamalia line, that featured a number of Black monkey-like creatures with exaggerated red lips. The controversy resulted in a lawsuit by a civil rights attorney in New York that forced the company to withdraw the goods and to launch a series of reparative initiatives, such as mandatory racial equity training in the USA, donations to charitable associations, the creation of scholarships and internships to support diversity in fashion and also of a diversity committee. It was reported at the time that the lack of diversity at the brand's HQ, where no Black individuals were present, was to blame for the scandal.

Gucci was also accused of racism in 2019, when it launched a knitted jumper covering the lower face, whose version in black was criticised as Blackface for its exaggerated red lips. The brand apologised and withdrew the garments, and launched a number of initiatives, from impact funding to scholarships, to try repair its reputation. Moreover, Marni in 2020 faced controversy because of a campaign for flip-flops. The campaign featured Black models adorned in tribal items, but those were unrelated to the brand's collection and moreover one model even had chains near their ankles, in what was considered a poor taste reference to slavery and colonialism. The campaign was withdrawn, and Marni apologised, stating that they had intended to celebrate Afro-Brazilian culture but missed the mark.

Moreover, Burberry was also embroiled in a scandal when it presented, in its AW2019 fashion show, a hoodie featuring a noose around the neck. The garment was supposed to be inspired by nautical themes, but was immediately criticised for making light of suicide. It was reported that models at the fashion show had actually raised concerns about the inappropriateness of the garment, but were not listened to. Moreover, in the USA associations between the noose, racism and lynching caused a furore. Burberry apologised and then launched a series of reparative initiatives, as, for example, in the UK the brand partnered with the Samaritans and other charities to support suicide prevention amongst the most vulnerable. In September 2019, Gucci made a similar gaffe when they had models wearing garments resembling straitjackets down the catwalk. This led non-binary model Ayesha Tan-Jones to stage a protest by walking the Gucci runaway and writing on their palms that 'mental health is not fashion', forcing the brand to apologise.

Another area that is becoming more problematic in the fashion industry is represented by the practice of using designs and traditional elements belonging to other cultures. Fashion has often been inspired by other cultures, but recently more and more controversies have emerged in this sense.

Pozzo (2020) discusses how in fashion influences can be reciprocal and result in motifs that are shared by different cultures, for example the 'roundel and pearl' motif can be traced back to China and Central Asia between the 6th and 13th centuries but also to Egypt and Eastern Mediterranean areas in the 1st century. Many fashion designers have been inspired by Eastern cultures, for example Paul Poiret proposed harem pants and tunics in the early 20th century, whereas Dior, for example, looked to India for inspiration for its 1988 collection by Gianfranco Ferré. However, more recently this practice has led to accusation of cultural appropriation.

Cultural appropriation is defined as the use of cultural symbols, traditions, or other cultural elements of a community by another community or entity without the permission of the former. Narratives concern power imbalance and focus on how cultural elements from marginalised communities are transformed into commodities and exploited for financial gain by a dominant culture without offering recognition or compensation.

Because, in this perspective, the other culture is not consulted or sufficiently researched, there is a high risk of desecrating symbols and causing offence in the original community. For example, in 1994 Chanel apologised for designing an evening gown featuring verses from the holy book of Islam. Karl Lagerfeld denied having knowingly done so and apologised, but the damage had already been done. A similar controversy involved Gucci in 2019, when the brand was criticised for releasing a turban called 'Indy Full Turban', desecrating a garment that is sacred for the Sikh community. Gucci ultimately pulled the item and apologised, but also launched a series of restorative measures, including the launch of a dedicated committee. In 2019, a number of luxury fashion brands such as Chanel, Burberry and Prada similarly established committees and initiatives with regards to diversity and inclusion as a reaction to a series of scandals concerning cultural insensitivity.

Cultural appropriation is also associated with the misrepresentation of subordinated cultures, further fuelling marginalisation and stereotyping. Cruz, Seo, and Scaraboto (2023) argue that cultural appropriation means using elements of another culture in a way that is perceived as inappropriate, using elements unacknowledged, and is associated to discourses of misrepresentation, decontextualisation and domination, as it involves inhabiting a cultural voice eroding its distinctive identity and fetishising it as a commodity or costume. On the other hand, cultural appreciation is associated to cultural diffusion, blending, adaptation and learning.

Lojacono (2022) observes that if in 2003 John Galliano was able to present a collection called 'Asia Major' for Dior, featuring direct inspiration from China and Japan and mixing different cultural elements, nowadays cultural sensitivities have changed and the public is less open to condone the use and appropriation of cultural symbols and the power imbalance it manifests. This leaves luxury fashion brands in a tricky position, as they have expanded internationally and aim to entice new customers through references to their culture, whilst also constantly searching for strategies to convey novelty and difference in the global market.

In the luxury fashion industry there are countless examples of cultural appropriation. Isabel Marant was accused of cultural appropriation for creating a dress that presented similarities with a traditional Mexican blouse of the Mixe people for the SS2015 collection. The Mexican community campaigned to have recognition and compensation, and the issue gained further media attention when Isabel Marant was sued by another label for copying that very same design, and the designer defended herself by stating that the design actually came from the Mixe community, leading the court to rule that none of the parties held copyright.

Later the design was withdrawn but the designer was accused of appropriating Mexican culture again in 2020 for a cape that was also subsequently withdrawn. Moreover, Valentino was widely criticised in 2016 for an advert campaign shot in Africa that saw members of the Maasai tribe used as backdrop to promote a collection heavily inspired by African garments.

Green and Kaiser (2020) discuss the case of Ralph Lauren, that in the mid-2010s was accused of cultural appropriation. Ralph Lauren has actually been employing the same aesthetics since launching the brand, mixing cowboy references with elements coming from different Native populations, creating a commodified and stereotypical mash up that decontextualises and marginalises communities further, depriving them of credit for their design and offering no compensation in return. However, the brand first came under fire for using historical photographs of Native people as props for a 2014–15 advertising campaign, and was then accused in 2015 of copying Native American design for a 'Cowichan' sweater made in China. In this case, however, the brand didn't stop selling the controversial garment, but simply renamed it as 'Cowichan-inspired', an approach that was criticised as exploitative and tone-deaf.

Another case involving Native American culture is represented by the controversy following the release of Dior's Sauvage perfume advert in 2019. Maiorescu-Murphy (2021) observes that the advert was withdrawn less than 24 hours after its release due to accusations of cultural appropriation. The ad, featuring Hollywood actor Johnny Depp, showcased the wilderness of the Utah landscape and Native American dances, but as soon it was released attracted controversy in the USA. Dior immediately withdrew the original advert (later a version that toned down references to Native American culture was released) but stated that it had been developed in collaboration with America for Indian Opportunity and that Depp had been adopted into the Comanche nation in 2013.

However, such elements had not been clearly communicated and therefore the advert was perceived by the general public as a case of cultural appropriation whereby a brand was capitalising on a marginalised community. Moreover, the situation wasn't helped by the fact that the very name of the fragrance was considered by some as derogatory towards the Native American community, although the French term actually can mean not only 'savage' but also 'wild', and the fact that Johnny Depp at the time was involved in a domestic violence scandal.

Other cases concerned the appropriation of traditional hairstyles. For example, the SS2017 fashion show by Marc Jacobs featured models (predominantly White) showcasing dreadlocks, a symbol of Rastafari culture, but in pastel-hued wool. A few days after the show the designer apologised, stating that the display wasn't meant to cause offence and that it had been intended as a tribute to music artist Boy George. However, a similar controversy surfaced for the Marc Jacobs SS2018 fashion show, as accusations of cultural appropriation of Black culture emerged when White models wearing head wraps walked the runaway. Later, the Comme des Garçons AW2020 fashion show saw models wearing cornrow wigs, the brand apologised for the display, although the hairstylist in charge stated that the display was meant to reference the wigs worn by pharaohs in Ancient Egypt.

Stella McCartney was also accused of cultural appropriation for the SS2018 collections, as it featured African styles, materials and methods, for example wax resist, but with no mention of where such techniques and styles came from. The brand simply stated that they collaborated with a Dutch company that had been using the wax resist method since 1846. Moreover, the lack of Black models to launch the collection further fuelled accusations of decontextualisation and exploitation of other cultures without recognition and compensation.

However, Lojacono (2022) also identifies good practices, when it comes to cultural references, within the luxury fashion industry. For example, Louis Vuitton for its 2018 Cruise Collection collaborated with Japanese designer Kansai Yamamoto and engaged with many cultural traditions, from Kabuki theatre to traditional prints, to create a sense of authenticity. Similarly, Dior's 2019 Cruise Collection was inspired by escaramuza, a Mexican women's equestrian tradition, both in terms of design and communication.

Lojacono (2022) argues that when cultural appropriation controversies emerge in luxury fashion, brands should avoid ignoring the issue, or rejecting accusations, as that could further suggest that they have a cultural gap and do not respect the marginalised position of the community offended, and that an apologise and intervene strategy is more appropriate. Moreover, Lojacono argues that to avoid accusations of cultural appropriation luxury fashion brands should showcase a deep understanding of local cultures, show respect and focus on authenticity, as exemplified by Dior's 2020 Cruise Collection, which saw designer Maria Grazia Chiuri celebrate Africa through engaging with local communities and experts.

The brand recreated iconic Dior prints in cotton that was grown, spun, woven and wax-printed in Africa, used local suppliers to provide props for the fashion show, and explicitly recognised the contribution of local communities, artists and artisans to create a sense of trust, respect and appreciation. However, in this sense it is essential to inform the public about respectful practices to support understanding and recognition of virtuous practices.

This was, for example, the case for Loewe, that widely disseminated information when it launched a collection inspired by traditional Chinese monochrome ceramics. The initiative was praised as it was perceived as an authentic tribute, which was supported by sponsoring the creation of a new monochrome ceramics educational program at the Jingdezhen Ceramic University. Similarly, to showcase respect and appreciation of Chinese craftsmanship, Hermès launched a joint venture with Jian Qiong Er in 2019 to create luxury brand Shang Xia.

10.6 Case study: Dolce & Gabbana

One of the biggest scandals to date concerning cultural sensibility, or lack of, is represented by the Dolce & Gabbana disaster of November 2018, when the company's attempt to appeal to the Chinese market spectacularly backfired due to an advertising campaign that was perceived as offensive by the very people it was supposed to charm. Moreover, the brand was slow and ineffective in taking action as the backlash raged on, so that Dolce & Gabbana alienated their target market further, losing revenues and negatively affecting brand image and equity.

The Chinese market is very important for luxury fashion brands, and therefore many have opened grand stores and launched spectacular events to capture consumers attention, increase awareness, prestige and loyalty, and to boost sales. To cater to this market and strengthen their presence in the country, Dolce & Gabbana in 2018 organised 'The Great Show' in Shanghai, a grand production that was supposed to involve over 360 people on the runaway and thousands behind the scenes, and to cement the brand's role in a country that at the time represented roughly 30% of the brand's revenue (Huang and Janssens 2019).

As discussed by Dallabona and Giani (2020), the grand fashion show was supposed to be a celebration of China, and was promoted heavily on social media through the

#DGLovesChina. Chinese celebrities, buyers and important clients were to attend and there was considerable media attention, but positive sentiments quickly evaporated when Dolce & Gabbana released three promotional videos on social media site Weibo. The videos were accused of portraying offensive stereotypes and, more broadly, of not being respectful of Chinese culture, and a fierce backlash on social media ensued.

The three ad series was entitled 'eating with chopsticks' and featured a male voiceover speaking Chinese that first incorrectly pronounced the brand's name and then instructed a young Chinese model, wearing Dolce & Gabbana clothes and jewels, on how to eat typical Italian foods. As the model struggled to cut pizza with chopsticks, or to lift a giant cannolo (a tube-shaped Sicilian sweet pastry), the voice made sexual innuendos, and appeared to mock her efforts to sample the 'great Italian cuisine' with her 'stick-shaped cutlery', comments that were perceived to be inappropriate and derogatory both towards the model and China as a whole.

The adverts were in fact also accused of being disrespectful to women and of using 'mansplaining'. People took offence as the adverts seemed to paint Chinese nationals as ignorant and lacking the refinement needed to understand foreign food whilst mocking their culture. Furthermore, critics observed that the Chinese folk music and the dark and outdated interiors used in the adverts also seemed to convey a backward image of China, and accusations of racism quickly spread.

Within hours hashtags calling for a Dolce & Gabbana boycott went viral, but the brand did not take decisive action, instead opting to post a message on its official Instagram page to thank the friends and guests who were planning to attend the fashion show and to reinforce that the event was intended to be a loving tribute to China and that the controversy was unfortunate for all those who worked with great passion to create the show. As many observed, no apologies were offered and this fuelled the scandal further, especially as Dolce & Gabbana removed the three videos from Weibo, but they were still available on the brand's Instagram account.

Things spiralled from there, and as accusations of racism and of portraying offensive stereotypes spread, the Dolce & Gabbana Chinese brand ambassadors resigned, and model agencies and celebrities started to distance themselves from the fashion show. However, the event was still planned to take place, and was only called off at the last minute as further controversial elements emerged.

In fact, screenshots of a conversation between a journalist of Diet Prada and Stefano Gabbana allegedly showing the designer making some derogatory remark towards China quickly went viral. Later the brand claimed that both the brand's and Stefano Gabbana's social media accounts had been hacked, and denied writing the offensive messages. Afterwards, Domenico Dolce and Stefano Gabbana finally recorded an apology video, stating that they never intended to cause offence and asking for forgiveness for the lack of respect towards China they showcased.

However, it looks like this was too little too late, the delay in apologising and taking strong action to control the scandal fuelled the controversy, and had little effect on the increasing calls for a boycott. People were seen destroying Dolce & Gabbana products in protest, customers were returning items they purchased and the pressure even led Chinese retailers and department stores to remove the brand from sale. Moreover, some Dolce & Gabbana stores in China were defaced. Since then, reports about Dolce & Gabbana's poor performance in the Chinese market, and low social media engagement in the country, have emerged.

It was estimated that Dolce & Gabbana lost €36 million in just one day, and whilst other luxury fashion brands have seen significant growth in China in the last few years, the label's revenues there have actually decreased in the aftermath of the scandal, in a sign that the controversy has not only financially affected the brand but also stunted future growth in a key market. The controversy lingered on and still affects the brand's image in China today.

In fact, as Dallabona and Giani (2020) observed, beyond the short-term consequences of the controversy, negative narratives surrounding Dolce & Gabbana can re-emerge in light of further scandals concerning lack of cultural sensibility that originated from other luxury fashion brands. For example, negative sentiments towards Dolce & Gabbana were brought to the surface again when Gucci was embroiled in a scandal in 2019, and similarly the Dolce & Gabbana fiasco in China was put in the spotlight again, continuing to damage the brand, every time another label faced a scandal about a lack of cultural sensibility.

Surely Dolce & Gabbana didn't intend to alienate such an important market. It has since been reported that the adverts were meant to be taken as tongue-in-cheek, but questions have been raised on how it was possible that a campaign like that could even see the light of day. In this sense, bad practices such as the lack of proper procedures to check the brand's message and also a lack of diversity in the brand's HQ have been mentioned, as many were baffled and theorised either that Chinese people were not consulted, despite the fact that the adverts were shot in Chinese, or that their concerns were not listened to, which are broader issues concerning diversity and inclusivity.

Moreover, by not acting swiftly enough and by failing to acknowledge the offence caused immediately, Dolce & Gabbana let the scandal fester and this further strengthened accusations of racism and lack of cultural sensibility, doing damage that is difficult to undo as it has offended and alienated the very market it was trying to entice.

Questions and activities

- What did the 2018 Dolce & Gabbana scandal involve?
- What strategy did Dolce & Gabbana adopt in the aftermath of the controversy?
- Compare and contrast the strategies adopted in this sense by Dolce & Gabbana with those employed by other luxury brands in similar circumstances.

10.7 Conclusions

Chapter Ten focused on issues that have become more and more relevant in the last few years and that are rapidly becoming major sources of scandals and controversies in the luxury fashion industry, contributing to reshaping the way luxury fashion brands operate from a variety of perspectives. First, the chapter examined the concept of diversity and investigated how luxury fashion brands are engaging with this dimension through a variety of strategies both in front of the camera and behind the scenes. In this sense, the notion of tokenism was also considered. The latter was also considered when it comes to inclusivity, exploring the steps undertaken by brands in order to foster change. Moreover, the chapter examined the issue of cultural sensitivity addressing how the growing internationalisation of luxury fashion brands and the role of new media have made labels more vulnerable to criticism concerning their practices. This phenomenon was also explored through the case study of the Dolce & Gabbana Love China scandal.

10.8 Revision questions

- How are narratives of diversity employed by luxury fashion brands?
- How has the luxury fashion industry tackled issues of inclusivity?
- Why do cultural references nowadays represent problematic issues for luxury fashion brands?

10.9 References

Barry, B. (2014) 'Expanding the male ideal: the need for diversity in men's fashion advertisements', *Critical Studies in Men's Fashion*, 1(3), pp. 275–93.

Cavusoglu, L. and Atik, D. (2023) 'Extending the diversity conversation: fashion consumption experiences of underrepresented and underserved women', *Journal of Consumer Affairs*, 57(1), pp. 387–417.

Cruz, A. G. B., Seo, Y. and Scaraboto, D. (2023) 'Between cultural appreciation and cultural appropriation: self-authorizing the consumption of cultural difference', *Journal of Consumer Research*, p. ucad022., https://doi.org/10.1093/jcr/ucad022

Dallabona, A. and Giani, S. (2020) 'The good, the bad, and the ugly: Dolce & Gabbana and narratives of heritage and national identity', in Amanda Sikarskie (ed.) *Storytelling in luxury fashion brands, visual cultures, and technologies*. New York: Routledge, pp. 38–50.

Green, D. and Kaiser, S. (2020) 'Taking offense: a discussion of fashion, appropriation, and cultural insensitivity', in *The dangers of fashion*. Bloomsbury Publishing Plc, pp. 143–60.

Huang, Q. and Janssens, A. (2019) 'Come mangiare un cannolo con le bacchette: the contested field of luxury fashion in China, a case Study of the 2018 Dolce & Gabbana advertising incident', *ZoneModa Journal*, 9(2), pp. 123–40. https://doi.org/10.6092/issn.2611-0563/9970

Lojacono, G. (2022) 'The fine line between localization and cultural appropriation in personal luxury goods: an exploratory study', *Strategic Change*, 31(5), pp. 487–96.

Maiorescu-Murphy, R. D. (2021) '"We are the land:" an analysis of cultural appropriation and moral outrage in response to Christian Dior's Sauvage scandal', *Public Relations Review*, 47(4), p. 102058.

Pozzo, B. (2020) 'Fashion between inspiration and appropriation', *Laws*, 9(1), p. 5.

Quarato, F., Cambrea, D. R., Lussana, G. and Varacca Capello, P. (2017) 'Top management team diversity and firm performance: empirical evidence from the fashion and luxury industry', *Corporate Ownership & Control*, 15(1-2), pp. 325–40.

Werner, T. (2020) 'Preconceptions of the ideal: ethnic and physical diversity fashion', Cuadernos del Centro de Estudios en Diseño y Comunicación. *Ensayos*, 78, pp. 183–93.

11 Sustainability and Ethical Issues in Luxury Fashion

Case study: Stella McCartney

CHAPTER OBJECTIVES

This chapter:

- examines social responsibility in luxury fashion
- addresses animal welfare practices within the industry
- considers how luxury fashion brands engage with sustainability

11.1 Chapter summary

Chapter Eleven examines a series of ethical issues that have become relevant in today's society and that luxury fashion brands cannot ignore in their quest to remain relevant and desirable, affecting a variety of areas from marketing and communication to management. First, the chapter explores social responsibility, outlining the different practices and strategies employed by luxury fashion brands in this sense. Moreover, the chapter addresses the issue of animal welfare and species preservation, exploring how fur and exotic skins, that used to characterise the luxury fashion industry, have become controversial and are being progressively abandoned, leading the way to new cruelty-free alternatives. Furthermore, the chapter examines how luxury fashion brands address the issue of the environmental cost of their products and the strategies they can employ to engage with sustainability. In this sense the case study of Stella McCartney is discussed.

11.2 Introduction

Nowadays, consumers are exposed to information about the impact of their consumption practices in an unprecedented way, and the fashion industry has been harshly criticised for not doing enough, as a number of scandals have emerged. However, initially controversies within the industry involved mass-market brands, like Nike, for example, that in the 1990s was accused of using sweatshops and child labour to produce its goods. Many mass-market

DOI: 10.4324/9781003264811-16

brands in fact moved production abroad, to countries where labour cost was lower, in a race to the bottom that saw them becoming associated with sub-contractors that did not necessarily follow ethical practices, exposing a lack of control over their supply chain that led to scandals.

Luxury fashion brands were initially shielded by the negative attention, protected by an aura of prestige, craftsmanship and quality. However, as brands expanded in the lower market segment, moving away from traditional craftsmanship, and started to use sub-contractors abroad in order to deliver cheaper goods, and due to changes in the mediascape brought by the Internet, that made it easier for news to quickly circulate worldwide, controversies about the production practices of luxury fashion labels also started to emerge more and more, leading to bad press, boycotts, and damage to brand reputation and equity.

In this sense, Karaosman et al. (2020) discuss a series of scandals. For example, some children lines by luxury fashion brands including Dior were found to contain hazardous chemicals, and it was also reported that some Louis Vuitton shoes that featured a 'Made in Italy' logo were actually made in Romania instead, as there labour costs are lower, before being shipped to Italy for finishing. Those examples showcase how the credibility and trust in luxury fashion brands can be eroded when questionable practices are exposed.

The world of fashion was again in the spotlight as it has been identified as the second most polluting industry in the world. Initially, luxury fashion brands were shielded by their reputation of craftsmanship and exclusivity, but as they expanded more and more in the lower market segment to launch large quantities of products more controversies emerged. Sustainability and ethics are nowadays being taken more and more into consideration by luxury fashion brands, but there is still considerable confusion, including among consumers, about what those terms mean and how to achieve more considerate consumption in this sense.

As sustainability and ethics involve different perspectives, consider different issues, and use different tools and metrics to measure the impact of fashion brands, reports in this sense can differ greatly and sometimes results can also be contradictory. For example, natural fibres such as wool or cotton have been associated with animal and human exploitation, but are better in terms of sustainability as they are biodegradable, however to switch solely to those would then cause more pressure on land and water and, therefore, lead to a high environmental impact.

On the other hand synthetic fibres are not associated with animal exploitation, but are often petroleum-based and can release harmful micro-plastics into the environment, polluting oceans and entering the food chain. People are exposed to confusing and contradictory information and are often unsure about the impact of their lifestyle, and accusations of greenwashing have further increased consumer scepticism towards companies' claims. Lack of clear information and grand claims having little impact have also been observed to negatively affect the adoption of more considerate consumption practices. Such concerns have been for example associated with the decision of Hermès to initially present, in 2010, their 'Petit h' project to recycle and reuse materials as a separate business.

In Western countries especially, people can feel the pressure to publicly voice concerns about how goods are produced, but research has shown that nowadays there is a gap between people's declarations of caring about the impact of their consumption in terms of the environment, communities and animals, and the actual adoption of more considerate consumption practices. In this sense a number of barriers have been identified, for example in terms of aesthetic appeal and cost. It has been observed that consumers expect 'virtuous' goods to feature the same good design of traditional versions, but they are not prepared to pay the same high prices for goods made with recycled materials, or materials that are perceived to be of lesser quality. However, consumers nonetheless expect luxury fashion brands to take care of sustainability, social responsibility and animal welfare because such labels are perceived to have the financial means to explore different practices and because of their leading role in the fashion industry, meaning that their adoption of more responsible practices would trickle down to other fashion companies and lead to broader positive changes.

Discourses of sustainability are linked primarily to environmental impact, although the word can also be used as an umbrella term to include animal welfare and social responsibility, which are examined in the following sections of this chapter.

11.3 Social responsibility

Luxury consumption has often been criticised for being inappropriate and intrinsically unethical as it symbolises the great wealth disparity between the many who cannot, or can barely, afford necessities and those who can access the finest and more expensive goods and services. This criticism has become more relevant in recent years, as reports have highlighted how wealth disparity has been increasing worldwide, but this concern has a long history.

As mentioned in section 1.3, inappropriateness has a longstanding association with luxury. For example, Berry (1994) observes that in Ancient Greece luxury was considered inappropriate from a political point of view. Philosopher Plato argued that it could weaken society and similarly Aristotle attributed the destruction of the Roman empire to the unethical luxurious lifestyle of the elites. Claims of inappropriateness were then put in moral terms by Christianity, associating luxury with corruption and sin, framing the debate until the pre-modern era.

Later, in 18th-century Europe, the notion of luxury lost part of his moral taint, but the debate over its inappropriateness returned in political terms. For example Rousseau argued that the poverty of the majority of the population was caused by the consumption practices of wealthy people and their indulgence in luxury. These themes are still topical today, as global economic crises and instabilities, alongside a growing awareness of socio-economic disparities, influence the debate, causing luxury fashion brands to come under fire for perpetuating inequality, also with regards to the exploitative production practices that have been used in some instances.

Social responsibility discourses focus on the work environment, health and human rights. Concerns raised in this sense are low wages and long working hours, impact over workers' health due to unsafe work environments and the use of toxic chemicals. Moreover, social responsibility also encompasses supporting and maintaining relationships with local communities and protecting traditional socio-economic structures. The UN has identified the fashion industry as the main source of workers exploitation and many groups, from the ETI (Ethical Trading Initiative) to a number of NGOs, have been asking for a more regulated and socially sustainable industry. Concerns have become more prominent as modern slavery is on the increase, fuelled by the rising demand of consumer goods, and fashion in particular.

Modern slavery is defined as the exploitation of workers (including children) whose freedom has been removed, as they are bound by debt bondage, or forced through violence, threats and coercion. As luxury fashion brands have moved production abroad, often in countries where worker's rights and labour laws are less regulated to lower costs, scandals have emerged. A number of luxury fashion brands have faced accusation of using sweatshops. For example, Celine has been reported to manufacture goods in factories in Eastern Europe that are linked to extremely low wages and poor work conditions. Moreover, Dolce & Gabbana and Prada have been accused of exploiting illegal Chinese immigrants to produce their goods in Italy. Also, Stella McCartney was criticised for partnering with Adidas as the latter was involved in a sweatshop scandal.

However, the whole industry has been associated to exploitative practices through networks of subcontractors and recruitment agencies. For example, WWD (2023) discusses how the luxury fashion industry had been ranking poorly in the Global Slavery Index, with claims of modern slavery in silk cocoon cultivations in Uzbekistan, whilst unethical cotton has been detected in Benin, Burkina Faso, China, Kazakhstan, Pakistan, Tajikistan, Turkmenistan and Uzbekistan. Moreover, it was highlighted how only four countries (Australia, France, Germany and Norway) have so far introduced compulsory human rights checks or modern slavery legislation.

Furthermore, Forbes (2021) examines the alleged human rights abuses in the Xinjiang region of China. Luxury fashion brands were in fact criticised for using cotton from that region, due to accusations of alleged unethical working conditions, but also suffered when they stopped doing so as a result of the introduction of international sanctions. In fact, when Western labels were banned from sourcing cotton from Xinjiang they were affected by a fierce backlash in China, as, for example, Burberry faced boycotts, was abandoned by Chinese brand ambassadors, and its clothes removed from the video game *Honor of Kings* only a few days after having been announced.

If many brands communicate their efforts on environmental sustainability, there is a lack of information on social responsibility in the supply chain. Luxury fashion brands are reluctant to clearly state where their products are made as labels aim to avoid courting controversies by declaring affiliation to areas and suppliers that may be using less than ideal ethical practices. Akrout and Guercini (2022) observed that as of 2020 the majority of companies published reports on their environmental impact, but those concerning the social dimension were still lagging behind. This situation was also attributed to the lack of common guidelines, as different perspectives focus on different issues, making it difficult to assess and compare the social sustainability practices of luxury fashion brands, and generating confusion in consumers.

However, the reluctance to declare where luxury fashion goods are manufactured is also related to the 'made in' effect. In fact, consumers of luxury fashion brands tend to respond negatively to the fact that luxury goods are not made in the country they associate with the brand, and labels, therefore, prefer to gloss over the issue to support their prestige and status. As a result, goods produced abroad, and particularly in countries associated with cheap labour and lacking the international reputation of the brands' country of origin, can affect brand reputation and equity.

Another element to consider is the fact that throughout the fashion industry many companies are reluctant to provide details as they worry about competitors accessing their suppliers and cutting them out. This is a concern that involves primarily SMEs, pivotal parts of the luxury fashion industry that are more vulnerable than bigger companies. If in fact many luxury fashion brands have implemented vertical integration strategies to gain more control of their supply chain, directly managing operations, such a strategy is not available to smaller brands, which lack the funds to do so and rely more heavily on contractors and sub-contractors. In this sense, Loro Piana, that in 2019 launched a new traceability tag showing where their garments came from, represents an exception.

In order to navigate the treacherous topic of social responsibility, luxury fashion brands have launched a series of initiatives such as creating ad hoc committees, rethinking their production practices, acquiring credibility by association with 'virtuous' brands and leading agencies, and creating wide-reaching programmes.

Nowadays a number of luxury fashion brands have established committees, for example Armani created a Corporate Social Responsibility department in 2013, whereas Kering has created a committee and two groups (in the Americas and Asia Pacific region) to monitor the group's ethical performance at all levels. They have also changed their production practices and banned some raw materials to protect people's health, as, for example, Armani published a list of restricted substances and Gucci decided not to use gold and diamonds sourced unethically anymore.

Moreover, luxury fashion brands can also foster a positive reputation in terms of social responsibility by acquiring companies that are recognised for their commitment in that area. For example, in 2009 LVMH bought a stake in ethical fashion brand Edun, a socially conscious clothing company committed to fostering sustainable employment in developing areas of the world. At the same time, luxury fashion brands can also create a sense of authority, credibility and trust by associating with leading agencies and associations for programmes or to develop charity ranges.

For example, in 2017 Louis Vuitton collaborated with UNICEF and released a new version of its Lockit bracelets, generating over $14 million for the agency. Moreover, Balenciaga in 2018 collaborated with the World Food Program to create a collection to support the cause and raise awareness of a spike in the incidence of global hunger. It has been observed that when luxury brands partner with charities, purchase intent and upselling increases whilst purchase guilt decreases, so that, in this sense, not only can labels improve their image by associating with worthy causes, but they can also reach new market segments and increase sales through such collaborations.

The most common form of collaboration with established agencies in this sense is represented by partnering on specific initiatives. For example, Prada in 2022 joined forces with the United Nations Sexual and Reproductive Health Agency to create a training programme for young women in Kenya and Ghana, where in addition to fashion training participants receive information on women's rights, gender inequality alongside sexual and reproductive health. Also, in 2010 Armani launched a charity initiative to promote access to clean water in collaboration with UNICEF and Green Cross International. Moreover, Gucci launched in 2013 its CHIME project, a wide-reaching initiative managed through an advisory board led by experts and activists that focuses on supporting vulnerable women and girls worldwide (in particular disabled and Indigenous individuals, those in the Global South, trans and non-binary people, young feminists and refugees), and collaborates with UN Women. Furthermore, Gucci also launched the Gucci Changemakers initiative in 2022 to support local communities worldwide.

Last, luxury fashion brands are also boosting their credentials with regards to social responsibility by adopting inclusive practices (see Chapter Ten), and supporting corporate volunteering, which sees employees allocated paid time to pursue worthy social causes. This strategy is employed for example by Stella McCartney, but also Gucci. However, luxury fashion brands have also faced controversies concerning how they manage their in-house staff.

In 2022 reports emerged concerning strikes in some factories owned by Louis Vuitton in France, as staff complained of low wages and long hours. Moreover, in 2023 it was reported that Gucci employees in Italy were planning strikes in response to plans to move the Design Office from Rome to Milan, among accusation of collective dismissals that echoed the ones that parent company Kering had to face when label Brioni underwent major restructuring. The controversial decision was even discussed in the Italian parliament, and news focused on the impact on the emotional and psychological well-being of the members of staff that would have to move, but also the loss of ancillary jobs, for example with regards to security or reception staff. However, the company defended the move, and emphasised that support and incentives were available to staff members.

11.4 Animal welfare

The luxury fashion industry is often ranked low for animal welfare, as it employs fur and exotic animal skins. If, in the past, this was not perceived to be controversial, nowadays more and more consumers feel uncomfortable with such practices, as media campaigns by associations such as PETA put the spotlight on dubious practices. Moreover, concerns over the preservation of some animal species that are endangered or dwindling in numbers have also been raised, as the growing demand has caused an increased pressure with regards to leather goods, cashmere and other fine fibres.

Fur and exotic skins have traditionally been associated with status and display of wealth, and luxury fashion brands have often used them in their products. Some, like Fendi, even originate in the fur business. If, in Western countries, the cruelty-free lifestyle is gaining popularity, on the other hand in many other countries demand for fur and exotic leather is on the rise, causing pressure on the supply chain and fuelling the illegal wildlife trade, that can lead to some rare species becoming even more at risk of extinction.

In the early 2000s, luxury fashion brands showcased a renewed interest in fur but a growing backlash caused many brands to stop using it. For example, in 2016 Armani stopped using fur in its products, a strategy also adopted by other labels like Gucci and Burberry, as scandals emerged. In 2017 Louis Vuitton received negative press for sourcing fox fur from farms that used unethical practices. In order to avoid potential controversies, in 2021 the Kering group announced that all of its brands would become fur-free.

In terms of exotic leather, popular animals used by luxury fashion brands are alligators, lizards, crocodiles and snakes. When it comes to exotic animal skins, concerns involve mistreatment of animals, cruel practices for killing and skinning, and the use of rare and endangered species. The use of such materials within the industry is probably more common than one might imagine, as, for example, it has been widely reported that between 2003 and 2013 thousands of goods made from illegal wildlife by luxury fashion labels were seized in the USA.

In view of scandals and consumer pressure, some brands have stopped the use of exotic skins altogether. For example, in 2018 Chanel declared that it would no longer use such materials as it was impossible to source them in a way that would satisfy the brand's ethical standards. However, many luxury fashion brands have bought farms (for example Hermès owns crocodile farms in Australia) in order to secure sourcing and provide better animal welfare by being able to implement more effective monitoring practices.

Despite the fact that a number of luxury fashion brands have launched initiatives to either ban or support a more ethical way to source fur and exotic skins, many still don't have formal animal welfare policies. In this sense, the case of Kering represents an exception, as the group has published a very detailed species-specific report, setting minimum levels of compliance and aiming to achieve best in class practices. For example, Kering states that it provides animals room to move around freely, access to clean, fresh water and a diet that is nutritionally appropriate to their species and age, for example offering a fibrous diet to calves to avoid anaemia.

Kering also give animals enrichments in their environment that are appropriate to their species, and the ability to perform their normal behaviours, for example managing species in herds or flocks where appropriate, and giving them the opportunity to graze, browse and forage. The group states that it guarantees that animals are handled carefully and calmly with no mistreatment or abuse, as, for example, when ostriches are moved, they are accompanied by handlers to make sure they don't fall and injure themselves.

Moreover, animals are managed in a way that promotes good health (for example, preventive measures are taken with regards to foot health in sheep), they are treated immediately should disease or injury be discovered, and are cared for by competent stock people, for example only trained workers are allowed to shear and comb goats. Furthermore, Kering is committed to the health, welfare and thermal comfort of animals, and a humane handling at end of life. When it comes to exotic animals such as crocodiles and alligators, the group also states that farms must also contribute to wildlife conservation.

Recently, as awareness of animal rights increases and both vegetarian and vegan lifestyles become more popular, leather and animal fibres such as wool have also drawn criticism. For example, Chanel has declared that it would only use leather and fur coming from the agri-food industry, so that no animals would be killed specifically for the brand. Also, in 2021 the Armani Group announced it would stop using angora in their collections and received a PETA Fashion Award for this. Luxury fashion brands are also exploring alternatives to leather, and recently mushroom-based mycelium has been employed by Hermès for handbags, whilst Stella McCartney, that pioneered the material, is now also offering garments.

Sometimes, sustainability and animal welfare concerns overlap, as in the case of cashmere. An increased demand from the mass-market led to increasing numbers of cashmere goats, this caused overgrazing and the degradation of the grassland in their habitat, which in turn negatively affected the quality of life of the animals and the attributes of the fibres. The quest to source high quality cashmere led many luxury fashion brands to decide to take charge of their supply chain, as, for example, Loro Piana launched a breeding programme in China with the aim to increase the quality of fibres and decrease herd sizes. Kering similarly committed to better animal welfare and to create a more sustainable cashmere production in Mongolia.

Loro Piana also launched a preservation project for vicuña, a small camelid, in South America. This helped save the species from extinction, doubling numbers since 1998 and supporting its natural behaviour and specific habitat by working alongside local stakeholders in this sense. Moreover, Gucci launched a series of initiatives to support regenerative agriculture, boost biodiversity and protect traditional practices, for example with two regenerative wool projects in Uruguay and Italy, where initiatives for silk and cotton were also launched.

11.5 Environmental issues

Sustainability is linked to environmental impact, and involves reducing consumption, re-use and recycle, and the general belief that present consumer practices should change to enable future generations to meet their needs, contrast climate change and avoid the disruption of ecosystems and natural resources.

Sustainability issues in the luxury fashion industry are varied and include habitat degradation, water use, energy use (including energy efficiency and the use of renewable resources), greenhouse emissions and toxic waste disposal during production, hazardous chemical waste from fibre and fabric production, and also issues related to the retail, care and end-of-life of goods. In fact, the impact of luxury fashion goods goes beyond manufacturing and can be seen in all phases of use and disposal, which are also influenced by design choices and the materials used.

It has been argued that the luxury fashion industry is inherently more sustainable than fast fashion for a variety of reasons. Luxury brands produce less goods than mass-market labels, and are associated with a slower production cycle, even though the expansion in the lower market segment has challenged this association. Luxury brands now produce more goods than ever before, and have abandoned the traditional two collections per year due to consumer demand for more regular drops.

Luxury fashion goods are generally considered to be better manufactured and more durable than their mass-market counterparts and are thought to better stand the test of time. They are often closely associated with notions of heritage and craftsmanship, and moreover longevity has also been observed to be linked to classical trends over short-lived fads. Also, the price of luxury goods might be an inherent barrier to overconsumption but, again, as luxury fashion brands expanded in the lower market segment and drastically increased the number of goods produced, the association is problematic.

Luxury fashion goods are not usually discarded, and more likely to be sold or passed on, including from generation to generation as heirlooms. In this sense, luxury fashion brands could emphasise emotional attachment to their goods and brands not only to boost sales and increase loyalty, but to support more sustainable consumption practices. For example, luxury fashion brands could foster notions of memories and heirlooms through their marketing and communication strategies.

As observed by Carrigan, Moraes and McEachern (2013), despite the fact that haute couture might never need to be reused or recycled due to their collectable nature, their impact can be significantly more than what people might think as they are often delivered and also flown by private jet to wealthy clients for fittings. On the other hand, sometimes luxury fashion brands are the first to dispose of their own goods. For example, scandal ensued in 2018 when it was reported that Burberry had destroyed goods worth over £90 million in the previous five years. Burberry declared that only goods carrying their trademark were destroyed, in addition to a large amount of perfumes as a new deal with Coty was signed.

Forbes (2018) observed how the disposal of large quantity of goods was to protect brand exclusivity, as Burberry experienced overproduction when introducing a see-now-buy-now model in 2016. Moreover, it was also reported that a financial incentive to encourage brands to export to the USA could be to blame, as by disposing of goods brands could then recover duties and fees. The scandal gained major exposure and Burberry was forced to announce that it would stop destroying goods whilst also launching a series of sustainability initiatives to try repair its reputation, for example donating leather off-cuts to be repurposed.

There are different elements than can drive the luxury fashion industry towards sustainability, as examined by De Brito et al. (2008) and Caniato et al. (2012):

- laws and regulations
- operational elements such as economic factors
- market benefits, for example improve reputation or attract more customers.

At the moment laws and regulations are not the most important element yet, but their role is perceived to be increasing in the future, as more and more countries launch initiatives in this sense. For example, France in 2007 introduced extended producer responsibility for companies making clothing, linen and shoes, making them responsible for end-of-life products, which drastically increased collection and recycling of goods.

Sustainability in luxury fashion is now being driven by operational issues. As prices of good-quality resources have increased due a combination of instability in the currency market, global crises, and the decrease of available materials (for example as a result of the degradation of the ecosystem as seen in the case of cashmere), economic pressures are driving luxury brands to explore more sustainable practices, for example by using recycled fibres.

Moreover, luxury brands are showcasing narratives of sustainability to attract consumers who care about the issue, promote a positive image, raise brand awareness and support brand equity. In fact, nowadays more and more people are exposed to information over the impact of their consumption and opt for more sustainable consumption practices. The demand for environmentally sustainable goods is on the rise, as is consumer acceptance of alternative materials. However, sustainability has also emerged as a means to convey status and privilege within society.

In this sense, some consumers use conspicuous consumption of sustainable fashion to express that they have the financial means (as sustainable fashion goods can be more costly to buy), the time and the knowledge to research and appreciate such items. Moreover, luxury fashion brands also use sustainability as a branding tool, to associate with positive narratives and improve their reputation, especially in response to scandals and controversies, as a way to generate buzz and increase brand awareness.

In literature, barriers in the adoption of sustainable luxury fashion have been associated with lack of information and awareness of such goods, low availability, limited choice and high prices. However, there are sometimes also legislative barriers, as, for example, Stella McCartney complained about how her brand was taxed up to 30% more for importing non-leather products into the USA, increasing prices and negatively affecting sales.

Moreover, scepticism and lack of trust towards brands' claims is also pivotal, as vague or misleading information and accusations of greenwashing can further confuse people. Nowadays consumers are more aware of sustainability and expect brands to do their part, driving demand for sustainable goods but also for information on sustainability, as it is imperative that relevant information reaches the relevant market segment. Initially luxury fashion brands that were engaging with sustainability did not share this information outside of the company, and still today many do not highlight this aspect in their communication strategies.

Cavender (2018) observes that LVHM was the first brand to create an environmental department in 1992, and among the first within the industry to launch a series of initiatives, such as acquiring tanneries to better control their environmental impact. The group also published yearly environmental reports but still in the 2010s LVHM did not communicate its sustainability efforts across consumer channels. Similarly, Louis Vuitton repair services for leather goods, or the use of refillable perfume bottles (also employed at Dior), are not widely communicated to consumers.

This could be attributed to the fact that brands are wary of being accused of greenwashing as it is difficult to convey authenticity, legitimacy and transparency with sustainability claims. One strategy in this sense, as discussed by Cavender (2018), consists in sharing both positive and negative information, as that is associated with increased credibility. However, this can be a risky strategy in the contemporary mediascape, as news travel faster than ever before and people are more vocal in their criticism, leading to negative consequences for brands.

However, there are many strategies that luxury fashion brands can employ to convey a sense of authority and trust with regards to their sustainability efforts:

- to establish committees
- to pursue certifications
- to partner with leading agencies and launch projects
- to launch scholarships focusing on sustainability
- to associate with 'virtuous' brands and companies
- to link financing to sustainability goals
- to release reports detailing their activities in this area

Pavione, Pezzetti and Matteo (2016) observe how, in order to show their commitment to sustainability, the Kering group has introduced a series of committees, both at the level of the board of directors and at executive level. However, many other luxury fashion brands have also launched such committees to showcase their commitment to sustainability and to implement responsible practices, for example Chloé created a sustainability board in 2021.

Second, luxury fashion labels have obtained certifications in order to convey that their sustainability efforts are credible and their results substantial enough to be awarded recognition. For example, Saint Laurent developed a new store concept in the early 2010s that focused on energy saving, resulting in the LEED Platinum Certification in 2015 and extensive positive media coverage. Moreover, Chloé became the first luxury brand to obtain a B Corp certification for its social and environmental impact.

Third, with the similar aim to acquire credibility, luxury fashion brands have teamed up with leading agencies, capitalising on the trust and authority they possess. For example, Louis Vuitton was one of the sponsors at the 2015 UN Climate Change Conference in Paris, and there it announced a commitment to cut its carbon emissions. LVHM supports the UNESCO 'Man and Biosphere' scientific programme aimed at safeguarding worldwide biodiversity. Moreover, Gucci created a special handbag collection with leather from Rainforest Alliance Certified ranches. Moreover, a number of brands have launched a broad range of activities, for example Chanel contributed to protect and restore rainforest in Sumatra (Indonesia), and Peru, whereas the Emporio Armani Green Project was launched in 2020 to promote reforestation in some of the areas where the brand operates. Similarly, Prada launched in 2023 the Forestami project, aiming to plant three million trees around Milan, the brand's city of birth, and a three-year training programme on urban forestry available to the public.

Fourth, luxury fashion brands have launched scholarships aiming to increase awareness of sustainability within the industry and the wider public. For example, the Kering group developed a sustainability award, launched in 2014 in collaboration with the London College of Fashion, that offered students £10,000 and internships at the groups' brands, including Alexander McQueen, Brioni, Stella McCartney and Gucci. On the other hand, Prada showcases its commitment to the preservation of oceans through training programmes aimed at schools.

Fifth, luxury fashion brands and groups have also pursued associations with sustainable brands and companies. This can be done through acquisitions, for example, in 2009 LVMH bought a stake in ethical fashion brand Edun, whereas the Kering group co-created the Stella McCartney brand to boost its sustainability credentials. Sixth, luxury fashion brands have linked financing to sustainability goals to further convey a sense trust and commitment. For example, Burberry used such strategy to showcase that the brand's efforts have substance and are not just a marketing ploy.

Moreover, to further support credibility and substantiate their sustainability claims, luxury fashion brands are also releasing reports detailing their activities in this area. Luxury fashion brands at the moment don't have legal obligations to publish their sustainability reports, and comparisons are made difficult by the adoption of different standards or models. The Kering group has gone further in this sense, and even developed its own tool to quantify the economic impact of its practices.

Another strategy used by luxury fashion brands to substantiate their sustainability claims and sharing them with the general public, whilst also conveying a sense of commitment and trust, is represented by the launch of exhibitions dedicated to the label's sustainability activities, like Salvatore Ferragamo in 2019, or to use fashion shows. In fact, fashion shows can offer luxury fashion brands a way to showcase their sustainability credentials in many areas at the same time.

For example, Chloé for its SS2022 collection referred to environmental and social sustainability practices, as items contained more recycled materials than any previous collections, guests sat on cushions made from the brand's stock fabric by women refugees, and the brand even donated leftover food to charity. The following collection by Chloé similarly used recycled materials, supported an Indigenous Women Fellowship programme cross the Amazon, and was shown in a venue covered in soil that would have been discarded but that had been made fit for use again for the construction industry, whereas chairs were to be donated to the We Love Green Festival to be reused.

Usually luxury fashion brands launch various initiatives that cover many different aspects. First, luxury fashion brands disseminate information on the more sustainable materials or processes they employ, which can take the shape of using more recycled content, limiting the use of more impactful resources, and the development of novel and more sustainable materials and processes to reduce their impact. Moreover, more luxury fashion brands are also working towards minimising waste by reusing offcuts and not sending them to landfill. Furthermore, initiatives related to packaging have also been launched. Also, luxury fashion brands have implemented wide-ranging initiatives concerning retail stores, offices and factories.

A number of brands have publicly declared a commitment to increase their use of recycled material, like Ermenegildo Zegna. Balenciaga used over 1000 metres of stock fabrics to create tote bags, moreover LVHM in 2021 launched a platform, Nona Source, that made the group's deadstock available for purchase. Moreover, Prada emphasises its commitment to sustainability through the use of recycled nylon originating from discarded plastic that would have been otherwise sent to landfill or that was found in the ocean. This is a promising area, as according to the Ellen MacArthur Foundation (2017) the fashion industry wastes more than $500 billion due to the lack of recycling schemes and other strategies to extract value. At the moment, a major issue is implementing strategies at the design level to overcome current technical limits, as, for example, fibre recycling processes shorten their length, impacting quality, and in many cases fibres can only be recycled once (House of Commons Environmental Audit Committee 2019).

Circularity has also emerged as a design approach, aiming to minimise impact in production and maximise the life of the product before it can be fully recycled and the circle can start again. The first attempt in the fashion industry was in 2013 with the the Puma InCycle collection. The collection comprised a shoe, a jacket and a backpack that used no toxic chemicals and could be easily disassembled and recycled, but the project was cancelled in 2015 due to poor consumer demand. Now, however, circularity is at the forefront of sustainability discourses and more brands are engaging with this dimension, but so far only with regards to limited goods. However, such a strategy can help brands to project a responsible image whilst they fare much worse with other products or lines.

Moreover, Gucci developed a tanning process that doesn't use heavy metals and reduces water and energy consumption by 30% and 20%, respectively. Gucci, like many other luxury fashion brands, has also introduced alternatives to plastic for their eyewear lines. The Kering group is also limiting the use of PVC whilst developing new materials characterised by less environmental impact. Furthermore, a number of brands have introduced recycled content in their packaging. For example, Burberry, Gucci and Valentino use recycled paper, whereas Chanel in 2021 introduced a biodegradable perfume cap.

Furthermore, initiatives related to retail stores, offices and factories have also been launched by luxury fashion brands. Many brands, like Saint Laurent and Hermès, have made changes to their retail spaces to make them more environmentally sustainable, changing lighting, sources of energy and materials used whilst also implementing rainwater collection systems. The Kering group is also committed to limit waste from shops, offices and warehouses.

One brand that has been launching a wide-reaching sustainability strategy in this sense is Prada. The brand gained considerable media coverage for purchasing certified renewable energy, installing photovoltaic systems, converting to LED lighting and developing staff training on a more efficient use of energy. Prada also announced that, where possible, they would restore existing buildings instead of constructing new factories, and that if no suitable ones would be available then they would build 'garden factories', landscape buildings to minimise land consumption and to offer aesthetic pleasure and foster a connection to nature to staff.

11.6 Case study: Stella McCartney

Stella McCartney, the daughter of Paul McCartney, member of legendary band The Beatles, has been in the limelight since her fashion degree shows at Central Saint Martin in London, where supermodels like Kate Moss and Naomi Campbell donned her designs. Only two years later, in 1997, she became creative director of Chloé, and in 2001 she founded her eponymous label.

The Stella McCartney brand was born as a 50/50 joint venture with Kering, and with a strong emphasis on sustainability and animal welfare, but also quality and design to avoid the negative connotations associated with sustainable fashion, that was at the time perceived by consumers as unstylish and frumpy. In this sense the Stella McCartney brand aimed to offer cruelty-free products that could be appreciated for their aesthetic appeal alone, therefore not speaking only to those that valued sustainability but widening the target market to include more generally the consumers of luxury fashion brands. Stella McCartney also aligned with other luxury fashion brands in terms of management strategies, for example adopting brand extension in the lower market segment through cheaper goods like accessories, lingerie, swimwear, eyewear and skincare.

As a vegetarian label, Stella McCartney never used leather, feathers, fur or exotic skins, which provided a unique selling point in a market that was not yet so engaged with animal welfare, social responsibility and sustainability in general. For example, in 2018 the Stella McCartney Cares Foundation was launched, focusing on sustainability (alongside breast cancer). The reputation of Stella McCartney also positively affected the image of the Kering group, that was lauded in the press and considered a trailblazer in the industry because of that association.

The ethos of the Stella McCartney brand helped put it on the map, and throughout the years its founder has become a poster girl for ethical fashion. In fact, after having acquired Kering's stake in her company in 2018, she then entered a partnership with LVHM and became a special advisor on sustainability to Bernard Arnault, founder and CEO of LVHM, and to the group's executive committee. In this sense, by associating with Stella McCartney the LVHM group boosted its sustainability credentials and improved its reputation. Similarly, in 2005 mass retailer H&M capitalised on the positive associations and sustainable credibility of the brand when launching a one-off special collection with Stella McCartney.

The Stella McCartney brand became synonymous with responsible consumption through a series of initiatives that covered a broad range of causes and issues, from animal rights to sustainability and social responsibility. When it comes to materials, Stella McCartney started to use organic cotton in 2008 and went PVC free in 2010. In the following two years the brand started to use plant-based resins and plastics, and bio-acetate for eyewear, and in 2020 also introduced bio-lenses. In 2015 they introduced recycled cashmere and regenerated nylon, in 2017 they moved to lower-impact metals, and in 2022 started using Recycrom dyes, pigments derived from used clothing and manufacturing waste, instead of perfluorinated compounds (PFCs) or azo dyes. Moreover, the brand also started to use biodegradable rubber and recycled polyester.

A material that is closely associated with the Stella McCartney brand is vegan leather, as for example the brand created the first vegan Stan Smith shoes with Adidas. Vegan leather has often been associated to low-quality and has a problematic status in terms of sustainability, as many types are petroleum-based and characterised by a high carbon footprint, and moreover can lose their aesthetic qualities quite quickly and cause significant waste and pollution issues by not being biodegradable and entering the food chain.

In 2013, the Stella McCartney label first developed Eco Alter-Nappa, a type of vegan leather, and in 2018 launched its first bag made of Mylo, a mushroom-based vegan alternative to leather, before debuting another alternative using grape waste in 2022. The brand also uses a number of other cruelty-free leather alternative, for example from banana plants and other bio-based materials.

As a way to signal a true commitment and avoid the vague claims associated with greenwashing, Stella McCartney has also pursued certifications to substantiate its claims.

For example, the brand uses FSC-certified paper (when not using recycled paper), alongside certified wood in order to not contribute to deforestation and to protect endangered forests. In 2016 they also started to use viscose made from FSC-certified pulp.

The brand also launched an initiative in 2014 aiming to encourage customers to take better care of their garments to extend their life, and to reduce their carbon footprint by wearing clothes more and washing them less. In 2017 the brand launched a resale scheme in the USA with TheRealReal to extend the life of their products, whereas in 2023 introduced a take-back and recycling programme making the brand responsible for its own goods after their end-of-life.

Current efforts are also targeting circularity and in this sense Stella McCartney obtained a cradle-to-cradle Gold-Level certification for its knitwear wool yarn. They also use a type of recycled nylon that can be recycled infinitely and launched, in 2023, their very first product designed for disassembly that can be fully recycled, a jacked that can be returned to become new yearn.

In order to achieve a lower environmental impact, in 2003 Stella McCartney started to use renewable energy for UK locations. Now all stores have LED lighting and the London flagship only uses renewable energy. The brand, when possible, also buys used fittings and office furniture, whilst giving away the old ones to a furniture refurbishment company that give them a new lease of life.

Stella McCartney does not test on animals and states that no animals are killed for its products, and is progressively abandoning some materials derived from animals.

For example, Stella McCartney stopped using angora in 2013, the company doesn't buy wool from farms that allow mulesing (a procedure performed on lambs to make them less susceptible to a lethal condition called flystrike, and that involves cutting flaps of skin from the animals' breech and tail to create a bare area where blowflies can't easily lay eggs and cause illness) and in 2018 it stopped using virgin mohair.

In this sense, however, the motivations don't solely involve animal welfare. In fact, the Stella McCartney brand uses the Environmental Profit and Loss model developed by Kering, that assesses the monetary value of the costs and benefits involved in the brand's operations in terms of sustainability impact. This, Stella McCartney claims, allowed the brand to realise that even though cashmere only represented 0.1% of total material used, it accounted for over 40% of the company's environmental impact, leading to the decision to abandon virgin cashmere and move towards regenerated content. Now the label uses much more cashmere, but the overall impact is just over 10%.

When it comes to social sustainability, the Stella McCartney brand emphasises how it follows guidelines set by the UN, International Labour Organisations and best industry practices to develop a series of policies that all suppliers need to adhere to. The latter are also audited to assess their practices in this respect. Stella McCartney doesn't source cotton from China, Syria, Turkmenistan, Uzbekistan, or other areas associated with risks of child and forced labour. Moreover, they don't sandblast denim, as the practice can cause fatal lung diseases, and only use distressing methods that are safe for workers. Also, in 2011 Stella McCartney developed a Fairtrade accessories collection to support artisans in Kenya. Moreover, in 2016 Stella McCartney started to analyse productivity and wages with the aim to raise workers' salary, and in 2017 a programme to build better HR management practices and improve workers conditions for their factories in China was launched.

Furthermore, Stella McCartney offers sustainable schemes with regards to pensions and staff rewards, and encourages staff to volunteer for at least three days a year (outside of holiday allowance) to support worthy causes. The label has also created products and raised awareness for a number of causes, for example breast cancer by developing compression bras to be worn after mastectomy. Other initiatives are represented by the creation of badges to celebrate the International Day for the Elimination of Violence Against Women and t-shirts to support charity War Child UK.

Questions and activities

- What values are at the core of the brand Stella McCartney?
- What strategies of sustainability has the brand adopted?
- Select a luxury fashion brand and identify the strategies it has adopted with regards to sustainability

11.7 Conclusions

Nowadays, consumers are more and more aware of the impact of their consumption practices and the fashion industry has been harshly criticised for not doing enough in a variety of areas. In particular, a number of scandals have emerged with regards to social responsibility, animal welfare and environment impact. The chapter addressed issues related to such notions and identified problematic elements but also opportunities for luxury fashion brands. A number of examples were provided, and the different strategies and approaches employed in this sense by luxury fashion brands and groups have been investigated. In particular, the powerful role of a virtuous reputation in this field was examined through a case study of the Stella McCartney brand.

11.8 Revision questions

- How do luxury fashion brands engage with social responsibility?
- What are the pivotal issues for animal welfare within the industry?
- How do luxury fashion brands engage with sustainability?

11.9 References

Akrout, H. and Guercini, S. (2022) 'Sustainability in fashion and luxury marketing: results, paradoxes and potentialities', *Journal of Global Fashion Marketing*, 13(2), pp. 91–100.

Berry, C. J. (1994) *The idea of luxury: a conceptual and historical investigation*. Cambridge: Cambridge University Press.

Caniato, F., Caridi, M., Crippa, L. and Moretto, A. (2012) 'Environmental sustainability in fashion supply chains: an exploratory case based research', *International Journal of Production Economics*, 135(2), pp. 659–70.

Carrigan, M., Moraes, C. and McEachern, M. (2013) 'From conspicuous to considered fashion: a harm-chain approach to the responsibilities of luxury-fashion businesses', *Journal of Marketing Management*, 29(11–12), pp. 1277–1307.

Cavender, R. (2018) 'The marketing of sustainability and CSR initiatives by luxury brands: cultural indicators, call to action, and framework', in Lo, C. and Ha-Brookshire, J. (eds.) *Sustainability in luxury fashion business*. Springer Series in Fashion Business, Singapore: Springer.

De Brito, M. P., Carbone, V., and Blanquart, C. M. (2008) 'Towards a sustainable fashion retail supply chain in Europe: organisation and performance', *International Journal of Production Economics*, 114(2), pp. 534–53.

Ellen Macarthur Foundation. (2017) A new textiles economy: redesigning fashion's future. Available at: https://www.ellenmacarthurfoundation.org/assets/downloads/publications/A-New-Textiles-Economy_Full-Report.pdf

Forbes. (2018) No one in fashion is surprised Burberry burnt £28 million of stock. Available at: https://www.forbes.com/sites/oliviapinnock/2018/07/20/no-one-in-fashion-is-surprised-burberry-burnt-28-million-of-stock/

Forbes. (2021) As Burberry faces backlash in China over Xinjiang cotton, other luxury brands could face boycott. Available at: https://www.forbes.com/sites/isabeltogoh/2021/03/26/as-burberry-faces-backlash-in-china-over-xinjiang-cotton-other-luxury-brands-could-face-boycott/

House of Commons Environmental Audit Committee. (2019) Fixing fashion: clothing consumption and sustainability. Sixteenth Report of Session HC 1952. London: UK Parliament. Available at: https://publications.parliament.uk/pa/cm201719/cmselect/cmenvaud/1952/report-summary.html

Karaosman, H., Perry, P., Brun, A. and Morales-Alonso, G. (2020) 'Behind the runway: extending sustainability in luxury fashion supply chains', *Journal of Business Research*, 117, pp. 652–63.

Pavione, E., Pezzetti, R. and Matteo, D. A. (2016) 'Emerging competitive strategies in the global luxury industry in the perspective of sustainable development: the case of Kering Group', *Management Dynamics in the Knowledge Economy*, 4(2), pp. 241–61.

WWD. (2023) Report finds 'disappointing' forced labor risks in luxury fashion. Available at: https://wwd.com/sustainability/social-impact/forced-labor-risks-luxury-fashion-walk-free-foundation-global-index-supply-chain-1235664090/

Index

For Product Safety Concerns and Information please contact our
EU representative GPSR@taylorandfrancis.com Taylor & Francis
Verlag GmbH, Kaufingerstraße 24, 80331 München, Germany